Praise for
Collateral Damaged
The Marketing of Consumer Debt to America

by Charles R. Geisst

"Charles Geisst is one of America's most talented financial writers. *Collateral Damaged* is a thoroughly readable account of the players, events, and history that brought us to today's financial debacle."

— THOMAS H. STANTON
Author, *A State of Risk*

"Just when and how did the American public get into such a profound consumer debt mess? *Collateral Damaged* takes on that very question by providing an impeccably researched and compelling account of the entire lending industry. Author Charles Geisst not only delves into the history of credit card marketing, but offers insightful suggestions on ways it can be improved and ultimately repaired. This fascinating and timely book will appeal to anyone who tears open a credit card statement and wonders, 'How did I get here?'"

— ERICA SANDBERG
Columnist for CreditCards.com
KRON-TV's money management expert
Author, *Expecting Money*

Collateral Damaged

Also available from
Bloomberg Press

The Audacity of Help:
Obama's Economic Plan and the Remaking of America
by John F. Wasik

Bonds:
The Unbeaten Path to Secure Investment Growth
by Hildy Richelson and Stan Richelson

Complicit:
How Greed and Collusion Made the Credit Crisis Unstoppable
by Mark Gilbert
(January 2010)

Investing 101:
Updated and Expanded
by Kathy Kristof

Making Sense of the Dollar:
Exposing Dangerous Myths about Trade and Foreign Exchange
by Marc Chandler

The Only Guide to Alternative Investments You'll Ever Need:
The Good, the Flawed, the Bad, and the Ugly
by Larry E. Swedroe and Jared Kizer

Pension Dumping:
The Reasons, the Wreckage, the Stakes for Wall Street
by Fran Hawthorne

A complete list of our titles is available at
www.bloomberg.com/books

Collateral Damaged

The Marketing of Consumer Debt to America

Charles R. Geisst

BLOOMBERG PRESS

NEW YORK

BLOOMBERG, BLOOMBERG ANYWHERE, BLOOMBERG.COM, BLOOMBERG MARKET ESSENTIALS, *Bloomberg Markets*, BLOOMBERG NEWS, BLOOMBERG PRESS, BLOOMBERG PROFESSIONAL, BLOOMBERG RADIO, BLOOMBERG TELEVISION, and BLOOMBERG TRADEBOOK are trademarks and service marks of Bloomberg Finance L.P. ("BFLP"), a Delaware limited partnership, or its subsidiaries. The BLOOMBERG PROFESSIONAL service (the "BPS") is owned and distributed locally by BFLP and its subsidiaries in all jurisdictions other than Argentina, Bermuda, China, India, Japan, and Korea (the "BLP Countries"). BFLP is a wholly-owned subsidiary of Bloomberg L.P. ("BLP"). BLP provides BFLP with all global marketing and operational support and service for these products and distributes the BPS either directly or through a non-BFLP subsidiary in the BLP Countries. All rights reserved.

This publication contains the author's opinions and is designed to provide accurate and authoritative information. It is sold with the understanding that the author, publisher, and Bloomberg L.P. are not engaged in rendering legal, accounting, investment-planning, or other professional advice. The reader should seek the services of a qualified professional for such advice; the author, publisher, and Bloomberg L.P. cannot be held responsible for any loss incurred as a result of specific investments or planning decisions made by the reader.

First edition published 2009

1 3 5 7 9 10 8 6 4 2

Library of Congress Cataloging-in-Publication Data

Geisst, Charles R.

  Collateral damaged : the marketing of consumer debt to America / Charles R. Geisst. — 1st ed.

    p. cm.

  Includes bibliographical references and index.

  Summary: "Collateral Damaged explains how America had turned from a nation of savers into a nation of consumers addicted to debt. Wall Street then used that addiction to create "toxic securities" that threaten to bring about the collapse of the global economy. How can America get its fiscal house in order again?"—Provided by publisher.

  ISBN 978-1-57660-325-3 (alk. paper)

  1. Consumer credit—United States—History. 2. Saving and investment—United States—History. I. Title.

  HG3756.U54G45 2009
  332.7'43—dc22

                                                    2009011735

To Meg and Ralph, many happy . . .

Contents

Introduction *1*

1 The Great American Credit Machine 11

2 Creating a Consumer Credit Society in the 1920s 35

3 A Self-Fulfilling Prophecy 59

4 The Rise of Credit Cards 85

5 The Mortgage Explosion 117

6 The Politics of Credit 153

7 Policy Implications 179

8 Prescription and Outlook 207

Statistical Appendixes *217*

Bibliography *259*

Index *265*

"Where I come from it's called collateral."

Introduction

Compound interest is the eighth wonder of the world.
—Attributed to Albert Einstein

THE STORY WAS HARDLY NEW. A head of state borrowed more than three times his country's annual revenues to fight a war abroad. His bankers, treated badly in the past, still agreed to lend him money despite a spotty record of being paid back. To their dismay, he finally reneged on the loans, driving several of them into bankruptcy. When pressed for payments, he simply walked away from the debts.

The basis for the lending was a commodity vital to his country's interests. Although he did not win the war, the head of state managed to establish precedents that survive. Even though his credit history was shaky, he assuaged his bankers by offering them jobs in his administration that provided them with revenues. In fact, the jobs were so important to the bankers that they tolerated occasional expulsions and even imprisonment in order to keep them. Currying favor and receiving lucrative fees were worth the occasional indignity.

If the outline of the tale sounds familiar, its main characters are not. The date was 1337, the head of state was Edward III of England, and the bankers all were from Italian banking houses. The commodity was wool, the major English export at the time, which provided many merchants with revenue from one of the first recorded English monopolies ever granted. The amounts that Edward borrowed ranged from as small as £100 to a multiple of his annual income. He would not be the first, or the last, to suffer from a debt-to-income ratio of 3:1.

At least one of the bankers reputedly had assets worth more than Edward's annual revenue. These bankers were the direct financial heirs of the Knights Templar, Europe's first truly international bankers. For two hundred years the Templars had amassed a sizable fortune, providing banking services to the crowns of England and France before being expropriated by the king of France on the infamous Friday the 13th of October 1307. The Italian bankers took the Templars' place and prospered.

Paying off debts had always been a problem for the Plantagenet dynasty (Edward's line), but Edward III had problems more unusual than most. To finance his war with France, he pawned the English crown jewels to moneylenders in return for cash. He made a claim to the crown of France based on his ancestry and, anticipating he would be crowned king of France in 1339, also pawned the crown he was having made for that occasion. Foreign moneylenders had learned years before to treat the Plantagenets gingerly because of their reputation for repudiating debts, dating back to Edward I. Edward III's financial plight continued and he kept on borrowing. But the strong hand of the moneylenders occasionally rose up to embarrass him. In the middle of his borrowings, they demanded surety for his debts incurred on the Continent. Being broke, Edward responded the only way left to him: He left his pregnant wife and children with the moneylenders in France as collateral until he could raise the necessary funds to ransom them. His travails continued, but he did have a few shining moments, especially when he paid another ransom for an administrator in his government. After Geoffrey Chaucer was captured by the French and held for ransom in 1360, Edward paid the amount requested (£16), ensuring that a long literary career lay ahead for the former page.

Indebtedness has been a central fixture in life since the time of the Plantagenets but has always remained primarily a government affair until recently. For centuries, tension existed between the need to borrow and the rates charged for the borrowing. Edward paid high rates to his moneylenders, for obvious reasons. But charging interest was more than a squabble about the rates. After the dissolution of the Templars, charging interest was proscribed as heresy by the Church, and anyone caught charging excessive interest could be punished by excommunication and occasionally faced worse consequences. That is not to say that interest was not charged on loans, because most monarchs and merchants were constantly in need of funds. But loans to individuals on a large scale did not begin until the early twentieth century and have been a central part of everyday life ever since.

The correlation between indebtedness and the average guy in the street has been the result of a collision of many factors. It has depended on the flow of information between borrower and lender, on the assessment of lending risk, and on the politics of the time. Subtle changes occurred over the years, but in the post–World War II period a debt explosion began that popularized debt and encouraged indebtedness on a scale never seen before. Ironically, usury still was being discussed, much as it had been in the fourteenth century, but it did not stop the mass buy-now-pay-later movement that has characterized society over the last fifty years. Like Edward III, anyone who would borrow three times his future revenues must be sanguine about either his future prospects or the righteousness of his cause.

The debt explosion was caused by an increase in wealth, rapidly improving information sciences, and most notably a political environment that encouraged borrowing as a way of fueling consumption. Once this horse was let out of the barn, there was no turning back. Unlike Edward III's bankers, contemporary lenders often were treated quite well, more often being rewarded for their foolish choices rather than being run out of town. And like his bankers, they too knew how to disguise excessive interest, not for fear of the Church but in order to lend as much money as possible, even to those who could not ultimately afford to pay it back. They were finally successful in destroying the last vestiges of the centuries-old usury laws. The statutes were considered to be standing in the way of progress.

• • •

THE AMERICAN EMBRACE of consumer credit began in the 1920s. Despite the intervention of the Great Depression and World War II, Americans became so enamored of consumer credit that many could not survive without it. In the postwar period, widespread borrowing by consumers and government became so commonplace that even constant reminders about its dangers went unheeded. When the bankruptcy laws were first introduced, there was no such thing as corporate bankruptcy; the laws were written for individuals only. Over one hundred and seventy years elapsed before debtors (by that time corporations as well as individuals) were protected from their creditors with grace periods allowing them to reorganize their finances and avoid liquidating assets to pay their debts. That change signaled a new attitude toward debt—personal debt in particular—for better or worse.

When the familiar national debt clock was first introduced in 1989, New Yorkers became familiar with its constantly increasing digits as a sober reminder of government borrowing. Ten years later in the 1990s, the clock was stopped as the debt fell dramatically during the Clinton administration, a cause for mild celebration. But the debt revolution had not ended; it was only taking a breather. It reappeared in 2002 as debt began increasing again during the Bush administration. Six years later, the inevitable happened. Perched high on a building at the corner of 43rd Street and Sixth Avenue, the national debt clock stopped its inexorable counting for repairs. The old clock did not have enough digits; so it had to be replaced, on October 9, 2008, to account for the increasing amount of the national debt. As the Treasury and the Federal Reserve scrambled to provide assistance to banks, insurance companies, and other sundry institutions during the financial crisis, the Durst family, who maintain the clock, decided to keep the tradition alive as conditions worsened. Americans did not need a reminder of the burgeoning debt burden facing the government, however. They too were facing a personal debt crisis of equally historic proportions.

The numbers on the debt clock tell only a part of the story of American indebtedness. The amount of private debt owed by consumers also is a considerable figure that is equally difficult to pay down. The approximately $2.5 trillion in consumer debt currently outstanding (mortgages excluded) represents $8,000 per person in addition to the $10 trillion displayed on the debt clock, for $40,000 per person. Mortgages outstanding add another $15 trillion to the bill, for $88,000 per person.

The problem is that consumer debt incurs higher interest rates than mortgage debt does and costs considerably more than the government pays on its debt. Even a crude estimate of how much interest is paid in the United States per year is a sobering number. If the consumer debt is charged at 10 percent per year, mortgages at 6 percent, and government debt at 4 percent, the total annual interest bill is $1.55 trillion, and this does not include corporate or municipal debt payments. An individual's personal share of this debt service is about $5,200, and this figure represents just the average interest charges that must be paid either as interest itself or in the form of income tax. Those payments must be made before one can consider principal repayments, and they do not include the increased government borrowing necessary for the bailout after the financial crisis began.

As the numbers grow, the question constantly asked is how large will they become in the future? That may be the wrong way of looking at the problem. The more important questions are how it got to this point and what must be done to ensure that it abates in the future. An immediate solution is not at hand. High debt levels cause impoverishment; they will in the future as they have done in the past. Interest charges have been viewed with suspicion for three thousand years of Western history, but within the last thirty years they lost their fearsome nature as large numbers of people felt so sanguine about their ability to pay that the odious nature of debt was forgotten. This will prove to be the most egregious error of modern culture.

In the seventy years between the Depression and the current financial crisis, most optimists thought that significant progress had been made in fighting high interest rates, loan sharking, and excessive debt. But that was not the case. Although lenders no longer charged 1,000 percent interest, rates exceeding 20 to 30 percent were not uncommon. The great irony was that state laws had been passed liberalizing interest rates that consumers could be charged. The old usury laws were weakened in an attempt to deal a blow to illegal lenders who charged exorbitant rates, destroying borrowers' ability ever to pay their way out of debt. The door was opened for consumer credit companies to fill the void with interest rates lower than those of loan sharks. Often, their rates were not lower and the consequences were similar.

• • •

LENDING MONEY has always been the second oldest profession and not always the most admired. No other business practice has been as thoroughly criticized for more than two thousand years. Presidents, finance ministers, popes, kings, and saints have labeled interest as a process that drains the life out of the economy, impeding progress at every turn. Historically, lenders have all shared a common trait in the eyes of their critics. Their purpose was to "beggar-thy-neighbor" by charging high rates of interest on loans.

For centuries, antilending feelings were so strong that Dante placed moneylenders in the inferno along with the inhabitants of Sodom. Scores of writers from the early church fathers to Shakespeare and Adam Smith spoke out against them, calling for an end to their evil ways. Smith actually favored regulating the hateful practice, and the Bard wrote famously about the pound of flesh as recompense for Shylock's services.

In a remarkable turnaround, today's lenders are not considered to be exploiting their neighbors but providing them with loans at a so-called market rate. The only true crooks today are those who covertly charge extortionate rates and use strong-arm tactics to make the borrower pay. When debt was something to be considered gingerly, rates of 30 percent were considered usurious. In today's markets, where the odious term "debt" has been replaced by the more complimentary sounding "credit," the borrower who is considered a credit risk is charged high rates of interest to compensate the lender.

A thousand years ago, lending was subject to strict restrictions far removed from today's world. When the lord of a manor lent a peasant two bushels of wheat and demanded two and a half bushels in return, the transaction was considered ordinary and lawful business. But when a moneylender demanded 25 percent on a cash loan, the interest was considered extortionate even though it was the same as the lord's percentage rate. If the peasant could not repay, there were ordinary legal remedies against him and the lender was protected. But the moneylender was in a more precarious position. Charging interest on cash loans was the province of the idle rich or minority groups in Europe, and moneylenders had to be careful because their activities, begrudgingly accepted as necessary in Europe, had little redress. Shylock did not win his case. Lenders could never be assured of protection under the law.

During the Renaissance and Reformation, debt became a more practical, commercial affair. The Italians made a good living from banking and became the best examples of the new leisure class that lent money while avoiding what was known as real work. The great banking houses became the first examples of making a living by investing in intangibles. When the modern banking houses of Rothschild and Baring were founded in the late eighteenth century, they capitalized on a tradition built by the Lombard bankers before them. It was now possible for heads of state to borrow money discreetly rather than hock the crown jewels for urgently needed cash.

For over a thousand years, the distaste for usury and interest remained in place. Ideas about indebtedness and interest then began to change in the early nineteenth century. Developments in the United States would prove crucial to the acceptance of debt in the twentieth century, especially with the long history of bias that had become deeply ingrained in Western European and American practice. The British perpetual war loans, incurred after the defeat of Napoleon, changed the perception of large-scale government borrowings. And the passing of bankruptcy laws in the early nineteenth century began the slow trend toward the general acceptance of debt as a necessary sin that could be remedied. Another subtle change was that usury was defined as *excessive* interest, not simply interest itself.

After surviving as a prohibition for years, the charging of interest underwent a profound change after World War II. A dramatic increase in population provided for easier credit for the masses, especially in the United States, and a relaxed attitude toward indebtedness in general. A subtle shift occurred. What previously had been known as the more onerous term "debt" now took on a positive note. Those in debt were referred to as having "received" credit. The newer version of the old concept made it more palatable to be in debt because now the borrower was being extended credit, as if being given a gift. Personal and corporate indebtedness grew to levels never anticipated fifty years before.

In the contemporary world, the debate still rages about usury but without the moral overtones. The levels of personal and corporate indebtedness in the United States have risen to historic highs. In the recent financial crisis, it finally has been admitted that the precipitous asset value drops were the result of the deleveraging of financial assets by borrowers. Although some originally believed that these levels of indebtedness were sustainable, the chance of a severe depression or recession caused by rising interest rates became more likely as the economic cycle shifted toward rising energy prices and slow economic growth, conditions similar to those last witnessed in the 1930s and 1970s.

The amount of debt financing began humbly but grew to be very large within twenty years. In the 1950s and 1960s, borrowing still was considered somewhat risky, depending on the income of the borrower. But when in the early 1950s Franco Modigliani and Merton Miller published their now famous hypothesis that a firm's debt levels were coincidental to its ability to make money, the old prohibitions began to crumble at the corporate level. The door now was open to higher levels of leverage in the United States. A revolution had begun. Corporate indebtedness increased, and the short-term commercial paper market grew rapidly. With it, consumer credit also exploded because the resurgent commercial paper was used to fund banks' activities in creating credit card debt, a uniquely American innovation from the start.

This credit revolution, beginning after World War II, took hold faster in the United States than in other industrialized countries. The general acceptance of credit cards and extensive corporate credit facilities helped fuel the world's largest consumer-driven economy and enabled it to maintain its premier position as the world's economic engine. America quickly was on its way to becoming a buy-now-pay-later society rather than the save-now-buy-later society it had been before the war. As a result, consumer and corporate indebtedness reached historic levels. Personal levels of indebtedness also became a factor when setting the course of monetary policy. Indebtedness now was an integral part of climbing the economic ladder.

The sheer size of the indebtedness acquired on corporate balance sheets eventually required a market where interest rate risks and currency risks could be laid off. As a result, the swap market was born in the 1980s. Institutional investors and corporations could exchange cash flows based on different types of interest rates. Most did this for hedging purposes, but others did it simply for speculation. Regardless of the intent, swaps proved that debt finally had become fungible and marketable. This marked another turning point in the history of debt. If the concepts had been around four hundred years earlier, Portia would not have had to intervene at the debt trial of Antonio in *The Merchant of Venice*. All she would have had to do was swap the onerous debt owed to Shylock for something based instead on Antonio's future cash flows. If that did not work, then that pound of flesh could have been securitized, sliced into tranches, and sold to other investors.

These new markets, especially the swap market, have made the wholesale trading of debt routine. Most of the old prohibitions against incurring debt were swept aside in favor of increased levels of leverage that could be traded in a secondary market, much like stocks or foreign exchange. As a result, credit became easier to obtain than at any time in history. Easy money found its way into the retail sector as consumption continued to be more important than indebtedness in driving the economy. With interest rates deregulated since the mid-1980s, trading debt-related derivatives was possible and quickly grew to become the fastest growing financial market ever witnessed.

The recent developments in the mortgage industry could not have been possible without securitization. The ability to bundle residential mortgage loans and other forms of indebtedness and use them as collateral for bond borrowing allowed banks to keep their balance sheets clear of many previously created loans and to continue generating credit. The original type of securitization, applied by Fannie Mae, Ginnie Mae, and Freddie Mac in the 1970s, became a standard tool for repackaging mortgages and consumer debt for eventual sale to bondholders. After 2001, the technique became so widespread that the value of the collateral was overlooked in favor of creating even more debt-backed securities, leading to the credit market crisis beginning in 2007. Securitization became the favorite way to fund subprime mortgages and other forms of debt, planting the seeds for the economic crisis that followed.

Securitization also helped create a new generation of mortgage products, many of which had never been seen before as retail financial products. Adjustable rate mortgages, many with sweetener grace periods; balloon payments; negative amortization loans; and reverse mortgages, to mention but a few, all became increasingly popular after the recession in 2001 as homeowners rushed to buy property or to "unlock the equity" in their homes. This great mortgage boom was propelled by a lack of fear for the consequences of potentially rising interest rates and personal debt ratios. Politics played a central role in minimizing the consequences of individual debt. Once interest rates started to rise, the damage to the mortgage market was widespread because many of the loans were originated under very loose lending practices. Then politics struggled to find an answer to the problem.

Although debt and interest rates have been thoroughly retooled and modernized over the last two centuries, the notion of usury is not totally dead in the contemporary world. It is rearing its head again as it becomes clear that many homeowners could not service the interest rates on their loans, creating collateral damage in the derivatives markets and the banking industry. Many of those same homeowners would be surprised to learn that the pesky adjustable rate mortgage (ARM) is only about twenty-five years old. Its appearance on the mortgage scene finally put an end to the usury laws because in twentieth-century America they applied only to fixed-rate residential mortgages. As the history of consumer and mortgage credit shows, the ARM is really an application of consumer credit applied to mortgages. Revolving credit, originally offered by credit cards, helped revolutionize the housing market and then nearly destroyed it.

Underlying these revolutionary trends in finance has been a practice that will be referred to as "cannibal consumption." This consumer practice helped destroy the housing market and consumer credit market because the links between them had become so intertwined. Consumer debt rose from what today seems a meager $6 billion during World War II to over $2.5 trillion today. When consumer debt became too onerous, many households used mortgage refinancing to continue their consumption patterns. Using long-term debt to finance consumption was finally the death knell for the buy-now-pay-later society. Consumers were not only eating out more frequently than in hard times, they were also eating the family residence in the process.

The old admonitions against debt and usury still ring true today. As Mark Twain once remarked, "If a man owes a bank a dollar and cannot pay, he has a problem. If he owes it a million and cannot pay, *it* has the problem." If that happened today, the lender's bank would probably sell some of that debt to another bank, which would buy it with money borrowed at 40 times its own capital. To Mark Twain's admonition we may add this: If a bank owes another bank a billion and cannot pay, *everyone* has a problem.

CHAPTER

1

The Great American Credit Machine

The time to save is now. When a dog gets a bone, he doesn't go out and make a down payment on a bigger bone. He buries the one he's got. —WILL ROGERS

THE STORY IS TOLD frequently, usually when some notable event or holiday is imminent. The Super Bowl is coming in a few weeks and a low-income person succumbs to local advertising and decides to buy a big-screen television to watch the game. Either the individual does not have a credit card or the credit line is not large enough to cover the purchase; so the television is bought from a local furniture rental store on an installment plan.

More often than not, a payment is missed or paid late, and the store repossesses the television. To get it back, the customer must make up the delinquent payment and pay a penalty before it is returned. Unlike unsecured credit card debt, the plan is a throwback to a previous period when consumer loans were collateralized. If one payment is missed or paid late, the television becomes the object of ransom payments. Rather than stop making payments and write the rental off as a bad deal, the customer continues until the debt is finally paid. It has become a matter of pride and has to be completed. By then, the cost is twice the original price or more. Raising the cost marginally is the money order the customer used to make a payment. Money orders are the third most common form of payment behind cash and checks and are used mostly by the poor who do not have bank accounts.

Another consumer walks into a used car showroom, usually located on the strip of a highway outside a city. He sees a nice six-year-old

11

convertible he really likes but it has no price on the windshield. A sales-person asks him how much he can afford to pay for the car per month and he replies maybe $300. The salesperson disappears for a moment and comes back saying that he can sell him the car for $280 per month, with a five-year loan, which is not mentioned immediately. Suddenly, the dream of owning that car has become a reality at less than the cus-tomer thought. He signs on the dotted line.

What the customer does not realize is that he will pay $16,800, al-though the normal price for the car is $11,000. An auto loan at a bank would cost 8 percent for four years, with forty-eight payments of $276 each, totaling $13,248. His loan is for an extra year at a rate of 16 per-cent. But the buyer considers the car affordable. The unwitting cus-tomer fell for the oldest sales trick in the book. Two years later, the stock-exchange-listed company running the used car showrooms, located in another state, is investigated by a major newspaper and even-tually goes out of business. Until that time, the company was a favorite of Wall Street analysts, but most of them admitted they never actually visited it; they only read its financials.

Too bad, most people say, but that is the price for being poor (or bad with numbers) or not understanding the credit process. Those in higher-income brackets are more sophisticated and do not fall into debt traps like that. They are smarter with their money and have more of it as a result. Most use credit cards, and the homeowners among them have home equity lines of credit. One-half of them do not pay their cards off immediately, and some will admit they "occasionally" make only the minimum payment. Others are interested only in how much their mort-gage loans cost them each month, never bothering to ask how much that house will really cost them over time. But they would never fall into the trap of the low-income person.

But they are unaware that they are committing the same faux pas as their lower-income compatriot. Their standard of living is higher, they claim, and their prospects are better; so purchases made on credit will be paid with future income, which, of course, will rise. Optimism about the future fuels present purchases. This is the implicit assumption be-hind modern consumption. When consumers are feeling good or want to display their status in life, they spend money. The sentiment is older than the modern consumer spending spree.

UNTIL THE SEVENTEENTH CENTURY, interest was never stated in terms of a percentage but only as an amount to be paid. Six percent was described as six in a hundred (pounds, florin, etc). Loans were made on the basis of adjusting a borrower's risk factor by altering that amount to perhaps eight per hundred for someone considered of lesser creditworthiness. Interest was quoted this way because most people could not calculate percentages in any event. In addition, not mentioning a true percentage made it easier to skirt usury laws; the calculations would have been known to only a few educated people. The habit of quoting it in payment terms continues today, especially when lenders do not want borrowers to know how much interest they are actually paying, such as the car salesperson or the television seller.

Over a hundred years ago, this was called conspicuous consumption. During the Gilded Age, many people wanted to emulate the rich and famous by spending as much as possible. Today, it has become cannibal consumption. Although the desire to buy goods and services on credit has not declined, the use of one form of credit to pay another has increased exponentially to the point where it has become a cycle of debt with no exit. Charging a minimum payment on one credit card to another or cashing out the equity in a home to pay off consumer debt has become a standard form of temporary payment by millions of consumers. Shifting funds from one account to another has become as common as paying off debt.[1]

In the last forty years, credit has become a commodity. Consumer credit is easy to obtain and expensive to repay. This is a reversal of its history over the last one thousand years when credit was considered a necessary evil but something that should be granted with some sympathy for the borrower, who must have been in dire straits. Why would anyone want to borrow money and be faced with the onerous task of having to repay it? In the past, the term "credit" was not used, however.

The American experience with consumer credit has changed those attitudes substantially. Past generations saw indebtedness for what it

ONE OF THE ORIGINAL models on which economist Thorstein Veblen based his idea of conspicuous consumption in his *Theory of the Leisure Class* (1898) was the Belmont family, known for the lavish lifestyles of father August and his son August Jr. August founded the New York investment banking firm of August Belmont & Company before the Civil War. Within a decade, it was one of the best-known firms on Wall Street, and August began to live a rich lifestyle. In 1849, he married a New York socialite who was the daughter of Commodore Matthew Perry, a hero of the Mexican War. Within a short time, Perry was down on his luck and his son-in-law hired him as the wine steward for his extensive cellar. Fifty years later, August's son was still at the center of the New York social scene, tending to the horse race named after his father and dabbling in banking from time to time. August Jr. was a major figure during the Gilded Age in New York City.

was: being *in* debt. Currently, the brighter side of the ledger is emphasized. A credit card offers $10,000 of credit, not debt. "Credit" has a friendlier ring than "debt." People feel that their financial position must be strong if they are offered that much. Their credit rating must be strong. They go shopping.

The situation was not always so upbeat. Until the 1950s, debt was handled more gingerly than it is presently. Companies borrowed to fund a capital investment project. Individuals borrowed to buy a home and a car. Borrowing had an objective in mind. But attitudes changed quickly. In the 1950s and 1960s, bankers discovered that new financial concepts were floating around that could be used to enhance their bottom lines. Merchants agreed because the concepts would help sales. Manufacturers realized the same. Medieval Italians understood long ago that banking was actually better than working and helped create a new leisure class of those who lent money for a living.

Regardless of the time period, all lenders have had to fight, circumvent, or evade the usury laws. The laws were one of the few universal codes transcending national boundaries, cultures, and religions over time. The Romans set the maximum rate of interest at 10 percent. The Elizabethans did the same fifteen hundred years later. The medieval church forbad interest but tolerated lower levels of 4 to 5 percent because, realistically, business was business. Muslims forbad all forms of it and still do. And the Americans in the nineteenth century adopted many usury laws as an early form of consumer protection. The conflict persisted because modern society is based upon production and production requires customers. Anything standing in its way needed immediate attention.

At the beginning of the twenty-first century, it is difficult to argue that several millennia of usury prohibitions are simply outdated and should be considered relics of the past. They are at the very heart of the experience with consumer credit over the last eighty years. The problem is that their Latin name (from *usuria*) does not connote the modern concept of interest. But as will be seen, every banker knew what usury was, especially in the late 1970s and early 1980s. The only problem was trying to determine how the patchwork of state laws prohibiting it could be circumvented.

The usury laws were designed to protect individuals from predatory lenders. Charging more than a basic rate of interest was considered immoral, uncivil, and criminal. But the old concepts of usury were not helpful. Was usury charging any kind of interest or excessive interest? Excessive interest was implied but exceeding what rate? Were there exceptions to the rule? The laws often were not applied and could easily be evaded by the clever application of simple finance principles or clever marketing. Actual definitions and distinctions made about usury did not help much because they were a minefield for legal arguments about what constituted interest and how it was calculated. The wide variety of the laws meant that some states became credit card centers while others tried to hold the line on what they considered excessive interest. This little-known battle changed the face of the American standard of living.

Being in debt was always the dark side of the American Dream or, before the term was coined in the 1930s, the American tradition of hard work and savings. But much of that tradition was myth. The first debt crisis in the country occurred when a former government official, William Duer, defaulted on speculative loans in the early 1790s, causing the old New York stock market to collapse. His subsequent financial problems and term in debtors' prison, where he died, precipitated the passing of the first bankruptcy law by Congress. Throughout the nineteenth century, being in debt was considered financially imprudent, but lenders could be found on every street corner. The legend held that financially sound people saved money; they did not borrow it. But subsequent revisions to the bankruptcy law proved that borrowing was growing. In its first century, the bankruptcy code dealt only with individual bankruptcy.

The advances made in consumer lending since the 1920s have occurred because of redefinitions of many basic, older concepts of credit plus the influence of new techniques designed to shift credit and counterparty risk from one party to another. The result has been an explosion of credit—and an accompanying explosion in the credit markets—that would have been difficult to imagine eighty years ago. Before the 1950s, being poor meant just that. Today, it means having several credit cards with limited lines and high rates of interest designed to reflect the shaky credit prospects of the cardholder. At the height of the property boom in the early 2000s, it even meant being able to obtain a no-document mortgage loan despite having little prospect of paying it back.

As a result, the poor, students with little income, and many others of limited means have been able to obtain credit during this credit explosion. In reality, the proper term is the "debt explosion." Credit carries a positive connotation, whereas indebtedness properly reflects the circumstances of the borrower. If credit cards were called debt cards, the point would be more striking. The facts that the average American household carries over 13 credit cards and that over six thousand different types of card are presently on offer suggest that this phenomenon is far more than just a trend. It is a way of life and an explosive social time bomb with insufficient regulatory oversight. Combined with the mortgage explosion of the late 1990s and 2000s, it carried the seeds of its own destruction, to paraphrase Marx.

Despite over two millennia of laws against excessive interest, it is clear that in the United States today the usury laws have been nettlesome to lenders but not necessarily prohibitive. Few prosecutions for charging usury were and are brought unless they are aimed at organized crime, usually in connection with illegal gambling. And a visit to any inner city or poor rural area quickly dispels the notion that excessive interest is a thing of the past. Pawnbrokers are still active, and check cashing services, offering the notorious payday loans, can be found on many street corners advertising their services, next to the fast food restaurants and the furniture rental stores. These services appeared in the 1920s and have remained a fixture in places where banks will not venture.

Their rates are simply whatever the market will bear, which in most cases means quite a lot. Pawnbroker rates can easily run as high as 50 percent, and payday loans are in the 20–25 percent range. Both clearly violate excessive interest laws, yet they are operating in the open, with no shortage of customers. Historical similarities are eerie. In the 1920s and 1930s, they were a common sight in American cities. Few could be found in Europe, however.

The payday loan had its origin in the post–World War I years. Workers would sign up to cash a check in advance of payday, receiving a discounted amount of the paycheck's value. When salaries were only $25 per week on average, the worker received around $20 for the advance cash service. Usually the people using this service did not bank at a depository institution but lived from check to check. The amount was clearly in violation of most usury laws at the time but open to interpretation nevertheless. Was it a loan or simply an expensive service? It was a

 MODERN CONSUMERS COULD take some tips from Ben Franklin. He amended his will in 1789 and bequeathed £1,000 each to the cities of Boston and Philadelphia. The money was to be used for the education of apprentices. But there was one catch. It could not be spent for one hundred years. It would have to be deposited in a bank, assuming a compound rate of 5 percent. Then a part could be spent and the balance again deposited for another one hundred years. Following his plan, the first hundred years should have produced a future value of £131,501 for each city, or $640,409. If the entire amount was compounded for another hundred years, it would have been worth £17,292,546 in 1989. The exchange rate enters the picture as well. In 1791, the first year the dollar had a pound value, £1,000 was worth $4,555. Today, the value of the pounds would be approximately $34,585,092. At the old exchange rate of around $4.50, it would have been worth $78,681,084. Unfortunately for the compounded value, the pound has declined over the centuries. And apprentices no longer exist.[2]

service, claimed the lenders, clearly wanting to avoid investigations into the rates charged. And where would the poor get legal advice about it in any case?

Over the last thirty years, much has been written about credit card growth and its effect on society. Most of the commentary tends to be concerned with the social effects of using cards, describing the demoralizing nature of getting into too much debt. Getting out of it is much discussed and has become its own industry, with debt counseling agencies offering their services to the beleaguered. The poison and the antidote have one thing in common: They both usually charge a fee. But the commentaries and studies somehow manage to avoid discussing the financial causes of these problems. One otherwise excellent study of the embattled American consumer devotes one paragraph to the financial roots of what clearly is a financial problem. As compelling as the stories of indebted consumers are, solutions cannot be based on social wreckage caused by excessive debt. Finance is responsible for this explosion but will not offer a solution unless coaxed.

Four Generations of Consumers

Although it is difficult to imagine, American life was materially different eighty years ago. In the 1920s, the gross national product began to be driven by consumption, reaching a level of 67 percent, where it has remained for decades before spiking even higher lately. But making consumer purchases was not as easy as it is today. Different credit rules applied, many of which have since been abandoned. In four generations, modern consumer democracy was born, reflecting a society in which credit is allocated more easily than ever. Four generations of the same hypothetical family can be used as an example of the best and worst that easy credit has to offer.

Following World War I, Joe Consumo returned from overseas military service at the age of twenty-one. Having graduated from high school, he easily found a job in a manufacturing plant as a production worker in an urban location. By 1922, his annual salary was $1,300 per year, enough to take care of his family (a wife and two children). A wide array of consumer products was being offered at the time. His home had a car in the driveway, a tabletop radio, and a few modern kitchen appliances. The major expense was his home.

His modest three-bedroom house cost $3,200 and had a 12-year mortgage of $3,000, the longest available. Any shortfall could be carried on a second mortgage, a common practice in the 1920s. The multiple of house price to his gross earnings (price to earnings multiple) was 2.46:1. The mortgage rate was 5.5 percent, costing him $348 per year in interest and principal repayments. Since no veterans' mortgage program was available, the interest was at market rates. The radio, costing $30, was paid for in cash and the car, costing $700, had to be paid for in four installments of $125 each over two years after a $200 down payment. The total cost of his consumer payments and interest was $49.85 per month, or about 46 percent of his monthly gross salary. In addition, he paid income tax at a rate of 1 percent, but all of his personal interest was tax deductible. There was no Social Security tax in the 1920s, and state taxes had not been introduced.

His mortgage rate was limited by state law to around 6 percent, based on the local usury ceiling. Consumer interest was set at 18 percent and was not limited by the same part of the usury law governing mortgages. For years, there has been confusion about applying the usury laws. In an attempt to finance manufacturing and consumerism, many states raised their usury ceilings to accommodate credit companies. A distinction was made between civil and criminal usury on one hand and between legal and statutory usury on the other. They were essentially the same thing and tried to protect only homeowners or borrowers who signed contracts for real property assets. Installment credit and later revolving credit were, and still are, included in the category of consumer credit. Corporate interest, usually interest paid on amounts over $250,000, remains in its own category.

Members of the second generation, born in the early 1920s, were ready to buy their first house in the early 1950s, after the Korean War ended. Joe Consumo Jr. had a white-collar job at a manufacturing company and a junior college diploma, which he earned after serving in the military. His job paid $5,000 per year, and similar houses to his father's cost $12,000, representing a multiple of 2.4:1. His mortgage was originally for 30 years, a term that was a postwar phenomenon. Because he also served in the military, veterans' mortgages were available to him, reducing the interest rate by about 0.5 percent, to 5 percent. College loans sponsored by the U.S. Department of Education were not yet available. Consumer installment loans could charge as much as 30–40 percent and required relatively short payback periods. All consumer and mortgage interest was tax deductible, as in the past. He would be eligible for one of the new credit cards only if he earned $10,000 per year or more. The tax rates had risen and now were about 20 percent in his income bracket. The average household paid approximately 45 percent of its income in debt payments. Social Security taxes also existed now, although state taxes did not.

His son, Joe Consumo III, was born in the 1950s and was the first in his family to graduate from a four-year college. Shortly after he entered the workforce, the average income was $23,000, and a similar house to his father's was $65,000, a multiple of 2.83:1. He did not serve in the military but did have guaranteed student loans totaling $10,000. (The Department of Education began offering the loans in 1957.) He already had changed jobs twice, although he was still located in Michigan in a finance-related job. Unlike his father and grandfather, he carried several credit cards, charging 18 percent interest, and had outstanding balances totaling $5,000.

The fixed-rate, $58,000, thirty-year mortgage was at an historic high of 12 percent. He qualified easily because his wife was working at the time, something his mother and grandmother did not do. She would give up her job two years later. Adjustable rate mortgages had not yet been introduced. The cost of carrying the mortgage was $600 per month, and the cost of the credit cards was $100 per month because he paid only the minimum payments (2 percent of the outstanding balance). Otherwise the monthly cost would have been $191. His tax rate was 30 percent of adjusted income, so his taxes were about $4,500 per year. His home and credit card debt was 47 percent of his after-tax earnings before property taxes or other bills had to be paid. After paying Social Security tax and state income tax, his debt and tax costs equaled 63 percent of his salary. When his student loans were added, the burden rose to 70 percent.

Joe Consumo IV presented a different financial picture than his father. Born in the 1980s, he acquired a graduate degree and moved to a large city to work. He remained single. In 2007, with two years' work experience, his salary was $100,000, and he lived in a $400,000 condo, which carried a $380,000 mortgage. The salary was $42,000 higher than the average American salary that year, and the condo was almost double the average house price. The multiple was 3.8:1, the highest his family had experienced. The mortgage originally had a 3.50 percent interest rate attached but that was for a three-year grace period, after which it would adjust to the appropriate market-adjustable rate, and the grace period was due to end in one year. Also, because the payment was interest-only, it was only $1,108 per month. But Joe IV is worried because if interest rates do not fall soon, he will be paying 6 percent and the loan amortization will begin, meaning that his monthly payments will increase to $2,400 per month.

Although the latest Joe's numbers are high, his multiple of 3.8 is also the national one, so he is in the same position as millions of others. But other financial problems lurk in the background. The mortgage company making his mortgage did not do a background check, so it is unaware that he borrowed the down payment from his credit cards. He carries ten cards, three fewer than the national household average, although he is single. His credit card debt amounts to $50,000, and he also carries $50,000 in student loans. Presently, his total debt burden is $38,000 per annum before his mortgage refixes. He is also paying only the minimum of 2 percent on his cards. Because he is in the 30 percent tax bracket, he pays 77 percent of his annual salary in debt payments and taxes before Social Security. If the refix were to occur tomorrow, this percentage would rise to about 87 percent.

Joe IV would like to get out of credit card debt but the task is daunting. His current average interest rate on his cards is 14 percent. If he were to pay the balances off together on a three-year program, it would cost him $1,800 per month, a figure he cannot currently afford. If he pays one of the cards late, he also fears that the card companies will declare him in universal default (that is, a late payment to one is equivalent to a default to all). That could raise his rate to 20 percent or more, in which case the monthly bill would rise to $2,000 per month, none of it tax deductible. The tax deduction for consumer interest was removed in 1986. But if he continues to pay only the minimum, his rates will rise in any event because the neural risk management programs used by the credit card companies to assess customer risk will pick up his behavior pattern and send out a signal.

Paying the minimum on his cards means that it will take 626 months to pay off the loan and cost $69,559 in interest. The fifty-two years needed amounts to lifetime interest payments and a substantial penalty for not being able to pay an extra $800 per month for three years. If the rate should rise to 20 percent and he pays the minimum $1,000, it will

THE WORST-CASE SCENARIO for someone in credit card debt can be seen as follows. A card customer owes $10,000 on a card that requires a 2 percent minimum payment. The card carries a 34 percent rate of interest because the customer has a spotty record of paying in a timely fashion and is classified as a high risk. At that rate, it would normally cost $485 per month to pay off the card using a three-year plan, which would actually take thirty-two months. But if the minimum is chosen, it will take 209 months to pay off, including interest of $12,914. If the card is still used, it can trigger an alternative scenario. The minimum rises to 5 percent, or $500 per month.

take 1,488 months to pay the debt and cost $248,114 in interest. All of this is perfectly legal because usury laws do not stipulate how long it should take to pay off a debt, only the interest rate involved. All of these rates fall well within acceptable guidelines.[3]

Joe IV realizes that he should take out a home equity loan and pay off his credit card debt. If he had done this before late 2007, his chances of approval would have been good, but after 2008 the picture was cloudy because of the credit market crisis. Banks are rejecting his applications because of his weak financial ratios. His condo is now worth only $320,000, well below his purchase price and mortgage levels, and he is now in negative equity territory.

One of the striking differences between the first two generations and the third and fourth is the nature of the working household. Until the late 1960s and 1970s, family income was based on the husband's earnings because most women tended to stay at home. When women entered the workforce in larger numbers, household income naturally increased, accompanying the great rise in inflation and interest rates that occurred in the early 1980s. High interest rates brought new practices to the credit card market, and they remained embedded long after rates fell. The annual fee and the minimum payment were both devised to help circumvent the usury laws.

The plight of Joe IV, when compared to the situation of his predecessors, is striking because the indebtedness of his generation is greater than the others. If he were to marry and add another income, his debt ratios would fall. In a weak moment, he also thinks about what it would be like to live in California. New forty- and fifty-year mortgages were just announced there recently. Perhaps the extra time could lower his payments.

Good Business

Putting credit into the hands of so many consumers has been facilitated by rapid developments in finance, especially since 1980. Credit card companies have been able to create credit with considerable help from techniques not existing in the 1970s or earlier. Once these aids were turned loose by Wall Street, they set off a chain reaction that benefited consumers in the end and could also be their end if not reined in.

Originally called "financial architecture," a new type of product design developed on Wall Street when interest rates were high. Its first notable success was the zero-coupon bond, designed for companies and the Treasury. The idea was simple: Bonds were stripped of their coupons and sold as deep discount securities paying a lump sum at maturity. The idea appealed to investors who were willing to forgo interest payments in favor of the future amount to be paid at maturity. Although the idea was simple, it allowed investors to realize something usually undetermined in investments. When they bought a stripped security at a discount and held it to maturity, they knew both the present and future value in advance. The same could not be said with any certainty for other investments.

Ironically, the zero-coupon bond demonstrated the virtues of compound interest that could work in favor of the investor. The success of zeros paved the way for other product design innovations. The architects quickly became known as "financial engineers" because the design called for advanced quantitative skills in designing instruments for specific purposes. Redirecting cash flows, changing risk profiles, and providing collateral backing for new financial instruments became known as "structured finance." Many Wall Street banks opened their own design boutiques dedicated to finding new ways to create new instruments, many times by dissecting and repackaging debt with derivatives, such as futures, or more recently by devising swaps.

Structured finance became the intellectual side of Wall Street, because grasping it required a fair knowledge of the intricacies of debt and the ways in which it could be manipulated. The designers were traders and corporate finance people with sophisticated knowledge of advanced math techniques used to design specialized instruments for investors and companies. In some cases, the designs became templates for others to follow. In other cases, they were ad hoc instruments known only to those immediately familiar with the reason for creating them in the first place. In extreme cases, the investment banks had the models copyrighted so that competitors could not use them.

The esoteric side of structured finance would create problems for Wall Street because it lacked transparency. Even their creators were not sure of what looming problems these one-off instruments had created for balance sheets and ability to meet future obligations once the subprime crisis began. There remains a fear that these sorts of instruments pose unforeseen problems for individual banks and the banking sector as a whole. Because of their lack of transparency, they have the potential to behave like an embedded computer virus, poised to spread throughout the financial system given prompting. But on the consumer credit side, their benefits were clear if not completely comprehensible. They helped fuel a revolution that was already in progress.

The minimum payment employed by credit card companies is a case in point. Seemingly harmless, the idea is deeply rooted in financial theory and practice. Crucial to the process of creating consumer credit is cash flow. Regardless of how it is generated, cash flow has been the primary objective of consumer finance companies for years. As long as cash continues to flow, either as a regular payment or as the minimum payment on a credit card, the lenders' objectives have been met. This causes customers to be in debt far longer than they may have intended.

Even what appear to be nonfinancial companies emphasize cash flow. Companies selling home security services, cable television services, or online services are good examples. Regardless of what service they provide, they are valuable to their shareholders for the steady income they produce. Potential buyers also view them enviously for the same reason. All those monthly payments provide an income stream that is open-ended. Not many businesses can claim that they have steady income on an indefinite basis. In the same vein, certain practices of credit card companies encourage what at first appear to be substandard practices.

The minimum payment option on a monthly statement is a case in point. Set at a percentage of the total amount due, it is too low to retire a debt in three or four years' time, as would be suggested by a standard amortization calculation. Although it extends the customers' payments if exercised frequently, it clearly provides a longer period of cash flow for the card company. It then becomes easier to securitize into a bond or note. Potential bond buyers want to know how long the pool of financial assets supporting the bond will last. If all credit cardholders paid off their debt in one year, that collateral would be less appealing than if it were to last three years or more. By offering customers the minimum payment option, the card company actually is encouraging a longer life for the pool of securities it creates.

Also, the minimum payment, if viewed in terms of a duration calculation, makes much more sense for a card company than for a consumer. Duration is used to determine a bond's sensitiveness to changes in interest rates. All other things being equal, investors normally prefer short durations on fixed-income investments rather than longer ones. But in the case of a credit card securitization, duration means little for the investor because the card company has the option of raising interest rates on the cards for a variety of reasons.[4] Investors are assured they are getting the maximum yield at any time and are less worried than if the bonds were fixed-coupon investments. And customers paying the minimum become favorites of the card companies because their behavior patterns suggest longer repayment periods, ideal for the longer-dated securitized bonds. Duration becomes less important than the traditional longevity of a bond. What is good for the card company and the investor in its bonds is much less favorable for the indebted customer.

Despite the complaints about credit cards that have been heard since their introduction in the 1950s, they do adhere to normal credit practices. Mortgage and consumer loans, like business loans, are tiered according to their standing in the event of a default by the borrower. Mortgage loans carry the lowest rate of interest because of the collateral underlying them. Home equity loans follow, being subordinated to the first mortgage. Auto loans and other forms of collateralized loans are next. Credit card loans are last and bear the highest rates of interest because they are unsecured and depend on the borrower's credit rating. But the lack of collateral is precisely what makes them inimical to the financial health of so many users.

Unlike secured loans, the unsecured types are easier to obtain and use. They also are the most competitive loans, being offered by hundreds of lenders. Because of these factors, they have helped destroy the traditional credit model based on collateral and used for centuries. The American debt model has undergone several distinct phases, but the most revolutionary have occurred within the last fifty years. The credit card phenomenon, based on contradictory notions of easily obtained and unsecured debt being made available to a wide portion of consumers, has created an enduring debt crisis spilling over into other areas of consumer credit and the credit markets overall.

Minimum payments on credit card balances originated early, almost as soon as revolving cards became popular. The payments were not derived by calculating a constant payment on an installment-type loan but were purposely set below a typical payment. For instance, if a payment on a $5,000 credit card balance was $180 per month (one of thirty-six equal payments at an annual rate of 14 percent), the minimum might be set at 2 percent of that amount, or $100. The minimum required by the card company only keeps the account in good order. Of the $180 payment, the actual interest amount is $58.33 per month on the original balance, and the extra $121.67 goes to paying off the principal amount. But if the minimum payment is chosen, then only $41.67 goes to paying down the principal, meaning that it will take much longer to pay off the loan. And, of course, interest is always due on the unpaid amount, so it is in the card companies' interest for customers to pay the minimum.

If the minimum payment is chosen, it will take the borrower 351 months to pay off this loan, adding $6,555 in interest to the bill. If the interest rate changes, then the payoff period will be longer. At 16 percent, it will take 428 months and add $9,328 in interest charges. As Benjamin Franklin once remarked, "Time is money." His other famous quip is equally to the point: "A penny saved is a penny earned."

The minimum payment is the credit card companies' form of an interest-only loan. The minimum goes to paying interest, and the residual is then used to amortize the loan. However, because the amount is small, the loan is extended beyond the normal three- or four-year term of an installment loan. This satisfies the card companies' need to claim the interest as revenue: The longer the interest stream can be extended, the better. Although consumers are aware of the implications of paying only the minimum, there is surprisingly little said about the practice except to warn consumers that it is not fulfilling their financial obligation to themselves. As will be seen in later chapters, the practice has been condemned for decades by consumer groups but continues unabated.

Annual fees on credit cards were introduced while usury laws were still in effect in the late 1970s and the beginning of the 1980s. Fees were assessed in states where usury ceilings were low and waived in others where they were higher. Card companies could then adjust their books accordingly. There has been considerable discussion about the nature of the fees and whether they are actually interest charges in disguise. No credit card lender will admit that they are in fact a disguised version of interest charges, but their history suggests otherwise. They have the added value to card companies of being a form of interest that is charged up front. Lenders do not have to wait for these charges to accrue on customer accounts over time.

Another amount that card companies frequently charge customers is the late payment fee. If a payment is received late, a fee of $25–$35 is added to the outstanding balance. This does not prevent the company from raising the interest rate on the consumer if it wishes. Again, credit card companies will not admit that this type of fee is really disguised interest, but many customers who complain to the card companies about the charges find that they are readily willing to waive them if challenged.

Although credit card companies often extend credit to marginal customers such as recent bankrupts and those with poor credit standings, they can be much quicker in raising rates or denying additional credit. The practice of declaring a debtor in universal default may occur if a payment is missed or received late. By declaring the default, all creditors may exercise their prerogative and penalize the cardholder if they choose. This raises the great irony of the current credit model in use. The granting of credit is assessed on an individual basis (usually by simply extending the offer of easy credit), but denying it later has taken on broader implications. In short, the beginnings of the credit process rely less on an individual's credit scores than do the more seasoned stages when the cardholder has developed a credit history. Then, ironically, procedures that do not apply when credit is first assessed and granted appear, adding more discipline to the process, which lacked it previously.

The actual format of monthly credit card statements also favors the card companies at the expense of customers. The most subtle form of concealing important information, the statements long have been suspected of lulling the cardholder into avoiding the fine print on the statement rather than reading it carefully. The Government Accountability Office (GAO) studied the matter and discovered that several techniques were used to obfuscate the information printed on the statements. Among them were using blurred font types, separating pertinent information that should have been grouped together, emphasis on less relevant information at the expense of important information such as annual percentage rates, and technical language that confused most cardholders. The clear intent of these practices was to provide disclosure as required by Truth in Lending while keeping customers in the dark at the same time. Formatting became another issue in the battle between those favoring credit card company reform and those favoring the old let-the-buyer-beware attitude prevalent in the 1960s and 1970s.

The Extent of the Problem

Despite the complaints about excessive credit card and mortgage debt, some maintain that the problem is illusory. The complaints, they contend, are based only on anecdotal evidence that the average American is in trouble financially or has the potential to be, very quickly; this concern is nothing more than a hysterical reaction to the recent credit market crisis. This view has some validity in official statistics.

But how valid is it? The Federal Reserve publishes a financial obligations ratio, or FOR, monthly. It shows the percentage that debt payments take of disposable household income, more technically called the ratio of debt payments to personal disposable income (after tax). This is published alongside the household debt service ratio (DSR). Both series of numbers are similar but the FOR is broader. The DSR includes the ratio of debt payments to disposable personal income, and debt payments consist of the estimated required payments on outstanding mortgages and consumer debt. The FOR adds automobile lease payments, homeowners' insurance, and property tax payments to the debt service ratio.[5]

According to the statistics, DSR in the first quarter of 2008 was 14.13 percent, and the FOR was higher at 17.82 percent. The numbers seem on the low side. If they are to be taken at face value, there apparently is no debt crisis and never was. In 1998, they were 11.94 and 15.22, respectively. They are now higher but still affordable. Going back another ten years to 1988, the percentages were 11.95 and 15.23, remarkably similar to those of 1998. Putting them into context underlines a problem with interpreting statistics.

According to these statistics, the average American family surveyed in 2007–2008 spends only 14.13 cents on the dollar for mortgage and consumer debt. If the extra items are added to the bill, the percentage rises to 17.82 cents on the dollar. Put another way, these households have between 82 cents and 86 cents after consumer debt and mortgages are paid every month. Renters faced higher percentages, with a FOR of almost 26 percent at the beginning of 2008. It does not require much thought to realize that numbers of that sort suggest that there is no debt crisis; perhaps only one of confidence.

How reliable are these debt service ratios produced by the Fed? The first and second generations of the Consumos cannot be compared to the numbers because the statistics only began in 1980. But the third generation had a FOR of about 14 percent, and the fourth generation has one of almost 18 percent. In the latest case, Joe IV appears to be an aberration with a FOR of almost 80 percent, whereas his fellow citizens appear to be much more frugal. Unfortunately, that is not the case. Even his great grandfather's generation had ratios weaker than 18 percent at a time when credit cards did not exist.[6]

Similar confusion can be found when discussing even what seems to be the simplest effects of card indebtedness. In 2002, the American Bankers Association (ABA) estimated, based on a survey, that 47 percent of existing cardholders were paying the minimum balance on their cards, 13 percent were paying one-half of their outstanding balances, and a further 3 percent had stopped making payments. The numbers improved in 2005 when 40 percent were paying the minimum but 5 percent had stopped. At the same time, 17 percent were paying at least one-half.

A year later, the Government Accountability Office put an entirely different spin on the numbers, claiming that one-half of all card customers paid no interest on their balances. That positive claim ignores what the other half are paying on their balances, if anything. Even more surprising is a recent GAO report that assumes the average American household has only 3 percent of its total annual debt bill in credit card balances. Slightly over 80 percent of its debt bill is devoted to mortgage payments and about 11 percent to installment loans such as autos. The report assumes credit card balances are not significant enough to cause repayment problems. The GAO concludes that "credit card debt remains a small proportion of overall household debt, including those with the lowest income levels . . . credit card balances as a percentage of total household debt actually may have been declining since the 1990s."[7] As will be seen later, that is true, but only because of cannibal consumption. Without an enormous increase in home equity lines of credit, the balances would have been much larger.

The card companies do not make the issue any more simple. Even what appear to be consumer-friendly gestures from them produce some unsettling problems. Some card companies raised the minimum payment required after the 2001–2002 recession from 2 percent to 2.5 or 3 percent. They claimed that this new calculation would help customers get out of debt earlier. (There had been complaints about the minimum payment at the time.) But the catch is that if customers cannot afford the new percentage, then more defaults will occur, casting shadows over the entire credit card industry. The card industry already has a political

STRETCHING THE SIMILARITIES between finance and consumption, *The Telegraph* (UK) once noted that "high finance differs from haute cuisine in at least two ways. The first is that bankers are better paid than chefs, and the second is that the customers have more difficulty understanding the complexity and variety of investment products than they do in interpreting restaurant menus. Moreover, whereas a meal is digested once, an investment product can be recycled many times."

problem, and additional consumer complaints will not alleviate it but only heighten calls for new regulations to police the industry.

High personal leverage and minuscule margins like the ones experienced by Joe IV remain stable only in a stable interest rate environment. Any small disturbance, like a decline in income or a rise in interest rates, can erode the ratios to the point where personal solvency becomes an issue. At present, Joe IV appears to have little prospect of getting out of debt unless he behaves like a bank. He either makes more money or sells some assets to make his financial ratios stronger. If he *were* a bank, regulators would close him down because his capital base is not strong enough.

This latter point is one of the problems with the current consumer credit model. He cannot be closed down unless he does so voluntarily. As will be seen later, the bankruptcy laws have become less friendly to potential personal bankruptcy filings since 2005; so if he were to file, the repercussions would be greater than in the period 1978–2005. More to the point, no one can force him to cut back on spending, nor is there any incentive for him to do so. As long as his lack of cash flow enhances some investors' portfolios, no pressure will be applied. And if he does eventually declare bankruptcy, it will mean only a temporary interruption in credit card offers in his mailbox.

Another more conservative interpretation of credit card use produces a friendlier conclusion for the consumer credit phenomenon. Much of the evidence against card use in particular is anecdotal in nature and assumes that consumers are not particularly rational when they have cards in their wallets and a burning desire to make purchases. This produces behavior that is inimical to their well-being, and, when the smoke clears, they find themselves overwhelmed by debt. But there is a rational side to the debate as well.

The consequences of credit card use have entered the debate about whether government should regulate the industry more extensively than it has in the past. This puts the argument in the traditional regulation-versus-antiregulation framework. Those who believe that consumers (some or all) use cards irrationally and that they are lured by card company offers of low teaser rates and other incentives eventually will call for government action to protect consumers from themselves. If you cannot use your card responsibly, then nanny needs to protect you. The old debate about whether legislation can change human nature is resurrected again.

On the other side of the coin is the rationalist argument that consumers are more rational and use cards (for the most part) prudently. A consumer who carries both a credit card and a debit card knows that the credit card usually offers up to thirty days of free credit if the bill is paid on time. So when the cardholder makes that next purchase, the credit card should be used and the debit card, which will be charged immediately, should be kept in the wallet. The consumer is acting rationally although the nannies will call the transaction nothing more than another needless credit card use.[8]

Taken one step further, this argument appears much weaker. If the customer charged $100 and did actually receive one full month's credit, the current rates of interest suggest that a grand total of 20 cents was saved because annual money market rates are at 2.5 percent ($2.50 on the balance divided by 12). Even if that shopper spent all day making purchases, it is doubtful whether the savings would pay the parking bill. The argument that credit cards are an efficient tool of personal money management is valid only when the balance is large or interest rates increase. Otherwise, the debt trap argument is still valid. Thinly disguised arguments about efficiency tend only to encourage more spending when simple math proves it is not worth the effort.

It is doubtful many consumers do the math when making a purchase, but some will be lured by this attractively constructed argument that could well have been written by a card company marketer. The argument is superficially appealing because there is an unproven suspicion that many consumers are not capable of doing the simple math needed to make a decision about their opportunity gains. And the matter of opportunity gains is even more problematic. Most consumers would assume they are gaining at the credit card interest rate in the example, not the money market rate available to them if they could somehow invest the money for one month.

The argument that credit cards offer consumers more flexibility is more valid and has greater appeal in describing consumer behavior. Some studies of consumers done in the 1970s demonstrated that they did understand most of the simple points of consumer lending, and many times better than they understood their other consumer rights such as purchase returns and lemon policies.[9] And more recent studies have demonstrated that the lack of a tax deduction for consumer interest has led many to borrow against the equity in their homes, especially since 2002. But what is not clear is whether this is something consumers understood or something that was simply sold to them by lenders eager to increase business. The education element is important because assuming rational consumer behavior means that consumers are acting in their own self-interest, which may not be the case with home equity loans.

Ultimately, arguing about interpretations of consumer behavior is fruitless unless an institutional element is added. This is where Wall Street enters the picture. When investment banks are involved, arguments about acting in one's own self-interest fade quickly. As will be seen, developments in consumer credit were not possible without the ingenuity of Wall Street banks, eager to encourage business with borrowers of bonds and commercial paper. To lure that business, banks developed many variations of the older practice of factoring accounts receivable, from asset-backed securities and structured investment vehicles to multitranche debt obligations with varying degrees of risk. Once bankers set their sights on credit card receivables, the consumer-credit-generating machine revved to new speeds, from levels that were already sounding alarm bells to the credit nannies.

The Great American Debt Machine encourages consumption because perpetual indebtedness benefits the investors who purchase it through securitized assets, relying on the cash flows it produces. A certain degree of default is normal and expected because there has to be some risk expected in the overall process. As will be seen in Chapter 3, these lenders are not behaving like creditors, and consumers are not behaving like borrowers. They are on opposite sides of a marketable investment. The holders of the debt depend on it for cash flow and smile when the portfolio extends itself. The debtors, on the other hand, smile when they can extend their payments with the creditors' blessings because they can avoid a nasty bill they cannot afford. As will be seen in the next chapter, this is a violation of the basic rules of the credit model used in the 1920s. This application of portfolio theory developed in the 1950s and 1960s, discussed in Chapter 3, has overwhelmed traditional borrower and lender behavior and created new credit relationships that have turned older, time-tested methods upside down.

Chapter Notes

1. Bank-issued credit cards are also called "general-purpose" cards and have become the most popular kind because many of the large banks offer customers more than one type and also service cards of other nonbank issuers.

2. The pound sterling remained in the $4 range until the early 1930s.

3. Calculations are based on the debt repayment calculators that can be found at www.Bankrate.com.

4. Duration calculations discount the cash flows expected by an appropriate rate of discount, weight them for the time period received, sum them, and divide by the total number to reach the average number of periods it will take to get back a portion of the price paid for those cash flows. A shorter number of periods suggests less sensitiveness to interest rate changes than longer periods.

5. Debt service ratios are taken from the Federal Reserve Board, "Household Debt Service and Financial Obligations Ratios," published monthly. These figures can be found at www.federalreserve.gov/releases/. The Fed notes that "the limitations of current sources of data make the calculation of the ratio especially difficult. The ideal data set for such a calculation would have the required payments on every loan held by every household in the United States. Such a data set is not available, and thus the calculated series is only a rough approximation of the current debt service ratio faced by households." Clearly, it omits amortization on mortgages, property taxes, and principal repayment on loans, all of which cannot be separated practically from interest.

6. Reading between the lines of statistics to ascertain the true plight of American households is one of the topics of Peter Gosselin's *High Wire: The Precarious Financial Lives of American Families* (New York: Basic Books, 2008). One of many points worth noting is the income levels of many American families. While growing at a slower rate than in previous years, the levels within the last ten years are solid but can be erratic because income is now derived from less constant sources than in the 1950s or 1960s. When a down year follows an up year in income and also coincides with an emergency or unforeseen effect, the effect can be devastating, but the statistics paint a more stable picture.

7. The GAO report referred to here is "Credit Cards: Increased Complexity in Rates and Fees Heightens Need for More Effective Disclosures to Consumers," U.S. Government Accountability Office, September 2006.

8. A summary of the rational approach to the matter of credit cards versus the behavioral approach can be found in Tom Brown and Lacey Plache, "Paying with Plastic: Maybe Not So Crazy," *The University of Chicago Law Review*, Vol. 73, No.1 (Winter 2006): 63–87. The authors use a broad survey commissioned by Visa to make their point.

9. An example of a 1970s survey of consumer knowledge and information can be found in William H. Cunningham and Isabella C. M. Cunningham, "Consumer Protection: More Information or More Regulation," *Journal of Marketing*, Vol. 40, No. 2 (April 1976): 63–69.

2

Creating a Consumer Credit Society in the 1920s

Nine out of ten people one meets in the street cannot even today go to a regular bank and borrow money.
—TWENTIETH CENTURY FUND, 1930

THE PERIOD LEADING TO World War I ushered in a new era in American business. From the Civil War to 1910, great investments were made in the American infrastructure and mass distribution systems. Railroads linked the country, electric power was becoming available, the telephone system was becoming capable of long-distance calls, and productive capacity in many industrial sectors was at historic highs. The United States had become an industrial nation within the brief span of a half century.

As many industries developed, capital was raised to help finance production. Wall Street developed alongside the new industries and raised capital to fund their balance sheets. Much of that capital came from abroad. Foreign investors, notably the English and the Dutch, provided much of the long-term funds by investing in bonds of the railways and the municipal securities of many of the larger cities. The United States clearly was dependent on foreign capital because the average American was not capable of saving enough to help fund these investments from home. This was referred to in the 1920s as the *period of production capital.*

When many goods were finished, more capital was needed to fund distribution systems so that the products could be moved to market. Investments in faster shipping and railroads were necessary to ensure that the goods made it to market in timely fashion, ushering in what was called the *period of distribution capital.* But what was lacking was a means of financing the purchases of this wide array of goods. The banking system was fragmented and mostly parochial. The Federal Reserve was founded only in 1913, and banking until that time was in the hands of state regulators who rarely permitted out-of-state banks to operate within their individual borders. What is today known as consumer credit was far less developed than corporate credit.

At the turn of the twentieth century, Americans began buying new consumer goods on an unprecedented scale. Prosperity followed the brief Spanish-American War, and President William McKinley's administration was marked by optimism for the future. Before World War I, the recently developed automobile and household appliances were in strong demand. Chain stores proliferated around the country, creating a nationwide system of consumer stores long before the country had a genuine national banking system. Former dry goods stores like Sears, Roebuck and Company and Montgomery Ward & Company were joined by chains of grocery stores like The Great Atlantic & Pacific Tea Company (A&P), capitalizing on the new mobility created by cars.

If consumer markets were to develop and allow workers to purchase the wide array of goods available, society would have to switch from the pay-as-you-go basis to which it was accustomed to one allowing consumers more latitude in paying for purchases. Making matters more complicated, the permanent income tax for individuals was introduced for the first time in 1913, although the rates were very modest for the average working person. Those most affected were those with higher incomes. More importantly, the first corporate tax had been introduced in 1909, and it would rise to high levels during the war. From the beginning of the income tax, interest payments were tax deductible for both corporations and individuals. Individual taxpayers could deduct interest payments made on cars and homes and would continue to do so until a tax reform was passed in 1986. But in the 1910s, it was felt that business had to find a way to stimulate more demand in the face of this new hurdle.

The wealthy classes always had been able to enjoy a high standard of living because they possessed equity, in terms of either real property or intangibles like securities. The working classes were not in the same position, many people living from paycheck to paycheck with little savings or property. Despite these apparent obstacles, business still developed methods to sell goods that people thought they needed. The average people in the street wanted to live as well as their wealthier counterparts. Consumption accounted for two-thirds of the U.S. gross national product by 1929. Economist Thorstein Veblen, a not-so-subtle critic of the carefree spending society, dubbed this attitude "conspicuous consumption" as early as 1898. Although his model was the lavishly spending Wall Street banker August Belmont Jr., within 20 years everyone wanted to behave as if they had a source of funds in excess of their wages. What was needed was consumer credit. In typical American fashion, it appeared quickly—and with a vengeance.

Part of the reason consumer credit would spread so quickly in the early twentieth century had to do with the American psyche. Society had long since become money centered, and Wall Street myths were already well established. American Society was characterized by a dualism that became conspicuous. Great wealth was admired and a worthy goal, a sort of Horatio Alger story for everyman. On the other hand, the very wealthy were usually assumed to be corsairs of commerce, deftly exploiting every loophole to be found, whereas the average guy in the street stood by helplessly. Wall Street was a long distance from Main Street, both geographically and emotionally, but it was deeply ingrained in popular folklore by the time the Panic of 1907 occurred. Then, as in a previous crisis thirteen years earlier, John Pierpont ("J. P.") Morgan orchestrated a bailout of the New York money market that helped the financial markets right themselves, avoiding further financial catastrophe. As a result, the legend of the Wall Street financier grew considerably. Bankers were able to save the country in its darkest financial hours, an impression that would linger for the next twenty-five years before government put a halt to it.

Thinking of bankers and financiers as pop culture icons is no longer as common as it once was. In the 1920s, they were highly popular figures, commanding attention from the press and the populace. Their thoughts on investments and politics were sought and widely reported. J. P. Morgan once even had a popular limerick written about him, describing him as a titan. Industrialist John J. Raskob of General Motors fame, and a chairman of the Republican National Committee, wrote a well-known magazine article entitled "Everyone Ought to Be Rich" that became the battle cry of the stock market frenzy. As 1929 approached, the attention turned toward adulation.

The president of National City Bank (today Citibank), Charles Mitchell, was the most popular of all bankers in New York City. Known for walking to his Wall Street office in the morning, he was photographed frequently, followed by members of his admiring public, and often joined by colleagues. His popularity was based on his business philosophy. National City was more of a retail bank than any other large city bank, serving retail customers with both loans and securities distributed by its affiliate, the National City Company. The bank was intent on becoming a financial department store, the Sears, Roebuck of financial institutions. If a customer needed it, he should be able to find it there. Mitchell considered New York his bank's oyster, and for a decade he was correct. All of this buoyancy was accompanied by a rash of new financial innovations.

Buy Now, Pay Later

The exuberance of the 1920s, like that of more recent decades, was based on a postwar prosperity that raised the standard of living substantially. All of the credit generated during the postwar years had improved the lot of workers substantially, and Mitchell was their hero, the symbol of what a banker should be: optimistic, cheery, and prosperous. Credit was easy to obtain, and the range of consumer goods available greater than at any time in American history. It was this sort of atmosphere that led people to borrow and purchase and then borrow more. The second mortgage was now popular because one no longer accommodated many homeowners' desire to buy more and more goods. Old ideas about the burdens of debt were quickly disappearing in the face of its more positive interpretation from the lenders' point of view—credit. *The New York Times* noted in 1923 that "it might be desirable to draw a line between credit and debt but it is difficult to find the dividing point."

Wall Street was at work helping to restructure American industry and infrastructure. Although the era of the trusts was finished, many mergers occurred, consolidating smaller companies into industrial giants. General Motors Corporation, American Telegraph and Telephone Company (AT&T), General Electric Company, and others had been reorganized and were more profitable than ever. Other auto manufacturers burst on the scene, offering a dizzying array of models and styles. Many urban homes had telephones and electricity. The electrical utilities were being consolidated into giant holding companies, under the assumption that economies of scale would help lower consumer rates. The assumption proved incorrect. It was not the first, or last, time that that sort of argument would be heard when arguing for the consolidation of goods and services.

Even before the war, when the boom was only a few years old, there was a feeling of unease about the new consumerism. There was fear that consumers were spending too much and saving little if any money. The fear coincided with concerns about the level of drunkenness and alcoholic consumption, especially among working people, that eventually led to Prohibition. But Prohibition and the ever present usury laws had one thing in common. During the 1920s, they would be violated repeatedly, to the point where both became almost useless. Lower Manhattan alone had more speakeasies selling alcohol than cops on the beat, and limits on the amount of interest charged were nothing more than a myth in many states.

Clearly, society was changing rapidly, and the level of spending became a national policy concern. Politicians, bankers, and clerics all exhorted the public to save for a rainy day, to little avail. Then a more formal campaign began. A film production company named Vitagraph Studios collaborated with the American Bankers Association to produce *The Reward of Thrift* in 1914, an eight-minute skit touting the virtues of saving and the results of profligate spending. The idea of the short film was to promote savings so that the country would not have to be dependent on foreign capital, which had been the case since before the Civil War. While the idea was commendable, another motive was not far below the surface.

Vitagraph was the same film company that had produced a short film supposedly showing American troops storming a Spanish installation in Cuba in 1898 during the Spanish-American War. That film had helped to inspire patriotism and support for the war although it was later revealed that it was filmed in Manhattan, not Cuba. Along with other silent films of the decade, its propaganda value was substantial. The motive in 1914 was similar. Bankers wanted people to save more money since the country supposedly was last in savings among industrialized countries. Bankers also recognized the potential of consumer demand, especially if they could channel it and make a profit.

During World War I, the thrift movement, as it became known, blossomed on several levels and urged citizens to save as much as possible. For its part, the government wanted people to channel their funds into government war bonds. Post office savings banks also were established, providing a convenience that many savings banks and credit unions could not match. Woodrow Wilson suggested that each dollar invested in war bonds would mean less competition for the government's fund-raising and would ensure success. Saving money became the patriotic duty of everyone, and the results were highly successful. All that cash also proved tempting to bankers.

The United States' long-standing affinity for consumer credit began in earnest in the 1920s, in the wake of the war. At the time, the changes in buying power and its implications for corporate America and Wall Street were clear, and a long boom began that only ended with the 1929 stock market crash. Like all booms, the 1920s produced a marked increase in the American standard of living that permanently changed lifestyles and attitudes toward debt. Consumer debt more than doubled in the 1920s, although the numbers were low by contemporary standards. A population of 60 million had about $7 billion in consumer debt before the 1929 crash, representing an indebtedness of $117 per person, or about 8 percent of the average annual income.[1]

With so much credit available, it was possible to become overextended by having too many lines of credit from different merchants or lenders. By 1925, over five hundred installment credit companies existed. To solve that problem, credit agencies developed that would keep manual tabs on account holders provided by merchants and lenders and take notes on them on a daily basis. One of the problems these agencies identified was the customer who took his own good time paying back a loan rather than adhering to a payment schedule. This especially was important because a repossession of goods purchased but in arrears often occurred as long as loans required collateral.

The years following 1921 surprised many commentators who were expecting rocky economic conditions. A recession occurred in 1920, and many feared inflation would follow, as is usually the case when pent-up demand for goods and services is expected to explode after several years of war and market distortions. Economist Irving Fisher and a host of congressional representatives and commentators fully expected inflation to raise its head, but the opposite occurred. Prices remained relatively stable, and the consumer trend built up even more steam.

The boom did not produce the anticipated inflation in part because it was fueled by savings. The huge amount of Liberty War Bonds sold during the conflict matured in the early 1920s, putting money back into the hands of the public. Much of that money found its way into the market for real estate, stocks, automobiles, and, most notably, newfangled consumer products like household appliances and tabletop radios. The Marconi device, better known as the "talking machine," developed by David Sarnoff and his RCA Corporation, became the must-have product of the decade. The American household of the period had to have its own car parked in the driveway and at least one radio set in the house. The house was financed by a longer-term mortgage than in the past. But the new consumer society was still markedly different from the one that would follow.

Despite the fact that many of these new purchases were financed by credit, it still was quite different from the credit that would develop after World War II. Credit facilities were available but they were hardly universal. A large percentage of the population continued to pay for goods and services when needed, and most did not have banking facilities. The credit phenomenon of the 1920s was all the more remarkable because it involved probably only 10–20 percent of the population. Most consumers banked, if they banked at all, at savings and loan associations, credit unions, or savings banks rather than at commercial banks. Banks with "savings" in their names existed since the early nineteenth century, whereas credit unions were founded later, in 1909. As their name implies, commercial banks dealt for the most part with companies, not individuals. The retail banking that did occur was marketed to the wealthiest 10 percent of the population. It was not until A. P. Giannini founded the Bank of Italy in California (later renamed the Bank of America), after the turn of the century, that a commercial bank actively sought retail business. Once the bank and others like it grew and began to expand, the consumer boom found institutional support. Previously, consumer credit normally was extended by merchants, happy to extend credit terms to buyers of their goods and services, and by other small, specialized consumer lenders.

Traditionally, merchant lenders allowed customers to put away money on a regular basis in order to make future purchases. That arrangement, typically called the "layaway plan," was marketed under a variety of names, the Christmas Club being one of them. A customer would begin setting aside cash with a merchant or bank in January, and by the following Christmas he or she would be able to spend the money.

The merchant set the goods aside but would not release them until payment had been received in full. The major difference between those plans and the contemporary ones is that the older ones required consumers to save *before* spending, not after it. Technically, the layaways were a method for funding a future purchase, not a means of retiring existing consumer debt. The horse was still pulling the financial cart in this case, not walking behind it, as it would later in the century.

While layaways would remain popular for several more decades, they were eclipsed by the new installment credit. The concept was simple but still somewhat radical at the time. Consumers were required to make a down payment on a purchase and then pay the balance in equal installments. Sears, Roebuck established its consumer credit operation in 1911, one of the first established retail stores to do so. Automobiles were the first big-ticket items to be bought in this manner. The Maxwell Motor Car Company was the first manufacturer to offer its cars on time in 1916. It required a payment of 50 percent down and the balance to be paid in eight equal installments. Most other car companies followed suit.[2] Big-ticket items were the first to offer standard installment credit, although eventually it would be offered on all sorts of consumer goods. The only qualification was that the items purchased had some relatively long lasting value so that they could be repossessed if the borrower fell behind on payments.

The concept of collateral was still a prerequisite for lending, indirectly if not directly. When customers wanted a home mortgage, they would normally use a building association with which they had built a relationship of savings over a period of time. Ordinarily, customers had to have a savings account at the small bank in order to apply for a mortgage. Often, the account had to be kept open after a house was purchased, so it was in the bank's best interest to do the math to ensure that the customer could afford the mortgage payments. In banking terms, the customer had to have a small compensating balance for the loan. And the mortgage terms were far less generous than after World War II. In the mid-1920s, a standard mortgage had to be repaid in three years. The building associations and savings banks offered more generous terms, stretching as far out as eleven years and seven months. Most mortgage financings actually were a blend of primary mortgages with second mortgages to produce longer repayment periods, although amortization periods of twenty years were rare. The smaller lenders clearly had the advantage over the larger ones because they knew their customers and did the majority of the residential mortgage business.

Those sorts of restrictions did not prevent residential housing from increasing dramatically. Housing starts quadrupled between 1921 and 1925 and tripled again by 1928. Outstanding mortgage debt followed suit.

The property boom also had its seedier side. Florida was the boom state and became a synonym for property speculation. The boom began after World War I when Charles Ponzi and other property promoters began touting the virtues of investing in hot scrub pine land. Many people bought parcels based only on newspaper ads touting Florida's virtues. Easy financing was made available. The publicity in the New York and Midwest newspapers helped prices rise. The Palm Beach area was being developed with $30 million. Small investors thought they saw their opportunity and followed suit. The boom continued for another seven years before reality set in. When the property bubble burst, scores of land speculators and promoters fled the state as quickly as they had arrived. Not all parts of the boom produced profits.

The average citizen's second largest cash purchase, the automobile, was facilitated by clever financing so that everyone could get behind the wheel. Immediately after the war, manufacturers quickly recognized the need for extending credit to customers. In 1919, General Motors created the General Motors Acceptance Corporation (GMAC), following in Maxwell's footsteps, to lend money to its dealers and customers. Within three years, the operation was a success, lending over $225 million for purchases. GMAC became the largest installment credit company in the country, lending money to both dealers and customers. The concept proved so popular that Citroën of France soon began using it to provide credit to buyers of its cars. The Ford Motor Company established its credit subsidiary in 1928 with the avowed purpose of helping everyone own a Ford at the lowest cost possible. Ford stated that it was not establishing the company to make a profit but only to provide finance for buyers. Its success was noteworthy. Within two years, it had provided $425 million in financing to 800,000 "time" buyers. At the time, the least expensive car cost slightly less than one year's salary for the average worker. Wages rose from about $1,100 to $1,500 over the decade.

Installment credit had become so popular by 1926 that many of the leading lenders joined together to form a discount company that would serve as a backup facility by purchasing the lenders' notes at a discount to provide liquidity. (There was a general fear that abuses by some companies could lead to problems in the credit market.) The American Rediscount Corporation was formed with capital of $31 million; it was touted as the Federal Reserve for installment companies. However, not all companies involved in installment credit wanted to remain involved. In 1928, General Electric sold its installment credit subsidiary to the Industrial Acceptance Corporation. Founded only seven years earlier, the subsidiary provided financing mostly to dealers of GE products. The company claimed that the installment business required the kind of expertise it could not provide and that a sale was the best way to ensure its continued existence.

By the end of the 1920s, installment credit had become the most popular type of credit granted. Of the approximately $4 billion credit generated annually, $2.5 billion was installment credit. The next two most popular sources were unlicensed lenders (including loan sharks) and pawnbrokers, representing $750 million and $600 million annually. The continued existence of these two demonstrated that, despite the advances made in consumer lending, society still was relying heavily on sources that had been popular in the past. Unlicensed lenders comprised a wide variety of sources, but the best known was one that had plagued American society for generations.

Swimming with the Sharks

In 1935, a man named Arthur Flegenheimer was shot on a Newark, New Jersey, street. During the dark days of the Depression, the event would have gone unnoticed except for his pseudonym. Flegenheimer was better known to the public as Dutch Schultz, a notorious racketeer who made a handsome living in crime. Only after the event did it become known that Schultz was the target of a wide criminal investigation in New York.

The New York Times remarked that "the ancient racket of usury, refurbished with the strong-arm methods of modern gangsters, was said yesterday to have been an important contributing factor which brought about the shooting." Indeed it was. Schultz was a loan shark, and New York authorities revealed that his racket charged unwitting borrowers a rate of interest on loans of 1,042 percent per year.

Even without the benefit of a financial calculator, it was not difficult to determine that loans of that sort could never be repaid. Schultz was only the most recent practitioner of the ancient art, as the newspaper implied. Disguised interest and its higher-rate cousin—usury—had been decried for centuries, even millennia, but were still being practiced overtly in Depression-era America.

During the 1920s and 1930s, organized crime captured the headlines. Producing illegal spirits during Prohibition gave way to loan sharking for mobsters in the later 1930s. A loan shark's services were in demand because the large banks still did not deal with the small saver, and when a loan was needed, many small-business people and individuals sought the services of a "private" lender. Tough economic times put their services in demand. The rate of interest exacted by the lender often was so high that any possibility of paying back the loan was only a dream. Loan sharking was therefore a major social and economic problem in the first several decades of the twentieth century. The high rates charged choked the ability of the unfortunate borrower to make any real economic progress. But there were other methods of exacting high rates of interest where the charge was taken before the loan was made. And not all loan sharks wore dark raincoats and did business in dark alleys. Many simply were unlicensed loan companies, some with branches, preying on the cash-strapped workingman. Besides making a mockery of usury laws, loan sharking became the target of legislation aimed directly at usury.

A 1928 example illustrates the problem that excessive interest caused small business and demonstrates how difficult it could be to decipher the claims of borrower and lender. A sad story emerged from the U.S. attorney's office for the Southern District of New York in Manhattan during a hearing on loan sharking. A cab driver in New York needed $100 to repair his taxi, did not have the cash, and applied to a loan company to meet his needs, signing a loan for $150, pledging the taxi as collateral. He began making payments when the cab broke down again and needed more work. He applied for another loan. The lender agreed if he used a repair shop provided by the lender, which the borrower agreed to do. The $70 in repairs cost $100 extra, but the lender required new loans and notes now worth $365. By this time, the cab driver could no longer afford to service the loan and had to move in with his mother while his wife left with their infant child and moved in with her family.

The saga continued when the driver refused to pay any more interest and the lender seized the car. The driver got a court order quashing the seizure and went to pick up his car, only to be told that it had been sold and the new buyer was already making payments. He could retrieve the car for a total of $567, which amounted to 567 percent of the original amount needed. Eventually, the sad story reached the U.S. attorney in Manhattan, who began an investigation into Manhattan loan companies. His office offered little consolation for borrowers in similar situations. "Once in the clutches of a loan shark," he noted, "release is very difficult and any man who gives as collateral any property far in excess of it is very likely to lose it."

 ONE FACT ABOUT medieval and ancient discussions of interest is that no stated rate of interest was ever discussed, only the number of units to be paid back. Although modern interest is discussed by the rate charged and the frequency of compounding, the concept appears to have been known to early mathematicians although not clearly mentioned. The first interest rate problem known to have been posed in Western literature was in 1207 by the Italian mathematician Leonardo Fibonacci. The problem posed is perplexing to modern finance because of a variable he omitted. In his *Book of Calculations,* Fibonacci asked how many denari a man would have in one hundred years if he began with 1 denaro, which would double in five years. His answer—1,048,576 denari—was solved not by compounding at a rate of interest but by simply squaring 2 nineteen times. His other well-known book was *The Book of Squares.* In more modern terms, 1 was compounded at 14.355 percent, compounded semiannually for a hundred years (or 7.175 percent for two hundred time periods). The answer is the same and more recognizable to modern finance.

The question becomes strategic. Why did Fibonacci state his problem as a solution to a squaring problem rather than ask the question algebraically, stating a rate of interest? Part of the answer has to do with decimals. Fibonacci was not familiar with decimals.

His contribution to Western culture was the introduction of Arabic numerals into mathematical use. Until that time, math used Roman numerals, which were cumbersome for performing more advanced mathematical calculations. Because he would not have been able to state 14.355 percent, the squaring solution to the problem was the only one available. When decimals and interest tables finally were introduced, interest could be stated in percentage terms, not in the older fashion, where 6 percent would have been stated as six in one hundred. It would have been feasible to state interest as 14.355 percent in Fibonacci's problem, but the tables would be stated only in whole numbers, 14 or 15 percent, as they still are today.

Fibonacci probably could have stated his problem using 14 or 15 percent without much of a problem. But either percentage would have been considered usurious by the church; so making the problem that obvious would have been tricky and possibly dangerous. And few people at the time were capable of determining the interest rate from the problem as stated. Medieval mathematicians knew how to be diplomatic while making their point accurately. His problem could also have been solved using fractions rather than decimals. By the time Simon Stevin introduced decimals 350 years later, the power of the church had waned considerably.[3]

Returning to the 1920s, the sleight of hand is still present. The New York cab driver took out a loan for $100, agreeing to pay back $150 in return. Clearly, the rate of interest is 50 percent but it was not stated as such. When the matter got to court, he was given relief, although temporary. But as Fibonacci demonstrated 720 years earlier, vagueness could save the day. In this case, the lender could always state that the rate was not as high as it appeared because of other calculations favoring the borrower, which just happened to be omitted from the discussion. The statutory rate was not in question; it was the legal rate, open to interpretation.

During the 1920s, consumer credit got a boost from unexpected sources. Because of the loan sharking problem, a movement began to make small consumer loans, usually of $300 or less, more widely available. Many states attempted to modify their usury ceilings to allow lenders to charge more for these loans under the assumption that higher rates would attract more legitimate lenders and fewer loan sharks. The idea became very popular, especially after several large lenders decided to enter the small loan market. The Russell Sage Foundation was instrumental in lobbying many state legislatures to liberalize their interest rate ceilings for small loans, and, as a result, two large commercial banks, in addition to the Bank of America, entered the market. In New York, the National City Bank (Citibank) and the Bank of United States decided to begin making small loans after recognizing that the market was ill served, and they developed buying "on time." Unfortunately, the market was well served by only one of them. The Bank of United States collapsed in 1930, having defrauded thousands of depositors out of their savings. It was the largest bank failure at the time.

In 1922, forty-three of the forty-eight states in the United States had usury laws on their books. There were not all the same. Some of them stipulated the maximum rate of interest that lenders could charge borrowers, and others were slightly more broad, designed to prevent what was known as "moral usury." In this latter case, usury was considered charging interest to someone who clearly could not afford it. In other words, lenders were taking advantage of someone in poor economic straits. Although these requirements sounded fine, infractions were very difficult to prove, especially with regard to moral usury.

The usury laws were products of eighteenth- and nineteenth-century legislation designed to protect borrowers from being charged excessive

 DURING THE REFORMATION in England, the Tudors attempted to come to grips with high rates of interest. A parliamentary act of 1545 established 10 percent as the legal rate of interest during the reign of Henry VIII. Anyone charging more was to be fined treble his profits. But the act was short-lived and replaced by another in 1552, which rescinded the 10 percent rate and made charging interest illegal again. After an uncomfortable hiatus, the 10 percent rate was restored by the Act of 1571, which stated that all contracts calling for more than the legal rate were rendered null and void.

interest. Generally, many states had statutory rates of around 6–12 percent, depending on the type of loan. The statutory rate was stated in the loan contract, but the legal rate was different. During the twentieth century, a distinction was made between civil usury and criminal usury. The terms were more clear and self-evident. And the remedies were different as well, with criminal usury carrying heavier penalties if proved. But in the early twentieth century, the older terms prevailed. The statutory side of lending was easy to monitor. The legal rate applied when no specific rate was established in the loan contract and was used to calculate the amount by which the loan could be discounted or when no specific repayment schedule was spelled out. The types of loans the

 ONE LENDER CAUGHT in the middle of the sixteenth-century usury conundrum was John Shakespeare, father of the playwright. A wool trader, he also dabbled in lending, as did many small merchants in England at the time. The Bard therefore had some firsthand experience with the practice before writing *The Merchant of Venice*. His father's experience with lending was uncomfortable, having been accused of usury on several occasions. In 1570 John, from Stratford-upon-Avon, was accused of usury by two informants. In one case, he exacted interest of 20 percent for a loan made in 1569 and in the other 25 percent. In both cases, he was charged with usury under the Act of 1552, in which usury of any sort was illegal. Within a year, the charges still would have been valid because the rate was higher than the 10 percent mandated by the 1571 act. Tudor era informants regularly hoped to receive about one-half the penalties charged to the miscreants when the usury was successfully proved in court. Shakespeare, however, went to court in only one of the two cases and settled the other claim without a trial.

His son's account of interest has become much better known. In *The Merchant of Venice*, all of the traditional attitudes and ideas about usury were on full display. Having approached Shylock about a loan, Antonio (the merchant) listens to Shylock's terms and readily agrees, fully realizing that potentially they could be harsh. Shylock demands strong terms and is about to collect when Portia's intervention saves Antonio.[4]

legal rate applied to were of lesser quality than those with contract rates, such as second mortgages or consumer loans. Despite the usury laws, it was recognized that they needed to command a higher rate because lenders would be frightened away from making loans without risk premium pricing of some sort. Generally, these rates could be as high as 18 percent by the mid- to late 1920s.

Although the statutory rates were fairly easy to monitor, legal rates were more problematic and often created the so-called moral usury. Usury was almost impossible to assess because it depended on a borrower's claiming unfair treatment. When dealing with an institutional lender, it was feasible if the rates applied to a loan could be shown to exceed the legal limit. But when dealing with a private lender or loan shark, proving that was improbable to impossible, to say the least. The loan shark in many ways was public enemy number one. The strong-arm tactics employed and extortionate rates of interest forced many employers to form mutual societies so that their employees could borrow money at more reasonable rates.

Some of the legal limit laws were passed during or after World War I. In 1915, the comptroller of the currency shocked the financial world by stating flatly that over two hundred nationally chartered banks were charging interest at usurious rates. High rates of interest were a problem, as they had been in the two previous centuries, and usury laws had been on the books for years. Why then was the debate still raging one hundred and twenty-four years after New Hampshire passed the first American usury law in 1791? Although the laws had been frozen in time, the techniques of finance discovered ways around them. Despite the usury ceilings, many finance companies were quickly discovering the virtues of lending money to the emerging consumer class.

In 1928, the Russell Sage Foundation estimated that commercial banks were charging between 13 and 35 percent for loans, small loan companies up to 42 percent, licensed pawnbrokers up to 60 percent, and the ubiquitous loan sharks up to 480 percent. Pawnbrokers ironically found themselves exempt from heavy criticism in the 1920s despite the fact that they effectively charged high interest rates. They were seen as a lender of last resort for workers who admittedly were overextended. But loan sharking and the rates charged would increase dramatically after the Depression began, when the nationwide credit crunch made less money available for borrowing.

Despite the distinction between statutory usury and legal usury, it is difficult to understand how the problem could have persisted after almost two thousand years of Western history. Was it not possible to detect usury and prevent its practice after centuries of prohibitions, condemnations, and excommunications? More to the point, why was it so easy to get around the prohibitions? Even the medieval church tolerated low rates of interest, around 4 percent, not far from the almost standard 6 percent prescribed by many state legislatures in the eastern United States five hundred years later.

Part of the discrepancy can be explained by the language of many state usury laws. They prohibited charging rates above a maximum stated rate as long as the loans were in written contract form. No one could charge a higher rate by written agreement. But when there was no written agreement, the complexion of the issue changed. It was generally accepted that contracts lasted for periods of one year or more, like mortgages, so the stated rate had to adhere to the usury laws. But when a loan was for shorter-term items like personal purposes or consumer purchases, then the rate was dictated by shorter periods, usually months. Then the rate could be stated in monthly terms, almost all of which would be below the annual usury limits. For example, 1.5 percent per month, in annual terms, is 18 percent, but the effective annual rate did not have to be stated until the Truth in Lending Act was passed in 1968. If the borrower paid back the loan in three months, the effective rate would be 4.5 percent. If it became a longer standing obligation, legal usury limits applied, but it is not clear whether the borrower could ask for relief from the courts unless the effective rate became outrageously high.[5]

Another common method of avoiding charges of usury involved what was known as "salary buying." This was simply a method used to lend workers money while avoiding charges of usury. A lender would require workers to sign over their weekly paychecks, for which the lender would make a loan, less a stiff charge. This essentially is known today as a "payday loan," although the contractual agreement led lenders to claim that it was not a loan but simply a service. Regardless of what it was called, the rates were high. A worker typically received $20 for the pledge to hand over his next $25 paycheck to the loan sharking company making the loan.

Despite the extortionate rates charged by payday lenders, little progress was made on finding a solution. In the mid-1930s, Mayor Fiorello

LaGuardia of New York City denounced them when it was discovered
that city workers, whose average paycheck was around $40 per week,
regularly paid 10 percent of the amount to get their cash as early as possible. "I have long since adopted the policy of protecting city employees
from loan sharks and usurers," he said, but to little avail.

Ironically, one of society's oldest lenders acquired some respect in
the 1920s even as installment credit became wildly popular. Pawnbrokers remained one of the largest lending sources in the country, behind
the installment companies and the unlicensed lenders, which also included some private pawnbrokers. Their business was not that different from an ordinary lender in that collateral was provided for the loan
and the rates charged were regulated in theory if the pawnbroker was
licensed by the state in which it operated. Pawnbroking was still very
much a local affair. The brokers were never consolidated into national
companies and remained small merchants, their businesses often being
passed down from father to son. Given that the average citizen was becoming stretched to the limit on credit, their facilities were often the
only relief for someone needing quick cash.

A pawnbroker remarked in 1928 that the average New Yorker probably did not have access to $100 cash in an emergency and often sought
his services. Since the Middle Ages, the profession had been identified
by three brass spheres hanging over the door of pawnbroking establish-
ments, not exactly a prestigious symbol. Most medieval societies considered pawnbrokers outcasts and forced them to restrict their business
to ghettoes. Before World War I, only one pawnbroker was reputed to
be doing business in France, charging rates of about 8 percent annually.
Yet in the United States in the Roaring Twenties, their services were
highly sought after despite the age-old stigma.

A piece of legislation called the Uniform Small Loan Law (USLL),
sponsored by the Russell Sage Foundation and the Household Finance
Corporation, which had been founded in 1878, began to be adopted
by individual states in 1928 as a way of making the usury laws more
flexible. Loans of $300 or less were made to individuals for household
items and were secured by the items themselves. The small loan law was
adopted in 28 states in 1928, and the usury laws were waived to provide
for higher interest, under the assumption that rates would eventually
drop. Many states were urged to raise the monthly interest a lender
could charge from 1.5 percent to 3.5 percent, indicating a rise in annual

interest charges from 18 to 42 percent. Not everyone was convinced by the argument that market forces would eventually intervene, however. Taking the more obvious interpretation, the governor of Wisconsin stated flatly that the USLL encouraged usury rather than discouraging it. But the horse already was out of the barn. As a result, Household Finance decided to expand its activities in 1928 and went to Wall Street for an infusion of funds, raising capital with a stock offering led by well-known investment bank Lee, Higginson & Company. Personal finance quickly was becoming mainstream.

Wall Street had a direct influence on the way consumers would finance their purchases in the future, although it was a long way financially and emotionally from Main Street at the time. The major change in both consumer and corporate finance developed in the mergers and acquisitions market in a deal that would have a significant direct impact on the market for automobiles. But when news of the deal was made public, it would not take long for all types of bankers to see its virtues for future lending. The credit revolution was set to explode.

Discounting the Future

Although borrowing money to finance consumer purchases was not new in the 1920s, the techniques used represented a stark change from the past. Buying now and paying later was a novel idea, but it would keep the repo man quite busy during the 1920s. The notion was supported intellectually by a technique that made the concept more palatable.

The idea of valuing assets on the basis of future earnings potential was not entirely new, but a buyout deal in the 1920s brought it to the foreground. A young banker, Clarence Dillon, was gaining a reputation as a dealmaker after the war when he was approached by the Dodge family in 1925, who wanted to sell their automobile manufacturing company after the untimely deaths of its two founders. They sought Dillon's advice because he had established a track record for mergers. This time the dealmaker had stiff competition. The ubiquitous J. P. Morgan was also involved in the deal, as he was in most of the postwar period's major transactions. To win the day, Dillon would need deep pockets and a clever way to beat back the challenge of the major Wall Street banker.

Until the 1920s, the traditional way of valuing a merger deal was to set the purchase price using the value of the target company's assets.

Financing for the deal then would raise more cash than necessary, with the excess going to pay the underwriters a handsome profit. Morgan used that technique when he created U.S. Steel in 1901 by merging his own steel interests with Carnegie Steel Company to form the world's first billion-dollar balance sheet corporation. Today, that excess is called synergy. At the time, it was still referred to as "watering down" a company's assets, a nineteen-century concept with its own colorful history. The differences in interpretation are reflected in the choice of terms. If something is sold for more than its asset value, its existing equity will erode, or be watered. If it is sold based on estimated cash flows, then its value correctly reflects investors' expectations about the future.

Morgan made his bid for the Dodge Brothers Company, offering $155 million based on asset value, with $65 million in cash and the balance in securities. Dillon did a more complicated calculation. Originally a bond salesman, he used the tried-and-true method of bond valuation to arrive at his own price. He estimated the future cash flows of Dodge and discounted them by his assumed cost of capital to arrive at the price, which happened to be $20 million more than Morgan's. The icing on the cake was that his offer was all cash. The Dodge family readily accepted, and Dillon scrambled successfully to finance the deal. The investment banker became a car manufacturer.

Dillon's coup also made him an instant legend on Wall Street, which quickly learned the lessons of discounted cash flows and net present value. His success as a car manufacturer was less impressive, however, and he finally sold the company to Walter Chrysler, the founder of the Chrysler Corporation. Although the newspapers were abuzz with the headlines of Dillon's coup over Morgan and his adept financial dealings, the technique he used gained general acceptance. The implications for consumer credit were obvious, and a change began in credit financing that would slowly change the face of and expand consumer society. It would now become acceptable to base a person's credit on the future ability to earn and service the debt.

The Depression and World War II would intervene before the consumer boom again picked up steam in the 1950s. When combined with Wall Street's embrace of Household Finance, the Dodge deal paved the way for institutional acceptance of consumer credit and valuation methods that would be used to assess credit risk in the future. But the 1920s still were removed from the more streamlined version of consumer finance that would prevail later in the century. If consumers missed a payment on an automobile or a household item bought on time payments, the security could quickly be repossessed. Collateral played an important role in consumer lending unless the buyer's personal financial ratios were very strong.

Invisible Revenue

Clarence Dillon's coup was not the only harbinger of things to come in finance in the 1920s. One of the banks' major revenue centers for two centuries has been float. Simply defined, *float* is the use of money by a payer or an intermediary until the funds clear. If a person writes a check dated the first and the funds do not clear in the payee's account until the fourth, the float is three days. The payer who knows the funds will not clear and needs a minimum balance in his or her account need not worry about falling below the minimum because the funds are still there until the fourth. If a bank is involved directly, it can benefit from the float if the payer's account has been debited but the payee is not credited until the later date. In the latter case, the bank can earn interest on the funds.

Before computers and high-speed communications, float was especially coveted by banks because of the long delays in clearing funds. The first well-known case of float in the United States occurred during the Mexican War when several banks were accused of floating U.S. government funds while being purposely slow in disbursing them to smaller banks around the country to pay for war supplies and materials. But the company that recognized the value of float while providing a service to customers at the same time was American Express Company. Founded in 1850, the company began offering travelers' checks to customers for a fee in the early 1890s as more people began to travel abroad.

Because the checks were paid for at the time of purchase, the company enjoyed particularly long float, especially if the customer was traveling to Europe or some other far-off destination. Money was paid out only when the check was presented back to the company by the merchant or bank. As travel increased during the 1920s, the company prospered with the checks, which were its major revenue center until the company introduced its credit card in the 1950s. It enjoyed float of up to $250 million at any particular point in time, earning interest on it by investing in municipal bonds.

All the advances made in retail financing during the 1920s did not match the banks' major source of lending: lending money to the stock market. Many banks lent call money to brokers, who in turn lent it to their margin customers, fueling the greatest stock market rally yet seen. The opportunities were substantial. Stocks bought or sold on margin required only 10–20 percent equity as payment, with the balance lent by the broker. Although loan rates varied between 1925 and the crash in 1929 from around 4.5 to over 7 percent and certainly were not as high as rates on installment credit loans, they were much easier to administer because the brokers did the actual work. After 1925, the banks were not the largest lenders to brokers. Large corporations such as the Standard Oil Company found that lending to the call money market was an efficient way to use their cash and actually lent more than the banks by a considerable margin. But it was that lending by the banks that diverted substantial money away from installment credit and opened the door for the nonbank lenders to establish a foothold in the retail lending market.

The success of travelers' checks and margin lending demonstrated to many other financial service companies that money could be made in retail finance, not just in wholesale finance and Wall Street. But the $2.5 billion being generated annually in installment credit took a serious blow during the dark days following the 1929 crash. Within a year, an estimated $900 million was in default annually, and the situation would worsen during the later days of the Depression. By 1932–1933, installment credit dwindled to half its 1929 level and would not recover until the late 1930s, before declining again during World War II. Brokers' loans also collapsed after the crash and within two years were only a fraction of their 1928 and 1929 levels. Installment credit continued to be generated during the Depression as installment companies marketed their services to those with higher, more secure incomes. One banker noted in 1932, "In spite of the subnormal business conditions and unemployment . . . installment selling and installment financing has [sic] justified its place in American business and demonstrated its essential economic soundness." The idea of spending the way out of a problem was developing. But speculation and buying on time would not return to pre-Depression levels until the war was finished.

Chapter Notes

1. Economic statistics from the early part of the twentieth century are not as reliable as they were after World War II. Because of the lack of hard statistics, the National Bureau of Economic Research was founded in 1920, with the strong support of Secretary of Commerce Herbert Hoover. The private research organization was founded to apply more rigorous analysis to economic data than had been done in the past. A year later, Hoover asked it to conduct "a careful investigation into the cyclical fluctuations in unemployment" and to investigate "the merits and defects of various remedies proposed."

2. Henry Ford agreed to establish Ford Motor Credit in the 1920s, although his company, privately owned, did not have any long-term debt on its balance sheet. Ford was opposed to borrowing because he feared the influence of bankers and wanted to keep them at a distance.

3. Although Fibonacci published his major works in manuscript form before the invention of the printing press, he still is remembered today in investment circles. Many traders use his theory of number sequence (Fibonacci sequence) as a guide to trading everything from stocks to foreign exchange. His *Book of the Abacus* (*Liber Abaci*) is available in only one English translation: Leonardo Pisano Fibonacci, *Liber Abaci*, translated by Laurence Sigler (New York: Springer-Verlag, 2003).

4. The account of Shakespeare's father is found in D. L. Thomas and N. E. Evans, "John Shakespeare in The Exchequer," *Shakespeare Quarterly,* Vol. 35, No. 3 (Autumn 1984).

5. Many of the state usury laws were amended or abolished in the 1980s and 1990s, although some remain today. Most of the civil usury laws were abolished, but prohibitions remain against criminal usury.

3

A Self-Fulfilling Prophecy

Frugality is for the vulgar. —FRANÇOIS RABELAIS

ALMOST A DECADE OF the Depression and the war years that followed put consumer spending temporarily on the back burners. Extraordinary measures taken by the Franklin D. Roosevelt administration during the 1940s diverted many national resources to the war effort, especially the country's financial resources. Wall Street was relegated to a minor position during the war because the commercial banks purchased bonds directly from the Treasury to assist in the massive war funding. Advances in consumer credit would have to wait for peace and prosperity to return.

When the war ended, consumer credit began to expand again. Once the horse was out of the barn, money became readily available; businesspeople realized that the best way to prompt consumers to buy was by making easy credit available, as they had done in the 1920s. The consumer revolution and the accompanying debt revolution, starting before the crash, quickly became the prescription for the economy, two-thirds driven by consumer spending.

The greatest economic expansion ever witnessed began after World War II. Similar circumstances to those in 1921 appeared, giving support to a revival of consumer credit. Once again, pent-up consumer demand was directed at consumer goods, and many of those goods were initially paid for with maturing Treasury bonds, used to finance the war effort. The result was much the same. All areas of the economy spurted ahead.

Inflation raised its head in the late 1940s but was eventually contained. Consumer finance companies were poised for the greatest gains yet recorded. A victorious America would celebrate the end of the war by spending its way to prosperity, setting a precedent for the future.

Old problems did not disappear but did recede from view. The usury laws still proved to be the underlying obstacle to consumer credit. They would have to be avoided if finance was to provide the demand element necessary for the economy to grow. Loan sharking endured, but consumers became more prosperous, and, although usury laws lurked in the background, ingenuity prevailed and credit became easier to obtain. Most charges of loan sharking were made against organized crime, through bookmakers and collection agents. Easier credit forced the loan sharks underground before they would appear in a more legitimate form.

Banking became a leaner, more concentrated business in the 1950s than it was in the 1920s. Before and after the 1929 crash, hundreds of banks failed because of their exposure to the real estate market and the collapsing stock market. Most were small or regional banks with too much exposure in one particular sector. Being undiversified, they fell quickly under the weight of bad loans and the market in late 1929. Law prevented banks from crossing state lines, and banking remained a local or regional affair. The same law prohibiting banks from crossing state lines (the McFadden Act of 1927) opened a bruising battle between state-chartered banks and nationally chartered ones that would persist intermittently until the next century. And it would also indirectly cause great confusion in interpreting existing usury laws.

The 1950s were to become the decade of home building, automobile production, general manufacturing, and the expansion of American business abroad. Home building reached new records; in 1954 one million new residential units were built in the United States for the first time, double the number produced annually during the 1920s. Suburban developments like Levittown on Long Island made homes affordable, and many were purchased by returning servicemen using veterans' mortgages. These subsidized loans were supported by the U.S. Department of Veterans Affairs (Veterans Administration, or VA) as a form of compensation for soldiers who served in the war.[1] After the war, the VA authorized the Federal National Mortgage Association (Fannie Mae) to purchase the mortgages, ensuring the expansion of the program. This organization became the underpinning of the housing boom.

Everyone wanted a car as well. None were produced for two years during the war so that the car companies could aid in the war effort. Once the boom began, auto manufacturing became a surrogate for the economy in general. The president of General Motors Corporation told a congressional committee that "what's good for General Motors is good for the country." Few disagreed with his assessment. As in the 1920s, cars became the second most important consumer purchase behind homes. General Motors announced that it was increasing the capital of GMAC by over $200 million in the mid-1950s in order to keep abreast with the demand for financing. A deliberate policy by the manufacturers of planned obsolescence kept production rolling throughout the decade as models of sometimes dubious quality and purposely changing styles appeared. The number of auto manufacturers was much smaller than the number existing thirty years earlier, but they more than compensated by producing record numbers of vehicles. The second family car was becoming a familiar addition to many residential driveways.

Other types of manufacturing underwent a similar boom, with many new consumer goods appearing. Televisions became as popular as radios had been in the 1920s, and the introduction of the transistor made many electrical appliances smaller and portable. The Federal-Aid Highway Act (Interstate Highway System) was created by Congress in 1956, beginning a building program spanning several decades and making travel by car easier than ever. The creation of a student loan program supported by the federal government in the wake of the launch of the first Sputnik made higher education more affordable, prompting more people to attend college than ever before.

The boom could easily be seen in the financings for the ten years following the war. From 1946, installment credit continued to explode, from $8.3 billion to $45.2 billion, an increase of over 500 percent. In the same period, noninstallment credit jumped from $4.2 to $11.1 billion, demonstrating that many Americans were buying consumer durables. As in the 1920s, they required time to pay them off, although the quick repayment of borrowed money still was popular. Notes outstanding from the car financing companies increased an astounding 1,500 percent, from $981 million to $15.4 billion. That was reflected in the explosive demand for autos, with better highways, suburban shopping malls, and cheap gasoline contributing to the phenomenon.

Financial services expanded considerably in the postwar period, with demands for insurance and retirement plans increasing substantially. Individuals began buying more life insurance and annuities. Stock brokerage again became respectable as memories of the crash faded and the new middle class tried its hand at investing. Brokerage offices popped up around the country, and it became fashionable to say that one had a stockbroker along with a minister or perhaps a psychiatrist. Sociologist Vance Packard, widely read at the time, dubbed this middle-class crowd the "Status Seekers."

Installment credit was as popular as ever, although a challenge to the way people paid off their loans was developing slowly. During the 1940s, a new marketing concept, initially designed for convenience, was introduced. No one at the time could have imagined the revolution it would cause in spending habits because the idea was simple. Brooklyn banker John Biggins introduced a plan called Charg-It in 1946, which has the distinction of being the first credit card. Used at local merchants, the card was limited to customers of his bank. A similar card was offered by the Franklin National Bank in New York in 1951 for its loan customers. Broader in scope, Diners Club International was formed in 1950. Originally, Diners Club cards were distributed to only a few dozen people in New York City so that they could pay for meals at restaurants that accepted them. Within a short time, the number of people using them had increased to over twenty thousand. Several years later, American Express entered the field, offering its own card. The cards were simple payment facilities: The balance had to be paid in full before credit was extended again. But both still involved float and benefited their parent companies' bottom lines considerably.

A significant new wrinkle was added when the Bank of America announced its own card, the BankAmericard, in 1958 (renamed Visa in 1976), allowing customers to pay their balances over time while being charged interest on the unpaid balance. At the time, cards were issued to those in higher income brackets as a convenience and were viewed as prestigious—a marketing idea that many card companies fostered for decades. In its first year, the card had sixty thousand cardholders and three hundred retailers signed up. Within a year, the numbers increased to 2 million cardholders and twenty-five thousand retailers. Numbers increased from that point, although the bank did not realize a profit on the operation for the first three years.

Credit companies in general could not have expanded their activities without the aid of computers. IBM established its clear leadership in computing in 1959 when it announced the introduction of its 1401 model, which used transistor technology. IBM sold over ten thousand units during the 1960s. When integrated circuits were introduced in the early 1960s, corporate installations increased from 240 in 1955 to almost twelve thousand in 1963. Consumer credit now was poised to expand exponentially in the number of transactions that could be managed by installment and credit card companies. More capability meant more transactions, and the modern consumer credit spiral was given significant impetus. The birth of the transaction-oriented society occurred quietly, and a long, often uncomfortable process would follow.

Faster, easier methods of payments of all types were necessary because the population was growing—and moving. Migrations of agricultural workers from the South and Midwest to cities began after the war, and many metropolitan areas witnessed increases in their populations. At the same time, city dwellers began moving to the rapidly developing suburbs in an attempt to escape the crowded cities. The United States was in the midst of demographic changes that would create new demands for consumer credit, based on an increasingly mobile population.

Freezing the Yield Curve

The levels of indebtedness assumed by companies after the war were based on an implicit assumption that interest rates could not do any serious damage to balance sheets and income statements. The immediate past had proved that interest rates were a paper tiger when compared with stock market volatility. Everyone feared another crash or a steep market sell-off, but what possible harm could rising interest rates have? And how often did they actually rise?

Since 1942, the short answer was not much. In that year, the Federal Reserve System (Fed) and the Treasury agreed to peg interest rates on Treasury securities, keeping rates stable for the course of the war. The plan was simple and froze the yield curve. Ninety-day bill rates were set at 0.375 percent and long bonds at 2.50 percent. The Fed stood ready to buy or sell bills at the stated rate, dominating the money market and keeping it settled. The most common bond financings were for intermediate terms, usually set at 2 percent. Banks were the major buyers and were induced to buy bonds because they could be used to satisfy reserve requirements. Most credit market operations were dominated by the Treasury, with Wall Street playing a very minor role. With the benchmark Treasury yields low, corporate bonds followed suit. Corporate bond issues had dwindled since the 1940s, and the lack of long-term funds curtailed capital expansion plans. Those that were issued yielded about 50 basis points more than Treasuries.

The peg lasted until 1951, when the Treasury agreed to allow the Fed again to pursue an independent monetary policy. After that date, Treasury yields began to rise, almost 90 basis points to 3.5 percent in 1957. Corporate bonds followed, their yields increasing to around 3.9 percent by 1957, a rise of about 100 basis points from previous levels. In either case, the nominal and real yields were still lower than in the 1920s. When combined with the tax deductibility for interest payments, the cost of issuing bonds and paying interest on mortgages and loans by individuals was cheap. Common stock financing began to rise sharply after 1954 during the bull market of the Dwight D. Eisenhower administration as well, but debt still held the upper hand in corporate financings. By 1957, the amount of publicly and privately offered bonds issued exceeded stock issues four to one.

Bonds had a distinct investment advantage until 1954 because the Fed kept margin rates quite high after the war and refused to relax its grip in the 1940s. The central bank was given the authority to set margin levels by the Securities Exchange Act of 1934 and used its new power quite liberally. Companies that previously lent money to the call money market did not return in the 1950s because the new margin requirements effectively excluded them from the market and lending was dominated exclusively by banks. As in the 1920s before the crash, complaints often were heard after the war about the rates charged in the call money market by banks to brokers. The usury laws did not apply here because call money, like corporate borrowing, was exempt from the usury laws.

The relative sleepiness of the bond markets and the low yields lulled many borrowers and investors into believing that interest rates were not a significant threat to their wallets because rates had been mostly docile since 1942. Another significant factor leading to complacency was that the interest rates attached to bonds and loans were fixed and did not float. Once the borrower agreed to a term, rates were fixed throughout and could not be adjusted. The wide array of usury laws in different states made adjustable rates impractical, especially for mortgages and term loans of more than one year stipulated by contract. And in the later 1950s, there were so many lenders in the marketplace that a borrower could afford to discriminate when seeking a loan; this was an improvement to the market for consumer credit when compared to the 1930s and 1940s. But installment credit still was beset with many pitfalls for consumers, a problem that never would adequately be solved.

Another precedent established during the war years would prove crucial in the decades ahead. As the yield curve was pegged, most attention shifted to the extraordinary war efforts made by industry and finance to ensure victory for the Allies. Auto manufacturers were concentrating their resources on vehicles designed for combat and related services. Shipbuilders were building warships in weeks rather than in months or years in order to satisfy Navy demands and replenish losses. Certain foods were in short supply and being rationed domestically so that the military could be fed. All of these extraordinary measures demonstrated that the war effort took precedence over all other business activity. Once hostilities ended and business conditions returned to normal, the Fed and other government agencies began to foster growth in the economy aimed at low unemployment levels. In other words, the role of government and its agencies was understood to be to support business, not hinder it in any way. As it did when providing veterans' mortgages for returning servicemen, government now was expected to help business prosper. The growth mantra of the 1960s assumed government would help business, not stand in its way.

Supporting the Debt Revolution

Despite the advances made in consumer credit following the war, much of it could not have been supplied without institutional support. Finance was now big business in itself, and all manufacturers of robust size, ranging from those producing capital equipment and machinery to consumer nondurables, wanted entry into the financing business. Auto manufacturers realized that they could enhance their profits with finance company profits even when car manufacturing was slow. They probably never anticipated that their finance subsidiaries would one day be the only profitable parts of their operations in lean years.

The revolution in consumer credit occurred relatively quickly, interrupted only by depression and war. And like all revolutions, it required intellectual support if it was to be long lasting. This was necessary in finance because there still were lingering misgivings about the levels of debt that companies were acquiring in the course of business. Finance had moved slowly since Clarence Dillon discounted the estimated future cash flows of Dodge in the early 1920s. More rigorous intellectual support was needed for the expansion of debt in the American corporate psyche.

In the wake of the war, the debt-to-equity ratios of manufacturing companies began to rise. After the war, they stood at a very conservative 27 percent, but by the 1960s had risen to 47 percent. The interest cover of these companies also fell as a result. By the 1960s, it was assumed that a debt-to-equity ratio of 1:1 or less was considered prudent on a corporate balance sheet. Despite the deductibility of interest for companies, the Depression had caused many bankruptcies, and memories lingered even twenty years after the fact. Too much debt would only put a burden on pretax income. Excessive leverage would create a drag on earnings and place too much risk on bondholders, who in theory should not bear as much operational risk of a company as shareholders. Balance sheet expansion should be created by equity, in the form of either new stock or retained earnings. Debt should be used for less risky projects in the capital budgeting process.

But in the years after the war, corporations were bucking this traditional notion. Manufacturing debt tripled, while new equity increased only about 40 percent. Retained earnings did increase 135 percent, however. Financial service companies showed similar proportions. Long-term debt in that sector increased 127 percent, while equity contributed a meager 14 percent. More importantly, short-term notes due increased 165 percent and accounts receivable shot up 300 percent. The more dramatic increases in the short-term items demonstrated that banks and other lenders were profiting from lending to consumers, relying less on long-term debt to finance their activities than manufacturing companies were.

Companies already were abandoning the older caveats about debt in favor of higher degrees of leverage when an academic journal article appeared supporting the notion that debt itself was neither good nor bad. It was only how it was employed that mattered. The authors, Franco Modigliani and Merton Miller, demonstrated that levels of indebtedness were not as important as the bottom line of a company. As long as the debt could be supported and profits enhanced, the financial structure of the firm was not as important as the fact that it was profitable.

The article, along with several that followed, became known as the "MM theory." In their paper, Modigliani and Miller showed that a firm's value is determined by its investment decisions rather than by its financing decisions.[2] In theory, as long as a firm's profits exceeded its cost of capital, its capital structure was not important. This flew in the face of the older accepted theory that there was such a thing as an optimal capital structure for each firm that should not be seriously violated for fear of its stock price declining. The new idea was highly appealing, especially since shareholder interest in stocks and in the market in general was at an all-time high in the late 1950s and early 1960s, when the idea began to circulate that profits could be enhanced by additional debt and not be endangered if employed properly. It found quick acceptance in academic circles and spread quickly to future generations of financial managers and chief financial officers.

A companion paper, written by Modigliani and Miller in 1961, extended the basic results by showing that, given a company's investment decisions, dividend policy is not as important as a firm's investment decisions. How the earnings are reinvested by the company is more relevant than how much is paid out to shareholders. In this respect, the theories owed much to investment research being done at the time and also influenced other theories in turn. The result was a critical period for finance. Older, accepted ideas of finance were being turned on their head by new ideas supported by empirical research. Years later, when Miller died in 2000, it was noted that dividends were in the range of 4–6 percent when they wrote their theory but that they had declined to around 2 percent in the interim. The decline dovetailed nicely with the increased use of leverage that many large companies had assumed over the years. Even Ford Motor Company, private in its heyday, had gone public in the 1950s and assumed a large amount of debt over the years.

Thirty years later, when Modigliani was awarded the Nobel Prize in economics for his work, the Swedish Academy succinctly summarized his work with Miller. In its introduction in 1985, the Academy stated, "Until the latter part of the 1950s, no viable theory of corporate financing of investment, debt, taxes, and so forth had been developed. It was not till Modigliani and Miller presented their theorems that more stringent theorizing began to appear in this field." The finance side had rarely been recognized in the economics awards to that point. Almost thirty years after the articles were written, it was clear that a significant contribution had been made to corporate America.

The MM theories became widely disseminated through graduate schools of business, which were becoming more respected at the time. Within thirty years, the ideas were firmly embedded in several generations of financial managers. Moving far from its original accounting base, finance now was a complicated discipline. The older version of finance relied on hallowed notions and untested theories such as simple portfolio diversification. Most MBA programs taught the MM theory with heavy doses of math, and it was spread among graduates at a time when the postwar stock market was booming on the back of the conglomerate and mergers and acquisitions trend. It provided a neat, complementary background for consolidation, using debt in particular to finance mergers and acquisitions.

The ideas helped fuel the growth trend of the entire period and appealed politically to Republican administrations naturally friendly to the growth of big business. The idea became affiliated with the Chicago School of Economics at the University of Chicago, which was in the foreground of growth-oriented research. Miller was a faculty member, although Modigliani was at Massachusetts Institute of Technology. After three decades, Miller was able to proudly proclaim, "At the theoretical level, we have won the day."[3]

The MM theory was supported in part by the experience of German and Japanese companies in the postwar period. Although their respective economies were rebuilding, their manufacturing and export efforts were highly successful, and it did not go without notice that they succeeded with high degrees of leverage on their balance sheets. The leverage ratios of companies were higher than those of their American counterparts, in part due to the fact that interest rates were low in real terms in both countries. As a result, they could afford to service larger nominal amounts of fixed-rate debt. In addition, stock markets in those two countries played a secondary role to the bond markets, so debt financing was more the accepted norm. Since the American experience with interest rates had been fairly benign due to the Fed's peg, the experience of foreign companies only added fuel to the debt fire.

Modigliani and Miller were not alone in the finance revolution. Other members of the Chicago School doing research in finance included Harry Markowitz, whose theory of portfolio selection and diversification became a cornerstone of investment theory and won him a Nobel Prize in 1990. His theory built on the older investment principle of diversity. The old idea of not putting all one's eggs in the same basket would now be refined and given empirical support. The multistock portfolio, taking the place of the one-stock portfolio, demonstrated that investors should build disparate holdings of stocks within their own comfort levels of risk and return.[4]

According to Markowitz, traditional portfolios were a selection of stocks chosen for their investment qualities. His basic idea was that investors were risk averse and that portfolios comprised of many stocks rather than just one would protect them over time. Although not maximizing gain as one stock could be expected to do, the investments needed to be chosen as portfolios, not simply as a group of individual stocks. Using mathematics to demonstrate his theory, he proposed that investors select their portfolios based on risk/reward characteristics of the group rather than compiling portfolios of individual securities assembled because they have individually attractive risk/reward characteristics.

One of the limitations in the theory was exactly how to measure risk. In 1964, William Sharpe developed another well-known and widely disseminated idea called the capital asset pricing model (CAPM). His work earned him a share of the same Nobel Prize won by Markowitz and Miller. Proceeding from where Markowitz left off, Sharpe broke risk into two components: systematic risk and specific risk. *Systematic risk* is the risk of holding the market portfolio. As the market moves, all assets are affected. All assets therefore have systematic risk. *Specific risk*, on the other hand, is risk unique to an individual asset. In equity investing, this is also known as company-specific risk. It represents the risk on an asset, and it can be diversified. Market risk cannot.

According to CAPM, the marketplace risk cannot be avoided and should be chosen carefully. Specific risk can be diversified. When an investor holds a carefully selected market portfolio, each individual asset in the portfolio carries specific risk, but through proper diversification, the net exposure becomes the systematic risk of the portfolio. Systematic risk itself can be measured by a beta coefficient, a measure of an individual

SHARPE'S CAPITAL ASSET pricing model formula shows that the cost of a company's equity capital (new stock or retained earnings) depends on its stock beta. So the more volatile the stock becomes in the market, the higher its cost will be—another implicit justification for using debt. The formula states the cost of equity as:

Cost of equity = Risk-free rate + Beta (Return on market − Risk-free rate)

stock's relation to the market. A beta of 1.00 means that a stock moves in tandem with the market. Higher or lower betas suggest increased or decreased volatility, risks that the risk-averse investor can then assess.

The growing use of debt was also reflected in another more practical theory, published in 1968. Edward Altman developed his Z ratio, a predictor of bankruptcy risk. Using a multivariate formula, he demonstrated how a company's probability of bankruptcy could be predicted about two years before it occurred by plugging its financials into his weighted formula. The resulting Z score then gave investors an indication of the company's solvency prospects, an important contribution given the increasing use of debt financing. Over time, the Z scores proved to be correct in about 75 percent of applications.[5]

The ideas presented by Markowitz and Sharpe, like those of Modigliani and Miller, were refined by the authors many times after the publication of the original articles, as well as by colleagues and former students. But the seed had been planted of assets being treated in portfolio terms rather than as individual assets, chosen for portfolio rather than for individual qualities. Within thirty years of the MM theories and those of Markowitz and Sharpe, the negative connotations of being in debt shifted to the more positive connotations of having credit. This was due to the idea that debtors are part of a credit company's portfolio of investments. Those investments can be managed as long as the return they provide is greater than the credit company's cost of capital, usually the commercial paper rate. In most cases, that spread is always in the company's favor, so the MM application is appropriate. Using the ideas of Markowitz and Sharpe, the credit portfolio should be constructed broadly because only diversification can offset the risk of a single asset, meaning that its pool of creditors should be well diversified. If portfolio guidelines are not followed, some consumers will be considered too risky and will not receive credit, and the portfolio's yield will be lower than if it were diversified. In theory, that would hurt both consumers and creditors and justifies granting more debt, not less.

The combination of the MM theory plus Markowitz's emphasis on diverse portfolios provided the intellectual basis for the debt revolution. Sharpe's notion of the CAPM also demonstrated that the more volatile the stock market is, the better it would be to issue debt because the cost of debt is traditionally lower than the cost of equity, in part because of the tax-deductible nature of interest. Although it is not the intent of the theories, they all nevertheless gave implicit support to the idea of treating a company as an investor in the market, not simply as a producer. Even pure producers like manufacturers could diversify somewhat and behave like investors rather than like classic providers. General Motors Corporation and Ford Motor Company already showed that they made a success of producing autos and financing them at the same time.

By the 1960s, it was accepted that credit should be extended to as many companies as possible in order to foster economic growth. The idea would spread to consumer finance shortly thereafter. Computers made the extension of credit and the management of credit facilities easier. Before long, credit card and installment companies would shift their models from lending to customers with high credit ratings to lending to those with lesser ratings, based on the assumed benefits of debt and a search for their own portfolio diversification. Credit was becoming democratized, a concept not in keeping with its own long, often agonizing history to date. Thirty years after the original MM article was published, Modigliani acknowledged the debt trend, noting that American companies were borrowing billions for acquisitions during the mergers and acquisitions binge of the 1980s. "But after you say leverage is the only way to do it, you have to realize that leverage is a source of instability," he acknowledged. The paradoxes in the theory were evident.

Structural Changes

The American experience with interest rates during the Depression and after World War II had been based on fixed medium- and long-term rates. For twelve years from 1942 to 1954, money market rates also were fixed, based on the Fed peg. As a result, the increasing amounts of debt assumed by corporations and individuals were predictable and manageable. If the situation changed, so too would the implications for the marketplace as a whole.

Most consumer debt, with the exception of mortgages, was based on short-term rates. Deposit rates at banks were set by the Fed, based on powers given to it in the Banking Act of 1933 (Glass-Steagall Act). According to Regulation Q, the Fed had the power to set deposit rates at banks in order to create a level playing field on which they could all compete. Because the deposit rates were set, the cost of funds was under control and the rates banks charged for loans would also be within a reasonable range. The usury laws were still in effect in most states, so this regulation was the closest thing to a national usury law, although it was indirect at best. Custom held that a bank would not charge more than 2.5–3 percent higher than its cost of funds for a loan. Only a strong dose of inflation would be able to break this range of relatively low interest rates.

Customers and businesses were charged interest at the prime rate, introduced by the Chase Manhattan Bank in the 1930s. The prime was fixed until further notice, rising or falling only when there was a substantial change in the underlying Treasury bill rate. This was as close as the banks got to charging customers an adjustable rate, although the prime was in theory subject to change. But most term loans longer than one year had fixed rates attached. The result was that interest rates were as predictable as they ever would be, especially when compared with developments that would follow.

The ultimate problem with fixed rates of interest was that they benefited customers if rates rose, putting the risk and opportunity losses squarely on the banks that made the loans. Before securitization became widely used, banks had to leave the loans on their books and manage their own interest rate exposure accordingly. These assets were not sellable and could pose risks to the lenders. Their lack of flexibility made them unmarketable to a third party.

This is why credit cards became so popular with banks. They were the first financial instruments that employed adjustable rates, even before adjustables became institutionalized in the 1980s. As a result, cards posed less risk in their original forms to banks than many other sorts of consumer loans. As long as they were offered to banks' more affluent customers, the credit risks were bearable, but the real test would come when they were offered to less affluent customers.

Before interest could be charged on a revolving basis, Congress intervened to pass the Truth in Lending Act in 1968, part of the Consumer Protection Act. For the first time, consumers had the right to be informed about the nature of charges they would pay when incurring loans. The power to enforce truth in lending was delegated to the Fed through Regulation Z. It requires lenders to inform all customers applying for consumer credit to fully describe the nature of the credit facility and the finance charges involved on an annual basis. The key part of the act was the term "consumer credit." The regulation applied only to installment loans and revolving credit granted to individuals for "household purposes." It did not apply to corporate credit or mortgage agreements.

The Truth in Lending Act was the only federal law ever passed dealing with interest rates. In a sense, it was the closest Congress ever came to passing a national usury law, although it fell far short. Passed during a let-the-buyer-beware period, it recognized that the patchwork of state usury laws could not be superseded and simply required lenders to state their terms clearly and fairly. The maximum rate of interest charged was a decision left to the states, but at least the consumer could make the choice among lenders offering credit.

A combination of finance theory worked together with the constant increasing demand for consumer credit to change the lending environment substantially. Theory could not become a factor without the proper market conditions, and market conditions required some theoretical justification for extending credit on such a widespread basis. Experiences outside the United States also contributed significantly to the credit-generating process and proved that high interest rates and inflation need not stand in the way of a consumer credit society.

International Influences

Since the mid-1960s, many international banks had been borrowing in the euromarkets in floating rate form. They often would borrow medium- or long-term bonds at a periodically adjusted interest rate, basing their coupon adjustments over the London interbank offered rate (Libor). This Eurodollar rate was a market rate, quoted daily, and reflected conditions in the credit markets, so it appealed to banks seeking to shed fixed-interest-rate risks. American banks began tapping the market for offshore dollars as well, often bringing the funds home for use domestically. But domestic uses were limited because of the domestic interest rate structure and the usury laws. Practically, these funds could not be used for retail lending.[6]

As a result, eurodollar funds were used primarily for corporate and sovereign lending. And offshore lending, not confined by domestic laws and regulations, was a better bet. The banks got their opportunity in the 1970s when many developing countries began borrowing dollars as a result of the oil price rises in 1972–1973. These countries borrowed large amounts through syndicated loans on a floating basis, at a risk-adjusted spread over Libor. Many of the early loans did not have caps, so the banks merely adjusted a rising cost of funds to an even higher lending rate. These large loans, made to countries as diverse as Brazil, Mexico, and the Philippines, were the first experiment in unregulated borrowing and lending in U.S. dollars on an adjustable basis. For about twelve years, they were an unqualified success as far as the banks were concerned, earning them high returns for what appeared to be limited risk.

Lending without restriction soon became as much of a problem as lending within the confines of usury laws or Regulation Q. After Paul Volcker and the Fed allowed the Fed funds rate and discount rate to rise to historic levels in the face of domestic inflation in the 1980s, Libor naturally followed and reached 24 percent in 1981–1982. Coupons reset to it forced many developing countries to pay interest at more than 24 percent, rate levels that were unsustainable. As a result, the Third World Debt Crisis arose, and many countries clamored to renegotiate their debts with the banks. Clear resolution was not achieved across the board until 1990.

Before the lid came off the developing countries, it appeared that adjustable-rate lending was coming of age. Domestic banks in the United States were having their own problems with the old fixed-rate structure, and the pressure finally led to changes in the way they were allowed to operate. Consumers also learned to react. When interest rates rose in 1979, many bank customers already had been accustomed to withdrawing deposits from the banks and placing them in money market mutual funds instead. The funds paid almost the prevailing money market rates, whereas bank deposits were still in the 6 percent range, the banks enjoying the protection of Regulation Q. In some cases, the differential was as high as 10 percent in favor of the funds. Banks were losing deposits at an alarming rate and needed more flexible forms of funding to remain viable.

By 1980, it was becoming apparent that parts of the financial system were in serious need of reform. That year Congress passed the Depository Institutions Deregulation and Monetary Control Act (DIDMCA), aimed at reforming the Fed and abolishing interest rate ceilings. Among other measures, the Fed's reserve requirement was extended to all depository institutions, not only Fed members. This was the first time that the central bank would have the power over all depository institutions, including thrifts, credit unions, and state-chartered banks. Extending the power was necessary and overdue because some banks were leaving, or threatening to leave, the Fed's jurisdiction, in order to avoid its requirements. This was a real threat to the authority of the Fed during a particularly tumultuous time in banking history.

The act also outlined a timetable to abolish Regulation Q interest rate ceilings. It planned to phase them out over a six-year period. But

DURING THE ITALIAN RENAISSANCE, many merchants and bankers sought to keep their consciences clear by donating part of their fortunes to good works, notably public buildings, churches, and funds for the poor. Ecclesiastical law allowed the Church to confiscate a usurer's estate after death, so in order for businessmen to remain in good standing, many gifts were bequeathed. Many of the great buildings in Florence and other northern cities were erected for this reason. Two hundred years earlier, when the cathedral of Notre Dame was being built in Paris, the bishop of Paris advised a usurer about saving his soul. He suggested that he donate his ill-gotten gains to the church so that the cathedral of Notre Dame could be built. When St. Bernard of Clarveaux saw the Gothic masterpiece, he discovered the virtues of what would become known as capitalism. He exclaimed, "Wealth is drawn up by ropes of wealth . . . thus money bringeth money."

a subsequent law, the Garn–St. Germain Act passed two years later, effectively allowed banks and thrifts to offer competitive rates of deposit interest, accelerating the phase-out period. State usury ceilings on mortgages also were abolished, as well as any state ceilings on interest that could be paid at banks and other institutions. But there was an exception. These usury provisions were set to expire in 1983 unless states reinstated their laws before then. The abolition of the many state usury laws was only temporary. The DIDMCA was written that way to allow the system to become deregulated, but ultimately the states' concerns about maximum rates of interest still were paramount.

The DIDMCA coincided with historically high real rates of interest in the United States. The act was one of the most complicated banking laws ever passed by Congress, but one clear point emerged in its wake. The path was now unobstructed for adjustable rates of interest on mortgages after 1983. But the yield curve would have to be positively sloped because no one would borrow at an adjustable rate based on money market rates if it was higher than the long-term rate. And the adjustable mortgage rate could not violate a state usury ceiling. The answer to that was simple. Caps were written into adjustable mortgages to provide some band of relief for mortgage holders. Those sorts of caps made many developing countries' finance ministers quite unhappy. If only they had them on Libor-based term loans incurred in the past, then maybe the debt crisis could have been avoided.

Within a few years, adjustable rate mortgages (ARMs) would become extremely popular among homeowners because they offered relief from very high fixed-rate mortgages, some approaching 15 percent in 1983–1984. Although the ARMs were set at around 12 percent, they offered the possibility of being refinanced later at lower rates. Once the mortgage-assistance agencies Fannie Mae and Freddie Mac began buying them, the market opened and ARMs accounted for 50 percent of all mortgages originated in the 1980s, especially when rates were still high. In a sense, the ARMs helped save the mortgage and housing industries from severe losses.

More importantly for future generations of homeowners and the banks, ARMs brought about a shift in risk from banks to homeowners. If short-term interest rates rose, the mortgage payments increased up to the legal cap. The increased cost of funds to banks was passed to homeowners. If rates passed through the cap, the risk shifted back to the bank. Below the floor at the other end of the cap, the risk was back on the homeowner, who was paying a rate higher than the market rate. The difference between the floor and the cap is known as a *collar* and can be managed by a bank much more easily than being stuck with a mortgage that may be lower than the prevailing market rate, as in the time before securitization and ARMs. Assets like mortgages are easier to manage if they have flexible features rather than fixed features, as in a traditional mortgage.

Forgive and Forget?

The consumer credit boom received aid from many quarters. Change in the law certainly was one of them although the changes in the 1970s and 1980s came from many different angles. One of the most profound changes was in the bankruptcy code.

Congress overhauled the bankruptcy code in 1978 in a sweeping change designed to make the existing code more flexible. The previous revision, the Chandler Act from 1938, was considered too cumbersome and unwieldy. One of the Chandler Act's noteworthy parts was the addition of the Chapter 11 idea that companies could be reorganized under certain circumstances, not simply dissolved to satisfy creditors, but complaints persisted. Cases took too long to get before the courts and then took too long to be resolved. Whoever claimed bankruptcy before getting to court certainly was bankrupt by the time the case was resolved. Yet the 1978 reform had its opponents furious.

 THE BANKRUPTCY LAWS have a long and sometimes tortuous history in the United States. After the first one was passed in 1800, amendments were added in 1841 and 1867, but both amendments were repealed several years after being passed. The 1867 version was the first to include protection for corporations before being repealed. Additions were again made in 1898, 1933, and 1934, all in response to periods of economic downturn, before the Chandler Act was passed in 1938. In a sense, all reflected the prevailing socioeconomic sentiments of their times. The most recent in 2005 also reflects a reaction to the previous law passed in 1978.

The bankruptcy code adopted in 1978 received little press, being overshadowed that year by New York City's financial woes. *The New York Times* called it imperfect but a good start on the road to reforming problems in the system. Critics thought otherwise. The new law provided corporations and individuals with similar sorts of remedies. Two types of bankruptcy could be filed. For corporations it was Chapter 7 and Chapter 11. For individuals, Chapters 7 and 13 were available. In either case, the outcome could be similar.

Under Chapter 7, a company or individual could liquidate assets to satisfy creditors, with any uncovered debts being discharged by the courts. That would enable a fresh start. Under Chapters 11 or 13, assets would be frozen and protection granted from creditors while a reorganization plan was worked out under court auspices. That usually required paying debts over a specified number of years and then being discharged. These latter two chapters were the parts that rubbed critics wrong.

Prior to 1978, bankruptcy filings had been rising constantly, choking the courts. By allowing reorganization, the courts were given the discretion to allow time for potentially viable businesses or individuals to get their houses in order while keeping their assets intact. What was to prevent anyone from simply filing Chapter 13 in order to dodge debts that he or she did not want to pay? Critics demanded to know. The law was too liberal and allowed individuals to ignore debt whenever it suited them.

Of all the causes of bankruptcy, the most common is having too much debt. For the consumer, this clearly meant too much consumer debt. In 1986 alone, over 400,000 cases of personal bankruptcy were filed, more than twice the number a decade earlier. Critics point to the increase as a direct result of the flexible new law. As will be seen in the next chapter, the same time period witnessed a continuing explosion in consumer debt that would be fueled by new innovations in securitizing consumer debt in the mid- to late 1980s. The combination provided powerful ammunition for those who thought that consumers were much too profligate in their spending, unwilling to face the consequences of debt.[7]

The shifting attitudes toward indebtedness certainly contributed to this bankruptcy trend. Were individuals discovering the beauty of the personal application of the MM propositions, while credit card companies reveled in the portfolio theories that would allow them to expand their portfolios without fear of too many defaults? Apparently, the theories had many real-world applications, although not necessarily the ones their authors originally intended.

Later in the 1980s, another significant change occurred in consumer financing that was to change the nature of indebtedness in the United States. For decades, consumers and corporations had enjoyed a tax deduction for interest paid. It was widely assumed that the deduction was embedded in the tax codes and would never change. But in the face of budget deficits, Congress passed the Tax Reform Act of 1986. One of its main planks was the abolition of the deduction for consumer interest, except for that paid on mortgages (technically not consumer interest). Suddenly, interest paid on credit cards, installment loans, and personal loans no longer qualified for the deduction.

Although the loss of the deductions helped Treasury revenues, it did not slow consumer spending as anticipated. The phase-out period coincided with a recession in 1991–1992, brought about by the aftermath of the savings and loan crisis and stock market collapse of 1987. As a result, it is difficult to attribute the recession to a reduction in consumer spending, although consumer credit did experience a rare decline in those two years. What the loss of the deduction did suggest was that consumers would seek another way to make their interest deductible.

That particular shift would be to home equity loans, still tax deductible. This would begin a 20-year period in which home loans would be used to finance credit card expenditures, all based on the assumption that home prices would continually rise, allowing the borrowing against the equity in the homes to remain intact. A home rising $100,000 in market value could be used to provide an equity loan that homeowners could tap in order to pay their bills. Equity as the mirror image of debt was now becoming accepted, as credit previously had been.

Despite these shifts in consumer financing and the acceptance of credit as a measure of financial worth, it was a crisis caused by the Third World debt problems that would provide the second and more substantive part of the debt revolution. Despite the introduction of adjustable rates on the consumer level, adjustables on the institutional level would have a deleterious effect on banks and thrifts. The first phase of exposure to adjustables would leave a painful trail of losses and bank failures.[8]

The great irony in the shift to adjustable rates of interest was that it did not prove the market-oriented experience that some had predicted.

The period from 1934 to 1985, which included the bulk of the Great Depression, provided a relative halcyon period for American banking, including thrift institutions. Within that fifty-year period, nine hundred and fifty banks and thrifts failed in the United States, but more than three hundred of the failures occurred in 1982–1984 alone. High interest rates, a very restrictive monetary policy, and the old Regulation Q had especially taken their toll on the thrifts, accounting for the high numbers in the early 1980s. But that was small compared to the problems encountered after 1985.

In the ten years beginning in 1985, over twenty-five hundred banks and thrifts failed. Those numbers had not been seen since the years before and immediately after the Great Depression began. A combination of the junk bond crisis and the recession that followed put the greatest stress on depository institutions seen in decades. The problems began in 1985, even before the stock market collapse of 1987. The revenues lost by restructuring developing countries' debt strained bank earnings, and the thrifts' liberalized portfolio policies proved disastrous. The DIDMCA and the Garn–St. Germain Act allowed thrifts to purchase corporate bonds for the first time in order to allow them to obtain higher yields than their older mortgage portfolios. But apparently no one warned them of the investment risks associated with junk bonds, which formed the majority of those new assets. When the market for them disintegrated after 1987, many had to be written off, leaving large losses in their wake.

Adjustable rates were not able to spare depository institutions the crisis of the 1980s and early 1990s, although their worth to banks could already be seen in the smaller credit card portfolios. But the coup de grâce for the banks of all sorts was a new series of capital requirements imposed on banks by the Bank for International Settlements (BIS) in 1987. Being weakened by the debt crisis, failing mortgage portfolios, and junk bond losses, many depository institutions' capital fell to dangerously low levels. At the behest of the Fed and Bank of England, the BIS imposed an 8 percent capital requirement on banks, forcing many of them to readjust their balance sheets. The choice was simple: Raise fresh capital by selling stock or shed assets. The requirement called for capital to be 8 percent of loans outstanding. If capital could not be raised, then the loans needed to come off the balance sheet in order to strengthen the existing capital base.[9]

The solution was ingenious but risky. Because loans were quickly becoming the bane of the banks, they decided to begin securitizing them in the future, dynamically changing their business models in the process. By pledging them against bonds as collateral, the banks effectively got loans off their balance sheets, avoiding the tighter capital requirements in the process. In the past, banks were known primarily as makers of loans. The new model suggested that they were transaction and portfolio oriented. Loans would always be a part of their business, but many of the loans would be made, securitized, and cleared off the balance sheets. Investors buying their securitized bonds would be brought into the process. How loans chosen for eventual securitization would be treated was relatively simple. When banks had created enough of them, they would be cleared. Over time, the loans would be created to be cleared immediately. The implications of that second stage in the history of securitization would have profound implications for consumer credit.

On the face of it, the process appeared to be foolproof. Since the early 1970s, Fannie Mae, Ginnie Mae, and Freddie Mac had been securitizing their bonds by purposely creating mortgages with the intent of selling them off to investors. But in those cases, the mortgages had to meet the specific agency's credit guidelines. Whether the banks would apply reasonable credit guidelines for loans to be securitized was not clear. The types they began using as collateral were car loans, credit card loans, and the like. In short, they were factoring their receivables to the bond market. The asset-backed security was born in the process.

This matter of flexibility is at the heart of managing a portfolio of financial assets. It is also the feature that attracted banks to consumer credit in the first place. Since the early 1960s, revolving credit as a portion of total consumer credit outstanding went from zero to about 35 percent. This increase aided banks considerably. But without proper consumer education, it does not necessarily aid the consumer because the abundance of credit makes the term "easy credit" sound as if it means easy to pay off, when in reality it only means easy to obtain.

In keeping with the advances made in finance theory, banks began treating revolving credit like an investment rather than an asset to be held to maturity. Once the ideas became firmly accepted, the consumer credit market established a link that would begin to grow and extend its tentacles in the years ahead. How much a consumer spent and how those purchases were financed were not simply matters of household expenditure any more. They now had greater and farther-reaching implications. Consumers seemed to be incurring more and more debt with impunity. How far they could take these easy-to-get credit facilities can be seen in the development of credit cards since 1958.

Chapter Notes

1. World War II had a profound impact on programs designed for soldiers and the populations suffering from the war. In Britain for instance, many social programs, including the development of social security and the national health services, could be traced to the immediate postwar period, when it was recognized that the sacrifices of many ordinary citizens needed to be addressed by government. The same generally is true in the United States. The interest rate stipend found on veterans' mortgages is one example. The student loan program came later, in the wake of Sputnik, but the housing assistance for low- and middle-income citizens did not develop fully until civil rights legislation and housing legislation were passed in the late 1960s after the urban rioting of 1967.

2. The original MM article, the first of several on the subject, can be found in Franco Modigliani and Merton H. Miller, "The Cost of Capital, Corporation Finance, and the Theory of Investment," *American Economic Review,* Vol. 48, No. 3 (June 1958): 261–297. The second, discussing dividends, is Franco Modigliani and Merton Miller, "Dividend Policy, Growth and the Valuation of Shares," *Journal of Business,* Vol. 34, No. 4 (1961): 34, 411–433.

3. Other members of the Chicago School, either educated there or faculty members, include Milton Friedman, Gary Becker, Eugene Fama, Herbert Simon, James Buchanan, Richard Posner, George Stigler, and George P. Shultz (also treasury secretary under Richard M. Nixon), to name but a few. Thorstein Veblen, who coined the term "conspicuous consumption," was an early faculty member before the school concept emerged.

4. Markowitz's original article was "Portfolio Selection," *Journal of Finance,* Vol. 7, No. 1 (March 1952): 77–91. Markowitz and Sharpe shared the 1990 prize with Miller. Sharpe's original article is William F. Sharpe, "Capital Asset Prices: A Theory of Market Equilibrium Under Conditions of Risk," *Journal of Finance,* Vol. 19, No. 3 (1964): 425–442.

5. Altman's original Z score article was "Financial Ratios, Discriminant Analysis and the Prediction of Corporate Bankruptcy," *Journal of Finance,* Vol. 23, No. 4 (September 1968): 189–209.

6. When banks lent floating rate funds to domestic and foreign companies, they correctly assumed that most of them understood how to hedge the risk of rising interest rates. That proved not to be the case for many countries that borrowed. Most of them assumed that any rising costs could be met by the rising cost of their major exports, usually commodities, that would rise with the price of oil.

7. A summary study of individual bankruptcy until the 1980s can be found in Teresa Sullivan, Elizabeth Warren, and Jay Lawrence Westbrook, *As We Forgive Our Debtors: Bankruptcy and Consumer Credit in America* (New York: Oxford University Press, 1989).

8. The number of bank failures since 1934 is recorded by the Federal Deposit Insurance Corporation.

9. Bank capital, as defined by the agreement reached at the Bank for International Settlements, called for 8 percent capital as a percentage of loans outstanding. This is also referred to as Basel I, recently supplanted by Basel II, which is a risk-based formula based on the value-at-risk (VaR) concept of how much market risk a bank incurs daily by trading. Ironically, banks pushed hard for Basel II only to have it whiplash them in the credit market crisis because it forced down their valuations of tradable assets.

4

The Rise of
Credit Cards

Money is a poor man's credit card. —MARSHALL McLUHAN

IN A TELEVISION INTERVIEW screened in the 1970s, then Prime Minister Ian Smith of Rhodesia tried to explain to an interviewer why his government required identity cards for its black citizens. He stated it was not unusual; in fact, many governments required them, including the United States. Puzzled, the interviewer asked him what identity card he was referring to. Smith's answer: the American Express card.

Ironically, Smith struck what would become a familiar chord. Since their introduction in 1950, credit cards had become status symbols, a matter of convenience and later of necessity; almost a national badge of honor in a sense. Perhaps he took the company's slogan, "Don't leave home without it," too literally, but in the twenty or so years since their introduction, the cards had become an essential accessory of the American consumer. They became identified with consumption on a massive scale. Whoever did not have at least one was in a very small minority indeed.

Although the first national credit card was issued by Diners Club in 1950, the idea was not entirely new. In 1888, Edward Bellamy's bestseller, *Looking Backward: 2000–1887*, was published amid great fanfare. An early futurist book, it purportedly looked back at the nineteenth century from the year 2000. One of his predictions was the introduction of paperless money, where buyers would have an identification card that they could use for purchases. Although Bellamy first conceived the idea, his concept of a card was not the modern credit card. His notion was more utopian, in keeping with his times. The single card would completely replace paper money or coin and be used for all transactions. Debits and credits would be booked to a government-managed account. The messy matter of printing, coining, handling, and accounting for money would be things of the past.

Although it would be over sixty years before the credit card was introduced, the idea gained some circulation, but it would require greater technology than the nineteenth century possessed before it would succeed. But Bellamy did not discuss how such transactions would be handled. This ideal payment form would have to wait until the technology became available to implement the notion.

The first credit cards were a step in the transition to a cashless society. They would take their place alongside installment loans as a bridge between older forms of paying for purchases and newer forms, allowing consumers much greater latitude in determining how much they paid and when. But greater consumer freedom in this respect meant problems that needed to be addressed.

In their first twenty years, credit cards were discussed mostly for their effects on banking and the Fed. The new, so-called plastic money was feared because it could easily circumvent monetary policy. Since bank credit card operations, like those of the nonbanks, did not depend on customer deposits, they effectively operated on a parallel plane alongside the banking system. And they were still able to create credit effectively. Even if the Fed decided to tighten credit, cards could remain unaffected. Its reserve requirements applied only to bank deposits, and cards usually were not funded by them.

The same was true of the effects on the money supply. Although the Fed may have wanted to drain reserves from the banking system to prevent banks from creating credit, card companies would not be affected. They were causing consumption while allowing customers to pay with future dollars. Combined, the two sides of the problem were serious concerns among policy makers, but the finance companies and bank credit card subsidiaries were not fazed. For them, credit cards were simply a new means of making a profit, something that regulators could not control directly. The Fed controlled bank subsidiaries through the Bank Holding Company Act but was inclined favorably to anything that would help banks make money as long as their activities did not violate existing banking law. As a result, no one interceded. Reserves and credit card companies would have only one encounter with regulators, for a brief time in 1980, and that experiment proved short-lived.

Credit cards also offered banks latitude that was rarely discussed publicly. Because the revolving credit card was the first American experiment with adjustable interest rates of any sort, its success was assured. To date, it was the only bank instrument having the flexibility to adjust interest rates if market conditions warranted. And when that flexibility was recognized, credit cards' growth became exponential. The banks wisely marketed this as a convenience to the consumer, an argument that no regulator would oppose, at least in public. The United States was thought of as a consumer democracy after World War II, and no one wanted to be seen interfering with the engine that drove 67 percent of the GNP.

Before the revolving credit concept was introduced, cards required full payment of the bill on a monthly basis. In this respect, the cards were more restrictive than the old layaway plan that was popular before the war. The major difference was that the purchase was recorded at the time with payment to follow. Most popular were cards issued by American Express, Diners Club, individual stores, and gasoline companies.[1] The banks were eager to join their ranks. Citibank purchased a 50 percent stake in Carte Blanche as early as 1966, but its competitors objected and the antitrust regulators agreed. The bank divested its new acquisition, but its plans were plain to see. Interest was not charged on these cards; the card companies made their money by charging merchants a small transaction fee and by float management.

In addition, the early bank cards required merchants to have a deposit account at the bank as a compensating balance. No interest was charged to customers if they paid the bill in full within the first month's credit cycle. If they did not, they were considered in arrears. The profit came from the merchants. When revolving credit was introduced, the interest rate charged to unpaid balances was about 1.5 percent in the early 1970s. The annualized rate of 18 percent per year was under most usury ceilings and lower than the rates charged in the 1920s during a previous consumer boom. And because the amount was tax deductible, individuals could build up interest charges and still get some relief on their tax forms. In fact, many early explanations of cards included the tax deductibility as proof that the real cost was less than the stated rate.

To obtain a revolving card, customers usually had to have a minimum salary or income of $10,000 in the early 1970s (about $50,000 today). Because they were introduced in the late 1960s, their number burgeoned. BankAmericard (today Visa) and MasterCharge both claimed about 30 million cardholders each, and Esso led the way with 45 million for its gas card. The amounts charged were significant. BankAmericard charges jumped from $1.7 billion in 1969 to $2.7 billion a year later. BankAmericard accounted for about half of all revolving credit outstanding late in 1970. Similar percentage increases were recorded by other cards. Many people already held more than one card, although two was the average number, much less than at present when many other sorts of cards exist.[2]

What differentiates these numbers from earlier comparisons is that this credit card debt was unsecured. The idea of collateral for consumer purchases rapidly became a thing of the past. The repo man was no longer a factor if the credit cardholder failed to pay, as in the 1920s and 1930s. Failures to pay now would be reflected in a consumer's credit rating and in the use of collection agencies. Initially, the card companies protected themselves by requiring those applying for cards to have a minimum income level deemed appropriate and by limiting credit lines. But record keeping had its problems. Complaints were constantly heard that billing from the revolving companies was poor, inaccurate, and misleading. Some complained that incorrect billings cost several billion per year in improper interest charges, although no one studied the amount lost on the other side of the coin if the card companies mistakenly charged less than required. The early cards were a disaster to administer, but the problem began to correct itself as newer computers arrived on the scene.

Lost in the innovation was the simple fact that revolving credit cards had driven a nail into the coffin of secured consumer debt for qualified cardholders. Secured debt would not disappear entirely, however; it found a home with companies offering credit to those in low income brackets, those who normally could not qualify for a credit card. Innovation in consumer credit usually begins by being marketed to those in higher income brackets, with the older concepts being relegated to those in the lower brackets. The result is that those in the lower brackets are still faced with methods thought to have long since disappeared: payday loans, very high interest charges, and punitive installment loans.

Funding the Boom

The boom in credit card debt was accompanied by a boom in funding, without which it would have not occurred so quickly or profitably. Considering credit card debt as a bank activity, the assumption was that the cards used depositors' funds to purchase the receipts from the participating merchants. But this was not the case. An even more profitable—and cheaper—cost of funds provided the ammunition.

Commercial paper became the popular method of funding the purchase of credit card receivables. Using a finance subsidiary of their holding companies, banks issued the short-term paper in the money market for periods of as long as 270 days, although thirty and ninety days were more popular. Unlike deposits, commercial paper was not subject to reserve requirements and was a cheaper source of funds than deposits until interest rates began to rise in the late 1970s. Not being protected by Regulation Q meant that commercial paper rates were subject to daily change. If rates rose, the banks had the flexibility to commensurately raise the rates charged to credit card customers. Market rates with no ceiling were not a problem because the card companies could charge as much as 18 percent while commercial paper rates in the money market had never reached double digits after World War II.

Many banks took a page from the auto manufacturers' book and began opening their own finance subsidiaries, owned by their holding company parents. They were still confined to ordinary deposit-and-lending activities, but the holding companies could issue the credit cards and fund them. The amount of commercial paper issued expanded exponentially during the 1970s, paralleling the rise in credit card balances. Exceeding the usury ceilings was not a problem because interest rates in the market never hit 10 percent until 1979. As a result, commercial paper issued by all sorts of finance companies and subsidiaries increased almost 20 percent per year through the 1980s and into the early 1990s.

The money market easily accommodated the finance companies' need for short-term funds. Along with GMAC, Citicorp became the largest borrower of commercial paper and required a rolling series of auctions conducted weekly to satisfy its credit card funding. Citi sold its paper directly to the money market, auctioning it much like the Treasury does when selling its own T-bills. As a result, Citi short-term rates became one of the bellwethers of the money market in the early 1980s, and the prime rate of interest became pegged to commercial paper rate rather than to Treasury bills. Many of the banks had AAA ratings at the time, so the relatively low spreads over Treasury bills that their paper enjoyed represented the cheapest cost of funds in the market. When these cheap funds were used to buy credit card receivables, the spreads could exceed 10 percent at time, much higher than the traditional commercial banking spread between deposit and loan rates.

Citi was joined by most of the major banks in tapping the market. Other nonbank finance companies regularly borrowing were General Electric Capital, Household Finance Corporation, American Express, and the auto manufacturers' finance subsidiaries. Some finance companies, like Household, managed other companies' cards because the largest borrowers with volume business commanded the best borrowing terms. Many merchants abandoned their own credit cards and accounts receivable operations and simply contracted the operations to a larger lender. And the banks were attracted to the card business because of the constraints placed on them by the existing banking laws.

One of those laws was the continuing prohibition against interstate bank branching.[3] Banks were confined to their home state and could not open new branches across state lines. The law had been challenged in the past, but the Fed effectively upheld it by restricting bank holding company operations. Banks could expand across state lines in financial services, however. Credit card operations fell within these acceptable operations, although the patchwork of state banking laws complicated matters with possible restrictions on out-of-state banks providing financial services. But interest rates were most important to bank expansion prior to 1994 when the Interstate Branching Act was passed.

In 1980 and 1981, rates began to climb into double digits because of Paul Volcker's restrictive monetary policy at the Fed. The yield curve had become negatively sloped, with short-term rates yielding more than long rates. Commercial paper rates soon were above 15–16 percent, higher than New York's usury ceiling by 4 percent. This was putting pressure on New York credit card operations because the maximum lending rates were too low compared to market rates. Citicorp had its credit card operations outside New York City on Long Island and was faced with a dilemma. The bank's margins were being squeezed, and Jimmy Carter's special credit controls, imposed in March 1980 for several months prior to the presidential election, exacerbated the situation.

The controls were the Carter administration's answer to high market interest rates and the lack of control over some forms of credit creation. The Volcker Fed had little choice but to accommodate them, although it was in the midst of its own battle with inflation. The administration imposed higher reserve requirements, along with reserve requirements against credit card lenders if they exceeded certain limits. This was done to prevent shoppers from using their cards by clamping down on the card companies. The control worked for a short period of time before being dismantled. From the late winter of 1980 until a year later, revolving credit declined and remained flat before resuming an upward course. This was the first time a decline of that sort had been seen since revolving credit card debt was introduced in 1968.

Fees and Minimum Payments

Before Truth in Lending was passed in 1968, credit card companies had been searching for ways to charge higher rates of interest on balances without appearing to do so overtly. Past experience demonstrated that adding fees to credit card balances could be justified by claiming that the costs of handling and administration were rising and that, by adding fees now, the card companies were protecting consumers from even more odious costs in the future.

Additionally, if card balances could be extended, the companies would ensure themselves of more revenue in the future. Customers who paid their balances promptly every month actually cut a card company's profits because no interest was earned on the balance due. If the length of the payment process could be extended, all the better for the bottom line. With these two objectives in mind, the annual fee and the minimum balance were born.

The annual fee was simply a $15 or $20 charge added to a customer's balance. The net effect was to raise the effective rate of interest charged, especially when balance and credit lines were smaller than they are today. A card charging a customer 18 percent interest on a $1,000 line could add 1.5 percent to that rate by charging a $15 annual fee, effectively raising the rate to 19.5 percent.[4] If that rate exceeded a usury ceiling before 1980, the company could always claim it was not interest, just a one-time

IS THERE SUCH a thing as zero interest? Many credit card companies offer zero interest on purchases made with checks they send prospective cardholders, claiming that they charge zero interest for a stated grace period. However, the customer must be aware of the fine print. For each check written to shift another card balance to the plan or for certain charges made under them, the companies charge a transaction fee, typically $25 to $45. Therefore, a $1,000 transaction costs $25 under zero interest, an effective rate of 2.50 percent. This is beneficial to the card company because the $25 is collected immediately and does not represent an interest charge. To avoid the 2.5 percent rate, a customer could increase his credit use to $2,000. Then the effective rate would fall to 1.25 percent but he would be in more debt.

The fine print does not stop there. The credit card states that the 0 percent will be changed to a much higher rate, around 20 percent, if any payments are received late. Therefore, if the payment is made by post and the mail arrives late, the company changes the rate to the high level, to reflect the increased "risk" the cardholder presents. The card usually will not revert back to the zero rate.

charge. And it had the extra advantage of being a present value charge. The card company did not have to wait months to collect it.

The minimum payment solved the problem of relatively short life spans for some credit card balances. Rather than treat card balances as installment loans to be paid back after three years, the minimum was devised as a way to keep customer credit in good standing while requiring less of a payment than the three-year payback required. Because the minimum was just that, the balance would be outstanding longer, and the effective interest rate higher. All of this was perfectly legal because the minimum was designed to "help" customers from becoming overburdened with monthly payments. The fact that it kept the customer in debt for longer periods of time meant little to the card companies as long as the balances remained in good standing. So by adopting the minimum payment policy, creditors ensured that customers would at some time choose that option, extending the time for repayment and raising the effective interest rate, all in one fell swoop.

Critics responded to the minimum payment practice in particular, especially after the Truth in Lending Act was passed. In 1970, Ralph Nader was highly critical of the comptroller of the currency, who he said was negligent when it came to investigating consumer complaints about credit card statements issued by national banks. His targets were Chase Manhattan Bank (JP Morgan Chase) and a small Maryland bank. He noted that the comptroller did not heed complaints about the vagueness of the minimum payment concept and of its effect on interest. "This is a classic case of bureaucratic negligence," he told a congressional commission studying the lending issues. He claimed that only the comptroller could influence the banks to change what appeared to be deceptive practices by diverting customer attention away from the interest rates ostensibly being charged and focusing on the minimum payment issue, which was doing more harm than just the rate charges alone.[5]

A year later, a consumer organization filed suit against the Bank of America, claiming that it misled customers on BankAmericard statements. The suit made claims similar to those of Nader: The charges were misleading, especially because they emphasized the monthly interest rate of 1.50 percent rather than the annualized rate of 18 percent. The bank responded by stating that the Federal Reserve saw nothing incorrect in its statements, and that, because the Fed was the executor of the 1968 act, the bank had done nothing wrong. The issue became bogged down in claims and counterclaims early in the history of credit cards. Thirty years later, the issue still was being discussed by the GAO, among others, but no resolution had been found.

Despite adding the extra charges, the combination of interest rates and usury ceilings forced Citi, Chase, and the other large banks with significant retail business to plot a new strategy for dealing with the situation. For over a decade, Citi had been aggressively moving into retail banking under its CEO Walter Wriston. Consumers were enjoying the benefits briefly because the maximum rate charged in New York for consumer loans was 18 percent for the first $500 borrowed and then 12 percent for higher amounts. At the time, Citi's prime rate for business customers was above 17 percent. Business rates were higher than consumer rates but were not subject to the usury laws. Consumers were paying lower-than-market rates and that was not helping the implementation of monetary policy. The usury laws were creating an arbitrage situation whereby consumers could borrow against their cards and, if their credit lines were large enough, take the proceeds and buy Treasury bills yielding about 4 percent to 5 percent more. When customers have the ability to act like banks, banking functions are disrupted. This was one of the unforeseen problems that plastic money and revolving credit had created.

Marketing prospects that could be mined from credit cards were also a strong motive for expanding operations. The millions of card accounts were a strong draw for Citi and for others expanding into retail banking. Those lists represented valuable cross-marketing possibilities because the bank was eyeing other forms of retail financial services. In this respect, Citi was both keeping and reestablishing an old tradition. Under the leadership of Charles Mitchell in the 1920s, Citi was one of the first banks that attempted to become a financial supermarket, a place where all sorts of financial services could be offered under one roof. The crash of 1929 and the securities acts of the early 1930s put an end to that vision but it was quickly reemerging in the 1980s. Credit cards were leading the charge, along with the other consumer banking services.

Because of the high interest rate environment, Citi claimed it lost $100 million on its credit card operations in 1979, stretching into 1980, despite the relaxing of the usury laws by the Depository Institutions Deregulation and Monetary Control Act (DIDMCA). As a result, it imposed a $15 fee on its card users and increased the interest rate on them to 19.80 percent. In addition, the bank required that all customers with outstanding balances pay one thirty-sixth of what was owed on balances above $720. That would require a $20 payment. Previously, a customer could have remained in good standing with a minimum payment of $5.

Ominously for the state, Citi also began seeking a new venue for its credit card operations. New York was aware of the problem and sought ways to allow Citi to keep its card operations on Long Island. Over two thousand jobs were at stake. Governor Hugh Carey's office acknowledged the problem, stating that it was "always concerned if we have an inoperative set of laws." But the outlook in the state legislature was bleak. Members of the assembly admitted that they were sympathetic to the bank but not sanguine about the prospects of removing the usury law. The New York legislature did rescind the rate limits on consumer loans. Technically, part of the civil usury ceiling had been lifted, but the criminal usury ceiling remained at 25 percent. Citi objected to the criminal law remaining because it was possible that interest rates could rise even further, setting off a string of criminal lawsuits.

Although the civil portion of the law was removed fairly quickly, Citi already made its plans to move and did not change them. As a result of the usury law, Citi, Chase, and others went shopping for new real estate in more friendly states. The banks always had been success-ful in finding financial centers of convenience and tax havens offshore. Could they find some closer to home?

American Lichtensteins

The banks' past experience proved useful in their latest round of ex-pansion. Because credit card operations were not a core banking activ-ity, the finance and credit card subsidiaries could be located anywhere in the domestic United States where they were welcome. Banks soon discovered that several states were willing to extend their hospitality even if it meant giving the impression that they were catering to Eastern money interests.

The states' different treatments of usury would provide an open-ing for high-interest credit cards offered on a nationwide basis. There certainly were precedents. During the Civil War, a suit in a New York court over loans carrying 26 percent interest rates, signed by the par-ties in Minnesota, was thrown out. The court stated flatly that the rates recognized in Minnesota were a local matter there and that New York had no jurisdiction over them. The law in the state where the contracts were signed applied, not that of another state. Almost one hundred and twenty years later, the principle would be put to the test again.[6]

Citibank found a reception in one of the least likely places. South Dakota had usury ceilings but was willing to forgo them in return for Citibank's investment in the state. Walter Wriston quickly saw the op-portunity. In quick fashion, the state legislature removed all trappings of the law with the banks' full support. At a 1980 legislative session, the state adopted new banking laws, allowing out-of-state bank holding companies to acquire a local banking charter. It then abolished the last trappings of its usury laws. The bank moved in. Citicorp agreed to base its operations in Sioux Falls late in 1980. The workforce was very com-petent, corporate and personal income taxes did not exist, and the cost of labor was inexpensive when compared to urban states. Initially, four hundred new employees were hired.

The investment was highly successful. By the end of the 1980s, Citicorp became the largest private employer in the state with over 2,800 workers. It spent $27 million on buildings encompassing several hundred thousand square feet of space in order to process 17 million of its 27 million Visa and MasterCard accounts. The state derived $20 million per year from the bank as a franchise fee, the only tax paid. The processing center collected over $1.5 billion per year in payments. Citicorp's experience also attracted six other card-processing operations to South Dakota, including Sears, The Goodyear Tire & Rubber Company, and United Air Lines. Although some complaints were heard about the state's selling out to big business, the increased employment was more than welcome because South Dakota's population was under one million and the local economy was predominately agricultural until the finance companies arrived.

South Dakota was not alone in attracting bank processing facilities. Closer to home, Chase and others also were successful in persuading Delaware to abolish its usury laws. This was a less surprising development because the tiny state always had been in the forefront of seeking business from large corporations. It was already known for its bankruptcy courts and liberal incorporation procedures. A former chairman of the Securities and Exchange Commission once referred to it as a "pygmy state, interested only in revenues." The local joke was that the state had three counties, but only two when the tide was in.

For over a century Delaware was dominated by DuPont (E. I. du Pont de Nemours and Company), which had its operations based there since the company was founded. In 1980, Chase began lobbying for the state to abolish its usury laws but met with a cool reception until several of the state's senior businesspeople were approached. A year later, the legislature passed its own version of a bank liberalization law, allowing out-of-state banks to open operations on the condition that they did not engage in retail banking, in order to protect the local banks. In return, a very low state tax rate was imposed that actually decreased to only 2.7 percent when the card subsidiaries earned more than $30 million.

Other consumer finance businesses seized the opportunity. Chase was joined by Manufacturers Hanover Corporation, Bank of New York

(Bank of New York Mellon), Chemical Bank, Citicorp, Bankers Trust Company, J. P. Morgan, and E. F. Hutton & Company, all seeking an operations base for securities clearing or for their credit cards. Among the stores, JCPenney and Montgomery Ward & Company also set up consumer credit operations. "We had no idea it was going to be so successful," said Delaware's governor. Most of the jobs and the building boom they brought occurred in Wilmington and its suburbs. Delaware was opportunistic and attracted ten thousand new jobs. It seemed that abolishing usury laws could be profitable indeed.

Other smaller banks followed Citicorp and Chase in requesting a rollback of usury laws. Twin City Savings and Loan Association, based in Minnesota, requested that the state rescind its usury laws so that it could offer card services in the state, based on its expanded powers under the Depository Institutions Act of 1982. Part of its argument was that it would then not have to charge the $25 fee it leveled against cardholders in the state as compensation for operating under the usury law. Citicorp's argument was beginning to be heard in many places, and not all of the requests were coming from big banks.

In Massachusetts, the case was slightly different. Two of the state's larger banks threatened to move their card operations out of state to avoid the state's 18 percent interest ceiling. Both government and community leaders protested and threatened a boycott. In this case, the banks lowered their rates as a sign of good faith. The problem for the state banks was simple. Citicorp and others not based in Massachusetts were actively soliciting their cards in the state and were charging customers 19.80 percent interest. The state banks wanted to do the same, but the official usury ceiling was lower. When Massachusetts did revise its usury law in 1985, it used a flexible market-based formula. It calculated the usury ceiling as twice the 91-day T-bill rate, which at the time was 8 percent. "In Massachusetts we're still feeling a lot of competition from out of state, like Citibank, which has been doing a lot of heavy solicitation," said one local banker, reflecting all banks' desire to raise interest charges to keep ahead of high commercial paper rates and Citi. By that time, the influence of cards was taken for granted. "We are a nation of credit card junkies," remarked Representative Frank Annunzio (Democrat of Illinois).

After an economic recovery began in late 1982, consumer debt as a percentage of household disposable income began to rise. Credit card debt also showed a strong increase, aiding in the recovery. But bank experiences with bad credit card loans also began to rise sharply, leaving banks with little choice but to write them off. The bank cards also had new competition. In the early 1980s, American Express began offering its Optima card, which offered revolving credit. Sears introduced its Discover Card, also offering revolving credit. The overall business was quite profitable, attracting new entrants despite the strength of the established leaders, Visa and MasterCard.

The logic used by the card companies seemed foolproof. Because credit cards were not collateralized, higher interest had to be charged to most customers. If write-offs could be contained at small percentages of the total, the business could grow. Then a new element was introduced. To enhance yields, cards were offered to those in riskier categories such as students or those in low-income groups. Soon, Wall Street would offer card companies a way to relieve themselves of some of the risk, opening the door to even more consumer credit.

Card defaults were increasing but in the late 1980s, the sky was the limit. Simple risk/reward ratios suggested that riskier cardholders could legitimately be charged higher interest. Without collateral backing, the argument was justified, and cards were being offered to individuals who would not have fit the lending profile ten years earlier. The portfolio concept was leading to a democratization of credit. But the expansion of so many forms of credit needed innovative financing techniques if the growth was to continue.

Sweeping the Sheets

During the years that the developing countries' debt crisis dominated the news, a major goal of banks was to keep their balance sheets as clear as possible. Although a bull market began to develop in stocks in 1983, it was far from clear at the time that it would last, and the banks' need for capital continued. In the absence of a strong new issues market, especially with their prospects cloudy, the banks were intent on creating fewer loans and finding new ways to make money. Citicorp devoted almost $200 million to developing credit card operations under John Reed, who succeeded Walter Wriston in 1984, in the first two years of his tenure. More innovation was needed from the banks' perspective.

A new wrinkle was taken from the government-sponsored enterprises (GSEs). Since the early 1970s, the three mortgage-assistance agencies had been securitizing successfully, but no private enterprise had attempted it. The reason was a simple credit matter. When a GSE securitized a mortgage, the assumption was that the agency was a better credit risk than the collateral. If the pool of mortgages failed, the agency would step in and make up the shortfall. And there was the implicit assumption that if the agency failed, the Treasury would support it. The formula and the guarantee assumption worked well for the first fifteen years that the agencies securitized debt. Quickly forgotten was the fact that the agencies were founded to assist the residential market with specific objectives in mind.

Ginnie Mae, the agency that remained owned by the Treasury, was mandated to intermediate in favor of urban housing for those in lower income brackets. Fannie Mae continued buying approved mortgages of the Federal Housing Administration, Veterans Administration, and other programs designed to help specific target groups within society. Freddie Mac was the mortgage arm of the Federal Home Loan Bank Board, the national regulator of the federally chartered thrifts. Freddie had less of a social purpose than the others because it intermediated on behalf of the small depository institutions rather than another government program. Securitization took the mortgages off the books of the lenders and transferred them to pools supporting bonds. The obligations of the agencies were off-balance-sheet liabilities (or contingent liabilities), reported not in the liabilities side of the balance sheet but only as a footnote. Would this concept work well when done by banks whose sole motive was to clear their balance sheets so that they could lend again?

Unfortunately, the banks were not in an enviable situation. In many cases, their balance sheets had been weakened in the high interest rate environment. Their loans often were of better quality than their overall balance sheets. In this situation, opportunity presented itself. If the banks could securitize their better-quality loans, investors would buy bonds backed by them when they otherwise might have eschewed the direct bank debt itself.

Although the mortgage agencies securitized long-term debt based on 30-year mortgages, the banks began securitizing shorter assets, such as credit card receivables and car loans (dubbed "CARs," short for certificates of auto receivables). Securitization can be applied to any pool

SECURITIZATION DEPENDS ON the creditworthiness of its collateral, but many older, traditional bonds also had collateral backing. The first well publicized case of tampering with bond collateral originated with Ivar Krueger, the Swedish Match King of the 1920s. His company, International Match, had exclusive rights to produce matches in many countries. His success eventually led him to finance some of his operations in the American markets. In one case, he borrowed bonds, collateralizing them with gold, only later clandestinely to switch the collateral with risky South American bonds, which eventually defaulted after the 1929 crash. His underwriters proclaimed ignorance of the matter, and the revelations helped bring about the end of his match and finance empire. As a result of the collateral switch, Congress eventually passed the Trust Indenture Act in 1939, designed to protect the integrity of collateral against swindlers and to define the role of trustees for bond indentures and collateral. Krueger died in Paris a few years after the crash, apparently of a self-inflicted gunshot wound, but the exact circumstances are cloudy.

of financial assets that investors are willing to accept as collateral. Key to constructing a pool is the nature of the asset. Real property assets like real estate or airplanes, locomotives, or automobiles may be used to back a bond, but the security would be classified as a first mortgage bond rather than as an asset-backed security (ABS). ABSs use only financial assets as collateral such as the lease on an airplane or locomotive or mortgages on property. In other words, investors are not interested in the property itself but only the income stream it produces.

The banks would remove the assets from their loan portfolios, sometimes overcollateralize the amount nominally pledged, get insurance for a portion of the pool of mortgages from one of the bond insurers, and then sell the bond or commercial paper based on the strength of the collateral. Investors bought the debt obligations based on the quality of the underlying collateral, not the banks' credit rating. The process began in 1984 with First Boston leading the charge into what became known as asset securitization. In the first year, First Boston underwrote over $1 billion in asset-backed securities.

Credit cards were not the first examples of asset securitization, how-ever. The first credit card ABS appeared in 1987. They were more diffi-cult to construct than auto receivables because more loans were included in the pool supporting the bonds. Typically, the early deals required rep-resentatives of the bond issuer, investment bankers, accountants, and lawyers to gather and hammer out a deal with some financial engineers, versed in structuring payment flows. After a couple of years, templates were devised making the issuing process less cumbersome—and faster. That speed would prove troublesome in the years ahead.

On paper, the new ABSs were the perfect answer to banks' need to clear loans off their books. How investors would react and how the new bonds would perform in the market was an unknown in the equation. One underwriter commented that "there is not a lot of history to how these instruments perform in different types of markets. We are approaching this cautiously." One of the reasons for caution came from bank inves-tors themselves. Clearly, banks were adding to their liquidity and clearing the balance sheets to engage in even more business, but at what cost? Another underwriter summed it up succinctly, remarking, "We may be disenfranchising existing shareholders by selling off the best assets and leaving them with what is left." Unfortunately, twenty years later when the crisis occurred in the subprime mortgage market, shareholders were disenfranchised along with a legion of unhappy investors.

The first auto manufacturing credit subsidiary to test the ABS market was GMAC, launching its first issue in 1985. Over the next several years, GMAC dominated the ABS market with a flurry of issues. The invest-ment banks took its acceptance as a seal of approval for the new debt instruments, and the market issued increasing numbers of new bonds in the years ahead. Quite often, asset-backed securities outnumbered more traditional varieties of corporate bonds. Their great virtue was that collateral could be chosen when it was in vogue in the market. The busi-ness opportunities were wide open again for many Wall Street firms to do underwriting on a large scale.

Not only bonds were being securitized. A large market opened for asset-backed commercial paper. A sponsor financial institution issued commercial paper backed by receivables such as credit cards or other loans, bought through a special-purpose vehicle (SPV). The number of these SPVs increased dramatically. From only three in existence in 1985, the number expanded to ninety by 1991. In that year, the SEC passed a new rule raising the ratings level on commercial paper that could be bought by money market funds. As a result, some issues never made it to market during the recession that year, although the standard protected investors in those funds from increased default risk.[7]

For the first twenty years, credit card ABSs stood on the credit of the pool of assets pledged to back the bond. Technically, the bank or finance company wanting to securitize would create a special-purpose vehicle, or trust in this case, which would issue the bonds and pledge the receivables as collateral. Because the assets were now off the balance sheet of the original lender, the trust was considered *bankruptcy remote*, meaning that, even if the bank or finance company went bankrupt, the bonds would survive standing alone and be paid off by the trust. After the debt crisis of the 1980s and banking problems of the early 1990s, this concept was appreciated by investors, but as banks grew stronger financially, it became less of an issue.

If investors still required additional assurance that the trust pool would pay in timely fashion, banks could overcollateralize it or obtain bond insurance from one of the monoline insurers. This became known as *credit enhancement* and would add to the costs of doing the deal. But most finance companies considered it a cost worth meeting because the ABS trust bond appealed to a wider array of investors than a traditional bank bond. As long as the bonds were well rated by the ratings agencies, investors had faith in the ABSs, and they became the fastest growing sector of the bond market. This provided an extra boost to the funding of credit card receivables in general.

Securitization transformed the credit card market like no other single innovation since cards were first introduced. In 1989, about 30 percent of all securitized consumer debt was revolving. By year-end 2007, the percentage had risen to 67 percent of the total. In the latter year, two-thirds of all consumer debt had been securitized. Lenders were no longer traditional lenders in the old standard banking sense. They now were nothing more than agents creating debt to be packaged and cleared off the books.

When securitization became popular among banks, it was billed as a win-win situation. The banks benefited, Wall Street underwriters benefited, and consumers benefited. The banks were free to create new credit card debt after clearing older loans off their books. Investment bankers had a new source of underwriting and packaging fees, and consumers got easier credit. Clearly, however, there had to be some downside to the process. There was, but at a higher level: The process was fraught with risk, to the banking system rather than to the banks. The problem was tricky.

The securitization process had put credit card companies in the credit creation process, and that process was outside the Fed's scope because any finance company with access to a cheap source of funds could enter the credit card business. Nonbanks were now fully engaged in credit creation, which was also taking place at the wholesale level of banking where nonbanks such as GE Capital were competing with the banks when making short-term business loans. Their source also was commercial paper, not deposits. The business was not as profitable as credit cards but was much cheaper to administer. Banking had gradually gained new members to its ranks that were outside the regulators' orbit.

One structural problem that posed a hindrance to securitizing credit card receivables was made much simpler by the minimum payment. Card balances paid off quickly would be difficult to securitize into a bond, and many were more suitable for asset-backed commercial paper. But as the minimum payment extended the life of card member balances, those receivables with longer assumed lives could be used to collateralize notes of three years or slightly longer to maturity, if the correct assumption was made about their life based on projected repayments. Again, market techniques were having a serious effect on the nature of consumer credit.

As the ABS market matured, it was slowly becoming obvious that the Fed had no direct control over consumer credit or was not willing to rein it in. Financial institutions outside its direct control were creating large amounts of consumer credit and were also creating business loans. Rather than exercise its influence through the Bank Holding Company Act, the Fed appeared content to fight the effects of inflation in the early and mid-1980s, unwilling to stand in the way of financial innovation. The price for that neglect would be paid at a later date.

Democratizing Credit

The net effect of securitization was to make banks more lax when extending credit to customers. If the receivables had remained on the books of the credit card subsidiary, write-offs would have eventually put a brake on the card business by forcing banks to reassess their policies toward unsecured loans. Enabling the banks to place them in a pool with other receivables meant that their portfolio characteristics were more important than their quality. A pool of $100 million of card receivables may have contained $10 million of card balances extended to students, not the most reliable payers. The risk was worth taking because the yield on that portion would be higher, assuming that student payments were timely.

Experience in other parts of the student market should have provided a clue to the risk of that sector. Banks regularly making student loans sold them to Sallie Mae or another loan purchasing agency precisely because student credit was poor.[8] Student default rates on government-guaranteed loans ran as high as 30 percent in the late 1980s and early 1990s, the highest default rate suffered by lenders. Yet banks still were willing to solicit students by mail, offering them credit. It seemed almost natural that those debts should be sold to a third party as well.

The 1990s became known as the decade of the preapproved card offer, regularly delivered in the mail to millions of homes. Credit was no longer simply easy to obtain. It had been commoditized. The credit lines offered to customers were exacerbated by the fact that many card companies offered similar deals. It was easy for anyone, even those with questionable credit profiles, to obtain much more credit than needed simply by obtaining multiple cards.

As cards were peddled to college students, the typical stories began to emerge about profligate spending created by the easy credit. Students were being offered cards without their parents' knowledge and accumulating as much as $25,000 in card debt. The typical charges included items such as alcohol, tobacco, vacations, and "self-mutilation" (body piercing). Also common were charges for traffic tickets and bail. One undergraduate at a Washington, DC, university ran up $20,000 in debt in 1998 on sixteen different cards and a $10,000 consolidation loan in addition to a $30,000 student loan already outstanding. He told a reporter that the student loan had to be separated from the rest because it was what he called "good debt" versus "bad debt." Another student at a nearby university ran up similar balances on thirteen different cards and filed for bankruptcy at age twenty-three. Many of them were able to keep their balances from falling into arrears by making the minimum payment only until the scheme ran its course.

Not everyone agreed with the assessment of profligate spending among college students. In 2006, a representative of the American Bankers Association told a congressional committee that 65 percent of college students paid their bills in full each month. Warning about reacting to anecdotal evidence, he claimed that the average student balance was only $452 and that the student payment rate was higher than that of the general cardholding population, which was only 40 percent that year. The numbers were producing very different interpretations.

Competition among the credit card companies led to too many cards being offered and mounting debt by consumers who could not afford to pay it back. The minimum payment was the only way that multiple card debt could be maintained. Similar stories abounded among all strata of society. The most surprising phenomenon to arise from the democratization of credit cards was the amount of credit made available to the poor. In 1983, about one in thirty poor families had a credit card. By 1995, the number had risen to one in eight. During the same period, household debt (including credit cards) rose significantly for poor families as a proportion of total income, along with continued bankruptcy filings for all levels of income.[9] This second stage of the postwar debt revolution was proving far more radical than the first. Only twenty years before, cards were offered to those who met income criteria. Now they were offered to the poor, who were the least prepared to understand the implications or the compound mathematics of credit card interest. Securitization was opening new windows of opportunity for the lenders. A similar situation was found in the 1990s when subprime lending developed, offering mortgages to low-income people who were the least able to afford the high rates attached. The American Dream was on offer, but at a very high price.

When a credit-card holder defaulted on the debt, intermediaries sprang up to take the loans off card companies' books. Many companies went into the business of buying what the card companies call "charged-off" debt at very deep discounts and then attempting to collect from the defaulted cardholders at higher prices. The first sale of charged-off debt came in 1989 when the Bank of America sold $35 million of bad card debt for 2 cents on the dollar. At the time of writing, the number of collection companies currently buying charged-off debt from card companies stands at 29, down from over 100 in 2000.

Securitization would not have developed without the aid of better, high-speed computers. Keeping track of the performance of a pool of

mortgages or credit card receivables is a daunting task without computing facilities. The three mortgage-assistance agencies could begin
securitizing residential mortgages only when computers were up to
the task. Without them, the errors would have wiped out any potential
benefits because bond investors needed to be repaid on time, without
any delay.

Credit or Commodity?

After Alan Greenspan assumed the helm of the Fed from Paul Volcker
in 1987, a number of changes occurred in the banking community.
Under his tenure, banks would be allowed greater latitude in their activities than at any time since 1933. Over the next 20 years, they would
gradually be allowed back into lines of business from which they had
been barred, namely investment banking and insurance. For those that
did not venture into those areas, credit card lending still provided one
of the highest margins in banking.

The Fed was lenient in its interpretations of bank holding company
activities. The pressure to engage in traditional nonbanking activities
became even greater than in the past. When compared to investment
banking or mergers and acquisitions, credit cards seemed more natural
for many banks because they had more experience in the area than in
the previously forbidden ones. As a result, credit card lending became
more aggressive in the 1990s, with new portfolios being created, consist-
ing of more loans to lower-income groups and those with questionable
credit histories. The 1990s became the decade of the aggressive card
lender and, as a result, of the increased use of cards in transactions.

Every trend the card companies established in the period to the early
1990s was continued after 1995 into the 2000s. Making credit available
to those with questionable credit histories continued unabated as lenders
bet that the revenues they could potentially derive from them at higher
interest rates were worth the effort and the risk. Although the losses appeared large, they seemed to have been proven correct. Since 1997, the
delinquency rate of general-purpose credit cards has averaged approximately 5 percent. Charge-offs were only about 0.5 percent higher.

The low default and charge-off rates became an excuse to offer even
more cards. A similar argument was used in the 1980s to justify the levels
of junk bonds being issued by noninvestment-grade companies. If only a

few percent actually defaulted historically, that risk was worth assuming by investors seeking higher-than-average returns on their investments. The portfolio argument easily won the day again. Credit card companies also employed sophisticated models of consumer behavior to help assess risk, including statistical methods of predicting defaults and charge-offs as well as neural risk management techniques. The latter, based on assessing each individual's credit risk factors, how they relate to each other, and supposedly human brain functions, could be used to assist a merchant in determining on the spot whether a customer should be extended credit by a computer for a purchase. This was basically the method the original Markowitz model of portfolio selection employed.

The credit card industry refers to itself as the "payments system" or as the "card payments system." This name became more of a self-fulfilling prophecy in the 1990s as card use rapidly increased, overtaking cash transactions for the first time. The value of cards to banks resulted in one major upheaval in the credit markets when Citigroup announced that it was abandoning its Visa cards in favor of MasterCard in 1999, claiming that it could use MasterCard in conjunction with its own payments system more easily and cheaply than it could use the Visa network. It followed by acquiring the Sears card and its membership list from the store in 2003. That acquisition ended the independence of the first retail store card, devised in 1911. Sears previously sold its Discover card to broker Dean Witter Reynolds, which was later acquired by Morgan Stanley.

Bankruptcy Reform

The paradox the card companies presented in their lending activities was clear. While creating easy credit on the one hand, they naturally wanted tough laws on the other to protect themselves against the problems they created. Credit card lenders were especially fearful of customers' declaring bankruptcy to avoid paying their balances. They mounted an intensive lobbying campaign concerning reform of the 1978 bankruptcy laws in 1999. The lenders wanted fewer people to be able to declare personal bankruptcy and imposed their will finally on Congress not to make the current law broader or more liberal. Their lobbying was crucial. Representative Henry Hyde (Republican of Illinois) described the power of the industry's lobbyists as "awesome," as his amendment to soften the bill went down to defeat. The bill died in the White House.

In 2004, Chapter 7 and 13 bankruptcies accounted for 30 percent of card charge-offs. Consumer bankruptcies were 1.56 million in 2004, down from 1.625 million in 2003. Congress finally reformed the bankruptcy code in 2005, twenty-seven years after the last reform was passed. The original critics of the 1978 law appeared to be correct. The code was being used to avoid excessive credit card debt. In the months before the new law became effective in October 2005, personal bankruptcy filings soared and with them credit card defaults. Before the act, filings averaged about 1.6 million per year. After the law became effective, they declined by a million cases. Although it may be argued that the new law inflated the numbers before October 2005, they began to rise again, even under the new code, after a brief respite. Part of the phenomenon can be attributed to publicity. The new law was widely covered by the print and broadcast media. Every major radio and television station, every magazine, and every newspaper ran stories on its eventual arrival, so many debtors knew of its potential consequences and the short time in which they had to act.

The Bankruptcy Abuse Prevention and Consumer Protection Act required filers to get bankruptcy counseling and increased the amount of court fees required (presumably, filers could not charge that amount to their credit cards). *The Nilson Report* analyzed the numbers before and after the act took effect, and the numbers appeared to confirm critics' greatest fears. The 1978 code was being used by credit card abusers who filed for bankruptcy rather than paying their debts. Before the new act, Chapter 7 filings averaged about 1.14 million per year and $41,000 each, causing a loss to lenders of $23.5 billion. After the act, the number of filings fell to 349,000 in 2006 for an average of $58,000 each and a total loss of $10.26 billion.

Chapter 13 filings were similar. Before the act, the average number of filings was 428,000, which immediately dropped to 248,000 in 2006. The average amount of a filing increased from $30,000 to $78,000, representing losses of $8.40 billion to $12.60 billion for the creditors. The law created a means test for those filing under Chapter 7 so the increase in Chapter 13 filings was not unusual. Several assumptions made about bankrupts also were confirmed by the results.

Most people filing under Chapter 7 had few assets to liquidate, so little was lost by wiping the slate clean. Others were clever enough to hide them so that it appeared that little was left to satisfy creditors in the courts. A procedure employed by credit collection agencies also seemed to be known to those in arrears on their cards. Collectors would not pursue a person in arrears who was unemployed. When many of those individuals did find employment, they then often filed for Chapter 13 to protect their assets immediately from the collectors who would pursue them again.

Consumers would need another outlet for all the debt that was tax deductible, offering some relief for the commodity they had so easily accepted. Consumer behavior regarding credit cards was recognized by critics but mostly ignored by policy makers before the credit market crisis began in the summer of 2007. With so many cards on offer and so much credit potentially available to even poorly rated customers, consumer credit was being treated in much the same way that automobile insurance was a generation earlier. Creditors and debtors alike treated credit as nothing more than a transaction, ignoring an individual's personal debt service ratios (pretax income divided by interest charges due). Auto insurance switched to a no-fault program when it became clear that establishing fault in the case of an accident was pointless after too many transactions swamped the auto insurers' systems in the 1960s and 1970s. The same had become true of consumer credit twenty years later. Now, consumer credit was no one's fault, just a minimum to be paid to be kept intact.

If customers defaulted and the balances were sent for collection, their other cards ordinarily would penalize them by charging higher interest, in the same way an auto insurance company would increase the premium for too many accidents. But even the so-called concept of universal default was changing. Citibank announced in 2007 that it would not change the interest charged to a customer who defaulted on another card. Other lenders were not as generous. Creditworthiness ultimately was not in jeopardy unless an egregious act of debt abuse or denial occurred. Even bankrupts were able to reestablish credit after a relatively short grace period. The credit card company would not attempt to tutor them in the ways of being better customers any more than an auto insurer would suggest that claimants attend driving school. Only Congress thought of that when mandating credit counseling for those filing bankruptcy under the 2005 act. Even after that date, it appeared that the courts were not actively enforcing that part of the law, presumably adding to the number of new bankruptcies being filed.

Although outstanding credit card debt increased each year after 2001, a bright spot occurred in 2002. The use of debit cards exceeded the use of credit cards for the first time. The amounts charged did not involve going into debt but simply using the card to debit a checking account. In this respect, debit cards were being used for many of the same reasons the original credit cards were: convenience, record keeping, and immediate clearing of transactions. They were simply the contemporary answer to writing a check or using cash. In this respect, they represented a real-time transaction as far as the consumer was concerned.

The trend is expected to increase in the near future as debit cards become even more popular. A similar trend appeared in Britain, where the use of plastic overtook cash in 2004 despite the fact that the credit card phenomenon appeared later in the United Kingdom than in the United States. The use of debit cards in Britain is less surprising because the United Kingdom traditionally has had a higher household savings ratio than the States. The use of plastic in general has now supplanted cash as the favorite transaction in both countries, although the proportion of debit to credit card use differs.

The trend has posed policy problems for years. From 2006 to the present, the U.S. money supply, as measured by M1, stood at about $1.37 trillion. Credit card spending (including debit cards, prepaid cards, and other sorts of pin cards) for purchases totaled $471 billion in 2007, with Bank of America accounting for 15 percent of the turnover with its various cards, followed by American Express (14 percent), Chase Manhattan Bank (12 percent), and Citibank (8 percent). The majority of the total was attributed to the cards of a hundred banks. The relative stability of the money supply is attributable to the use of cards at the expense of cash and checks, unlike the early 1980s when money supply growth was an inflationary problem requiring serious attention from the Fed. Even at that time, Jimmy Carter with his special credit controls recognized the problem that card credit had on the administration's ability to restrain inflation and financial stability. The motives for issuing as much plastic as possible were obvious. Credit cards rapidly were becoming part of the payments system, threatening to quickly doom cash and checks to obscurity.

In the forty years since they were introduced, credit cards and their other plastic cousins—prepaid cards and debit cards—have proved to be the most successful financial innovation in American history. The

IN 2006, THE TOP TEN most profitable U.S. credit card issuers were Bank of America, Citigroup, JP Morgan Chase, American Express Company, Capital One, Wells Fargo, HSBC Bank USA, Discover, U.S. Bancorp, and Washington Mutual Incorporated. But the differences in net income earned from cards was significant. Bank of America earned $5.64 billion, Citigroup $3.89 billion, and JP Morgan Chase $3.21 billion, whereas U.S. Bancorp earned $970 million and Washington Mutual $750 million.

numbers they have produced are staggering. At the end of 2007, customers used bank-issued credit cards to pay for $4.34 trillion worth of purchases worldwide, with the Americans and Europeans accounting for 75 percent. To achieve that total, over 64.5 billion transactions occurred, with Americans accounting for almost half of them. Over 2.38 billion cards exist, with slightly over a billion in use in the United States alone.[10] That represents three credit cards for every person in the United States, whether they actually had a card or not. In mid-2008, $954 billion in revolving consumer credit was outstanding in the United States, along with $1.6 trillion of nonrevolving credit, for a total of $2.55 trillion.[11] This did not include home equity loans. Of the revolving credit, statistics suggest that around 40 percent of credit card bills are paid when the first bill arrives, with the balance financed on a revolving basis.

THE MEDIA ALWAYS report consumer credit numbers around the Christmas holiday season as an indicator of the health of the economy. Usually, the amount of revolving credit increases sharply from November to December and then declines in January and February before resuming an upward climb in March. That pattern has been evident ever since the amount of revolving credit was first recorded in 1968.

Collision Course

While securitization was trumpeted as something for everyone, a down-side to the practice rarely caught attention. As well constructed as the pools of assets underlying ABSs were thought to be, what would happen if there were defaults among the pools? What effects would they have on the individual bond trusts? For decades the questions were thought to be purely academic.

The mortgage market provides an example. When banks began sell-ing pools of residential mortgages to one of the GSEs, there still were residual benefits for them. The mortgage-originating bank continued to collect the mortgage payments made by the homeowner every month and passed them to the agency, minus a collection fee for its efforts. Those fees were not particularly high but were still profitable for the bank. If they slowed or stopped, the bank would lose that source of revenue. And there was the other matter of the ownership of the ABSs themselves. Who were the investors buying them? And how would they react if the income streams stopped?

Securitized bonds issued by the mortgage assistance agencies were a variation of the covered bond, an instrument used in Europe for over two centuries. If the collateral began to fail, the institution that issued the bonds in the first place stood ready to assume the payments so that the bond did not default. This was the most prominent feature of the mortgage-backed security (MBS). That feature gave the MBS a privi-leged place in the bond markets, trading at very small spreads above Treasury obligations despite the fact that two of the three GSEs were traded on the New York Stock Exchange.

But ABSs were different because the bond issued by the SPV trust stood on its own. If the collateral fell in value or defaulted, so too did the bond. It was not covered by the original issuer. This was true of the private label ABSs supported by subprime mortgages issued dur-ing the mortgage boom after 2001. They were nothing more than the long-term version of an ABS backed by credit card receivables, auto loans, or leases. When their collateral began to deteriorate, there was no recourse.

Of the nearly hundreds of billions in losses incurred by banks and investors during the subprime crisis, these subprime-backed bonds were the main culprits. Then in 2008, the large banks began announcing losses on their ABS holdings as well. Credit cards were falling into arrears, and the banks were feeling the pinch, announcing losses on both the value of the bonds and the fees they earned by continuing to collect the receivables.

The problem was compounded by interbank relations. Many banks bought other banks' asset-backed securities with the intention of holding them as investments. Many foreign banks especially bought large amounts of subprime mortgage-backed securities from American banks, hoping to cash in on the mortgage explosion that began after September 2001. Others bought similar packages of collateralized loans designed with specific cash flow purposes in mind. Most were collateralized by debt instruments designed for specific purposes. The same was true of credit-card-backed bonds. Banks with no exposure to the American mortgage or consumer lending market incurred some exposure by buying ABSs, with less than the desired results.

Cracks were appearing in the consumer credit market almost from the day revolving credit was introduced. Practices such as noncollateralized credit card debt and securitization (when applied to the cards) helped develop fault lines in the system that had the potential to crack given the proper circumstances. The potential for collateral damage in other parts of the credit markets was now gaining significant strength. The most vulnerable area was that of home equity loans.

Since the Fed began allowing commercial banks greater latitude in their activities beginning in the early 1990s, old distinctions between investment and commercial banking had blurred. After the Financial Services Modernization Act was passed in 1999, the old lines of demarcation officially fell and commercial banks could now engage in investment banking and insurance. A bank holding company technically could own these types of subsidiaries. The old dream of Citibank, born in the 1920s, finally became a reality after 75 years of waiting. The financial department store was born again.

Early experiences with the concept, especially the combination of commercial and investment banking under one roof, were not fruitful. When Enron and WorldCom collapsed under the weight of fraud in 2002 and 2003, many of the large banks were forced to take losses based on loans and investment banking services performed for both companies. To win their investment banking business, the banks made them short-term loans at fine terms that later had to be written off. Under the old Glass-Steagall regime, they could not have performed the investment banking functions.

The same problem was evident during the subprime crisis and the credit market crisis in general. Many banks had made mortgages to customers and securitized them in order to clear their books. But many banks also kept the ABSs created by the investment banks, sometimes their own subsidiaries, on their books because they now were securities, not just simple mortgage loans. In their great haste to participate in the mortgage boom, the banks were acting as bankers, investment bankers, *and* investors, not a prudent combination of activities. When asked at a congressional committee hearing why his bank rushed headlong into many areas of the mortgage market, former Citigroup CEO Charles Prince responded simply, "because the investment banks were doing it."

Securitizing all sorts of assets subjected banks to one of the greatest dangers that the old banking laws tried to prevent: overexposure to closely related risk. In this case, it was the combination of credit card debt and mortgage debt. When banks securitized, they moved in the right direction by sweeping the assets off their balance sheets. But when they bought ABSs for their own investments, they simply reexposed themselves to the same risks in a different package. The counterparty risk still was present, although the ABSs were more liquid than the loans themselves, at least in theory. If the two major sectors of the ABS market ever collided, the repercussions would mark a new point in finance.

The collision began in 2007 and continued into 2008. After 1996, the growth rate in credit card use slowed although it still managed to reach new highs each year. The main reason was the use of home equity lines of credit. Homeowners began paying down card debt through the lines, using lower-rate, tax-deductible debt in place of the higher-interest-rate card debt. In that respect, the strategy was successful. According to a Federal Reserve paper coauthored by Alan Greenspan, from 1996 to 2006 home equity of almost $800 billion was used to pay off consumer debt, including credit cards, installment credit, and other loans, along with financing home improvements, education, and other purposes.[12] It is not possible to tell how much of the total was used to pay down credit card debt, but that category of debt as a percentage of overall debt outstanding declined to slightly under 3 percent of the total U.S. debt bill of $30.5 trillion in late 2006.[13] This is the point where conspicuous consumption can be seen turning into cannibal consumption: using home equity to pay off unsecured credit card debt.

Consumers were using the rising equity in their homes, fueled by the rising housing market, to "cash out the equity" in their homes, a favorite mortgage banker phrase. But the actual percentage of equity in their homes was not rising as a result of these refinancings; it was falling, replaced by more debt. That strategy worked tolerably well as long as the housing market rose. But most home equity loans are made on an adjustable basis, so if interest rates rose or if the market stopped rising or fell, the strategy had the potential to backfire. When the subprime crisis began, it was clear that it would extend to other parts of the mortgage market because prices were falling sharply, eroding the increased equity many homeowners had borrowed against.

As consumers faced increasing interest bills on their revolving consumer debt and as many adjustable rate mortgages began to rise, consumers were faced with the most difficult choices in several generations. With home equity declining and credit card debt at an historic high, if consumers under severe financial pressure were faced with stretching their limited financial means, they were looking at a nasty prospect. Which would become more valuable under such circumstances: the home with negative equity or a functioning credit card line? The potential for collateral damage in the markets would be substantial.

Chapter Notes

1. In the 1970s, some well-known credit cards such as American Express, Diners Club, and most of the oil company cards initially did not offer revolving credit and were classified as nonrevolving.

2. Two period accounts of credit card operations in the 1970s can be found in Robert A. Hendrickson, *The Cashless Society* (New York: Dodd, Mead, 1972), and Lewis Mandell, *Credit Card Use in the United States* (Ann Arbor: University of Michigan, 1972).

3. Banks were not permitted to cross state lines and open a new branch because of the constraints placed on them by the McFadden Act of 1927, originally aimed at banks with national charters. The act effectively fragmented American banking until the Interstate Branching Act was passed in 1994, allowing banks to expand geographically.

4. There was considerable legal discussion about the fees charged by credit card issuers and whether they constituted a form of interest. This issue was confused even more when card companies began issuing elite cards, sometimes charging an annual fee of as much as $2,500. For the price, the cardholder was entitled to special treatment at sporting events, private airplane hires, and other services not available to the average cardholder.

5. In 2006, minimum balances and other practices of credit card companies were addressed in a paper by the GAO. See "Credit Cards: Customized Minimum Payment Disclosures Would Provide More Information to Customers but Impact Could Vary." Government Accountability Office, April 2006.

6. The New York court case challenging the Minnesota usury law was *Joshua Balme v. Henry Wornbough,* 1862.

7. The SEC rule that raised the quality ratings for money market funds was Rule 2a-7, which became effective in June 1991.

8. Sallie Mae, the student loan intermediary, did not securitize its loans because of their notoriously poor reputation for being paid on time. In the late 1980s, it was discovered that many higher education loans, eligible under the federal loan guarantee program, were being made to students at trade schools, beauty academies, and the like that charged high fees but did little to place their graduates in jobs. As a result, many of those students were left without cash and jobs after graduation, unable to pay back the loans to Department of Education lenders.

9. An article tracing the rise of lending to the poor can be found in Edward J. Bird, Paul A. Hagstrom, and Robert Wild, "Credit Card Debts of the Poor: High and Rising," *Journal of Policy Analysis and Management,* Vol. 18, No. 1 (Winter 1999): 125–134.

10. The credit card industry statistics cited here, as in previous chapters, are found in *The Nilson Report.*

11. The amount of consumer credit outstanding and the major creators of the debt are supplied by the Federal Reserve in several publications, most notably the *Survey of Consumer Finances* and the *Federal Reserve Statistical Release.*

12. The article concerning home equity financing and consumer debt is Alan Greenspan and James Kennedy, "Sources and Uses of Equity Extracted from Homes," Finance and Economics Discussion Series, Federal Reserve Board, No. 2007-20, 49 pp.

13. The total U.S. debt bill of $30.5 trillion includes all debt outstanding in the United States, including government debt and all personal and corporate debt.

5

The Mortgage Explosion

The law against usury is for the protection of creditors as well as debtors; for if there were no such check, people would be apt, from the temptation of great interest, to lend to desperate persons, by whom they would lose their money. —SAMUEL JOHNSON

SINCE CREDIT CARDS were introduced in the 1950s, consumer credit and mortgage credit have been considered two different categories of indebtedness. The latter was considered more senior on an individual's personal balance sheet, whereas the former was considered a short-term item that was subordinate to mortgages. Although those facts have not changed, altered perceptions triggered a crisis that would shake the foundations of finance and American society.

In the aftermath of the stock market collapse of 1987, many new mortgages were created and old ones were refinanced. The Tax Reform Act of 1986 retained the interest deduction paid on residential mortgages while disallowing credit card interest. Consumers awoke to the fact that the home now was one of the few places left where a tax subsidy could be found, and they responded by beginning a twenty-year mortgage boom. Unfortunately, the boom ended in the largest bust in American history. Somewhere in those twenty years, mortgage financing had undergone profound changes, leading to the largest defaults in history.

A traditionally conservative approach to the problem of consumer debt simply always assumed that consumers would not be as cavalier about home mortgage debt as they have been about consumer debt. If the most senior sort of debt an individual had was treated in this manner, then a major credit crisis would occur. But that would never be possible because a home is one's castle and the castle is never abandoned except in the worst-case scenario.

Were credit card loans and auto loans made with less oversight than home mortgages? One need only to listen to the radio or TV before 2008 to realize that "easy credit" was generously on offer. Offers abounded from those sectors. But mortgages were never commoditized as was consumer credit, so the housing finance sector was safe. The foundations remained strong even if consumer credit was being abused. But that time-proven assumption began to be challenged in the early 2000s.

When the dot.com bubble burst in 2001, the major Wall Street indexes retracted, and it appeared that the financial community was set for a quiet period after years of unprecedented growth. Hard on the heels of the dot.coms, the Enron and WorldCom scandals caused investors to be even more skeptical of their investments than they were in the 1990s. Yet a new bull market developed, and it was unforeseen and unprecedented. Although investors became skittish after Enron, Wall Street still managed to find a new source of investment money to be tapped. As in many booms before, the new boom thrived because of a lack of regulation and dubious practices that could not be proscribed.

For years, complaints have been heard about the rate of household savings in the United States. The reasons for the low rates were explained in part by the uniqueness of the American financial and taxation system. Only municipal bond interest was tax exempt, whereas all other forms of investment and savings were taxed at ordinary tax rates. The consumer had been conditioned to spend rather than save. And finance had not helped the savings mentality by showing time and again that present value was preferable to future value, especially because present value was certain, whereas the future was not. But soon a bird in the hand was not worth two in the bush. Consumers would demonstrate that they wanted the two for present consumption. That particular emphasis fitted well with the desire to consume as much as one's budget—or credit card—allowed. But little was left to invest. Any new potential boom after the dot.com bust would have to find new sources of investment money to tap.

Home ownership grew steadily in the twentieth and twenty-first centuries. In 1900, about 47 percent of Americans owned their homes. By 1950, that percentage had risen to 55 but it jumped dramatically to around 67 percent in 2000.[1] Home ownership had always been encouraged because it was the central part of the American Dream. Politics also played a factor in the mortgage boom that began after 2001. George W. Bush repeatedly stated that he envisioned an "ownership society," in which more and more people owned their own homes. After the September 11 attacks, many appeared to take that advice, and they began buying, and selling, homes on a scale never before witnessed. The new boom gravitated toward the one area that still provided tax breaks for the individual with the promise of capital appreciation. This latter factor began to fuel the rise in prices.

Real estate booms had been seen before. A significant one occurred in the 1920s, and others occurred at least once a decade. The income tax deduction had been kept intact on home mortgage interest, and even the interest deduction on home equity loans was preserved. When all factors were considered, the home was considered the best investment an individual could have made in the post–World War II period. Despite the constant comparisons with stocks over the same period, most individuals did not have accounts with brokers and at best only dabbled in the markets. When larger numbers of individual investors were attracted to the market, based on a fad or trend, it usually ended badly, as the dot.com implosion proved. Housing was inviolate: the one investment an individual could make with some assurance of safety. But residential housing had never been treated as a potential source of consumer credit.

The major pitfall for housing and the homeowner was the onset of so-called negative equity. Through almost all of the postwar years, house prices had risen, increasing the equity in the home. Everyone knew the stories of homes selling for $5,000 immediately after the war that were sold forty or fifty years later for $400,000 or more. A basket of stocks behaved well during the same period but could not match that performance unless it was professionally managed. And the stock portfolio was taxable. The home provided numerous deductions and, if sold at the right time, had a considerable tax break on the capital appreciation as well. These factors alone helped prices appreciate. During that time period, the idea that a house could be worth less than its mortgage was almost unheard of.

But not all parts of the real estate market could make the same claims. Wealthy suburban and urban areas saw steady price increases, but other less populated areas saw very gradual price increases based more on standard price inflation than heavy demand for housing. The average price of a home in a city in Alabama, Ohio, or Michigan was around $200,000 in 2006, whereas prices of similar homes in the New York metropolitan area or California could be three or four times as high.

Negative equity does not present a problem for the homeowner unless the home needs to be sold before prices recover. Traditionally, the increase in equity meant money that could be used for some future expenditure such as a larger home, retirement, or investment. But when home equity loans allow an individual to convert that hypothetical increase in equity into cash to pay for current expenditures, the entire outlook changes. This is as radical as the change from layaway plans before the war to credit card purchase since the 1960s. What used to be a store of value for the future is consumed for present purposes, robbing the future to pay for the present.

Innovations on Wall Street helped the mortgage market beginning in the 1980s and helped fuel the boom to follow. The financial turmoil of the late 1970s and early 1980s had sparked a debate about present and future value that was a hangover of the high inflation that subsided in 1984. The first example of financial engineering in the debt market is a case in point. When zero-coupon bonds were introduced in the early 1980s, a debate began about their relative financial value. Despite the attractiveness of the new instruments, Congress would not allow the Treasury to borrow zero-coupon bonds (at a deep discount) because it would require a much larger lump sum payment at some future date to redeem them. Why mortgage a future generation to pay for present expenses? The fiscal conservatives won that argument and would allow the Treasury only to strip the bonds of their coupons rather than issue original-issue zeros.

Both sides of the argument had validity, but it was the fear of abuse that won the day in Congress at that time. For instance, if the Treasury borrowed an original-issue zero for $500 million at 7 percent for twenty years (then), it would have raised $129 million with the promise to pay back the $500 million at maturity. In those twenty intervening years, no interest payments were required, so the Treasury cash flows were helped. The argument had its supporters. But as was pointed out, the future burden was large, and experience with federal budgets showed that the $371 million difference between present and future values would not be amortized systematically and that a future administration would be faced with finding the sum to make repayment. The natural inclination was to put off retiring the debt as long into the future as possible, and many in Congress could be quoted as saying that they were not willing to place that debt burden on future generations.

The same argument was used against the Treasury's borrowing floating-rate debt. In its history, the Treasury had borrowed only plain-vanilla fixed-coupon debt in addition to discounted bills. The idea of paying an adjustable rate could be appealing when interest rates started to decline, saving the government interest at a time when interest payments had become the largest item in the federal budget. The concept clearly collided with monetary policy that required money to be in shorter supply during times of inflation rather than being indexed to it. And the developing world debt crisis of the 1980s demonstrated the dangers that floating rates presented to borrowers. As a result, government borrowing was treated very conservatively by Congress at a time when it was running large budget deficits and when financial innovation would have provided some quick relief.

The same conservatism was not found at the retail level, however. These two institutional developments would resurface in the market for residential mortgages over the next two decades. Adjustable mortgages were introduced in the wake of the Depository Institutions Deregulation and Monetary Control Act (DIDMCA), and a variant of the lump sum due in the future would make its appearance later in the 1990s. Ironically, they were both ballyhooed as innovations that would allow homeowners greater latitude in paying their mortgages. Mortgage

THE NAME "CHARLES DICKENS" does not usually come to mind when thinking of financial commentators of times past, but the author of *David Copperfield* and *The Pickwick Papers* made some pithy comments about indebtedness that have stood the test of time. Concerning the behavior of people during the Christmas holidays, his Ebenezer Scrooge observed that "Christmas is a very busy time for us, Mr. Cratchit. People preparing feasts, giving parties, spending the mortgage money on frivolities. One might say that December is the foreclosure season. Harvest time for the money-lenders."

lenders would package both concepts into a variety of mortgages that required more financial acumen to understand than many mortgage holders possessed. The results began to be felt during periods of interest rate uncertainty.

Many of the mortgage variations introduced after the advent of adjustables employed the car seller's pitch to a customer described in Chapter 1. Mortgages were presented to consumers as requiring a monthly payment that was affordable while ignoring the future repayment risks. A $300,000 mortgage that normally would have cost 6 percent over thirty years was offered on an "interest-only basis" for the first five years. Customers might be unaware of the fact that the money market rate attached for the first five years, say 3 percent, was only a sweetener and would be adjusted into a fixed rate for the last twenty-five years of the mortgage's life, with amortization of the principal only beginning then. These sorts of problems began to appear as early as 1993 when the Fed unexpectedly allowed short-term interest rates to rise. Orange County, California, and its huge derivatives portfolio were victims at the time. It was later discovered that the county portfolio contained all sorts of adjustable swap rates, including reverse floaters.

For the first five years of a typical adjustable rate mortgage (ARM), the customer paid only $9,000 per year (simple interest). The $750 per month payment—advertised by the lender under the banner "Why Rent When You Can Buy?"—misled the customer because it was only partially correct. The detail was left to the fine print of the mortgage contract, which often was not read correctly. The customer went through a kind of future shock when his monthly payments rose to $2,050 per month as the rate was fixed at (say) 6.50 percent. By the time that bill became due, it may well have been unaffordable and house values had already plummeted, triggered by the subprime crisis. If the price drops had wiped out the existing equity in the home, it was worth perhaps less than the mortgageable amount, and the customer was faced with a harsh decision. If he or she could not afford all the monthly debt payments, which one or ones should be allowed to default? If there was also a home equity loan on the property, it may have been used to pay down credit card debt. Which was more useful to the consumer, the card or the home?

The boom in home equity loans also contributed to the marginalization of the homeowner, especially in the post-2001 boom. Home equity loans are made on an adjustable basis, and any rise in interest rates did double

ONE OF THE MAJOR changes in the attitude toward a second mortgage was the idea of funds for a rainy day. Before the home equity loan became popular in the 1980s, borrowing against the increased equity in the principal residence was popular occasionally but for different reasons. In times of tight mortgage markets, second mortgages were used to prop up limited financing if the original mortgage did not fully cover the cost of a home. That worked when the individual was less leveraged than he is today. And if a home appreciated in value over time, the increased value was viewed as a potential cushion, not a source of cash for spending. If an unforeseen event occurred requiring extra funds beyond an individual's savings, the second mortgage was often the answer in emergencies.

damage to the homeowner with an adjustable first mortgage. Television commentator Jim Cramer, commenting on the phenomenon during the subprime crisis in May 2008, complained, "What bothers me is that the banks did no due diligence and don't seem to know the collateral," adding, "If you bought a home with little or no money down and you attached a home-equity loan to it, the loan's going to fail."

For decades, the housing market had been remarkably stable, producing some periods of temporary discomfort but generally advancing in value. How the mortgage market came off the rails so quickly during the subprime crisis after so much stability is a phenomenon that parallels the credit card problems of the same period. In the credit card business, problems were always assumed, but real property was considered the first, and last, bastion of a individual's creditworthiness. When mortgages became commoditized, as did consumer credit, the stage was set for a market collapse of historic proportions.

"Revolving" Mortgage Credit

The complexion of the residential housing market began to change when banks began to receive assistance in granting credit to potential homeowners. Until the early 1970s, home loans were similar to credit card loans in one fundamental respect. Loans were made by banks, and payment was expected per a repayment schedule. Mortgage loans were not yet considered an investment by the lenders or by investors. Once they were, the market would change substantially.

When there were only two mortgage-assistance agencies—Ginnie Mae and Fannie Mae—both originally were considered institutions capable of assisting fiscal policy. Because housing is directly tied to the construction industry and to producers of consumer durables, stimulative housing policies could help the economy weather slow periods by encouraging construction of new homes with interest rates designed to encourage ownership. The Depression years proved that government intervention was useful to keep the housing industry stable despite poor economic conditions.

During and after World War II, the two original housing agencies— the Federal Housing Administration (FHA) and the U.S. Department of Veterans Affairs (Veterans Administration, or VA)—kept a tight lid on the mortgages they guaranteed, setting a national mortgage ceiling. Rates stood at 5.75 percent when the Kennedy administration took office in 1960; it lowered the maximum rate to 5.25 percent a year later. Private lenders often added extra charges to their mortgages for those not eligible to be purchased under either program, but the agencies effectively imposed a usury ceiling on mortgage loans.

In 1968, Ginnie Mae was created and Fannie Mae was privatized, and more flexibility was found in the mortgage market as the two agencies sought ways to clear mortgages off their books in an attempt to provide a flow of constant liquidity to the market. Both agencies adopted the issuance of pass-through securities, originally intended to be sold to institutional investors, not to the general public. Ginnie attempted this in 1969, although the first issues were postponed several times until the market was ready to accept the concept. Pass-throughs were the first attempt at securitized mortgages. A bond was issued backed by a pool of mortgages, and each month, as interest and principal were paid by homeowners, the payments were passed through the agency directly to investors, making these the first bonds to pay interest and repay principal (if any) on a monthly basis.

The government cleverly was trying to establish a niche for the new bonds that the agencies had created. Almost forgotten is the fact that in 1969, Treasury bonds with terms longer than five years from original issue were capped with a maximum coupon of 4.25 percent, a limit that was established in 1918. Yields in the secondary market were higher, and the bonds necessarily had to trade at a discount. The new mortgage securities would not be subject to that limitation and were designed to appeal to the institutional investor needing a higher coupon and monthly cash flows. Because monetary and fiscal policy were conducted differently than they were ten years later, Treasury and Fed officials were more worried about the deleterious effects of high long-term interest rates than they were on the short- and medium-terms. In 1959, Dwight D. Eisenhower told Congress that "there is no statutory maximum on the interest rate which can be paid by the Treasury for marketable borrowing of five years or less . . . the Secretary of the Treasury should have similar flexibility with regard to Treasury bonds (which run five years or more to maturity)."[2]

Ten years later, conditions changed. The mortgage bond concept was novel and slowly began to succeed. The bonds remained as off-balance-sheet liabilities of the agencies, and each issue was a stand-alone obligation, unlike any other. The agency stood ready to make up shortfalls of interest if the pool should partially fail. Since Ginnie was owned by the Treasury and Fannie (after being privatized) bore its implicit guarantee, investors realized that these obligations stood right behind actual Treasury debt in seniority. Adding to the new bonds' popularity, the FHA rates were raised to 7.5 percent in 1969.

Packaging sometimes obscures the basic concept of a security. This was the case with the original Ginnie Mae obligations. By creating constant liquidity flow for mortgage lenders, the agencies brought the revolving credit concept to the mortgage market. Traditionally, a bank made mortgages and kept them on its books until the loans were paid off. Now, it would securitize them, receive cash, and be free to create more mortgages. The only discipline to prevent a bank from creating mortgages with loose lending standards was the requirements of the agencies: They would purchase only mortgages made using their own guidelines regarding down payments, mortgage insurance, and the like. If the agency guidelines ever broke down, the process would become similar to credit card creation. But in the beginning, that was not the case.

The agencies had to securitize mortgages into bonds in order to keep their books clean. Because Ginnie in particular was wholly owned by the federal government, any mortgage assets on its books would be de facto assets of the Treasury and would contribute to the national debt. But because the securitized bonds it issued were off the balance sheet, their amounts were not counted and the federal debt remained untouched by them. So the government could intervene in the mortgage market without having to suffer the pain of finding mortgages on its own balance sheet, something that successive administrations had disavowed in the past.[3] The free market ideology of Wall Street was kept intact at the same time that mortgages were being created with implicit government help.

In a period of rising interest rates, mortgage rates eventually would collide with the usury laws in some states. The economic turmoil of the 1970s put upward pressure on rates, and a collision course was inevitable. In 1979, the Housing Act relieved some of the pressure by exempting the FHA from usury ceilings, allowing it to raise rates, and it did so immediately. This was the longest period of rising rates witnessed in the twentieth century and would culminate with the Paul Volcker Fed pushing the Fed funds rate to over 20 percent by 1981. The pressures soon provided the second round of ammunition for abolishing all of the usury ceilings except for criminal usury.

By the middle to late 1970s, Ginnie Mae and Fannie Mae trading had become extremely popular on Wall Street, especially among fixed-income investors. Freddie Mac (Federal Home Loan Mortgage Corporation) was created in 1975 to perform similar functions for its parent, the Federal Home Loan Bank Board. Being a part of the board, its mandate was to buy mortgages from thrift institutions, allowing them to remain liquid. Fannie Mae's mandate was wider, and Ginnie Mae's was confined mainly to urban housing mortgages, but the three operated in similar fashion in the marketplace. All three created what came to be known as mortgage-backed securities (MBSs).

The pass-through security proved extremely popular among investors because it remained ultimately an obligation of the agency that created it.[4] Once Wall Street discovered its virtues, other variations of the concept appeared, including the asset-backed securities backed by credit card receivables, among others. But these were not pass-throughs, but pay-throughs. The pay-through paid its interest and principal from the trust created by the securitizer and was also a stand-alone issue, no longer tied to the original asset seller. Banks realized that the ABS formula would allow them to offload many loans into the market.

ONCE ASSETS SUCH AS mortgages were securitized, the interest and principal payments still had to be serviced. On pay-through securities, the responsibility for collecting the payments and passing them along to bond investors was the job of servicers, institutions that earned a fee by servicing mortgages or other paying assets. In some cases, banks provided the services; in others, private companies performed the task, which was always complicated by the fact that any missed payments in the cash flow stream between mortgage holders and bondholders could mean a technical default of the bond itself.

Mortgages were the main asset banks decided to securitize in the 1980s along with credit card receivables. After the 1988 decision by the Bank for International Settlements (BIS) to raise primary capital requirements for all banks under its jurisdiction, securitization became a valuable tool. Many banks were not able to raise fresh capital through retained earnings or by selling stock; so the next best thing was to reduce assets while continuing to make loans, a process that securitization facilitated. Of all the assets in their portfolios, mortgages were the prime candidates for the process because of their long-term nature. Once banks and other institutions were able to make mortgages solely to sell them, a new chapter in consumerism would open.

The Savings and Loan (S&L) Crisis

Critics of regulation of financial institutions, as well as supporters, both have a difficult time explaining the lessons of the S&L crisis of 1988–1989. The legislation passed to clean up that mess was prompted by earlier deregulation in the form of the Depository Institutions Act (Garn–St. Germain Act), passed in 1982 in the wake of DIDMCA. Cleaning up one mess led to another, costlier mess that almost destroyed an industry that had been the backbone of the mortgage business since the early nineteenth century.

Inflation in the 1970s led to severe pressure on the thrift industry. Until that time, the thrifts had been protected, as had the banks, by relatively tame interest rates and Regulation Q of the Fed. The interest they paid on savings deposits could exceed those offered by banks by 0.25 percent, and the slight differential attracted many deposits, especially from potential homeowners. When short-term interest rates began to rise, especially after 1979, thrifts began to suffer withdrawals as savers withdrew their funds in favor of higher yields in money market funds. As the yield curve became more negatively sloped, the problem worsened, and a liquidity crisis forced many thrifts to the brink of ruin. This was one of the several problems leading to the passage of the DIDMCA in 1980.

But the legislation did little to help the thrifts. The original intent was to raise the interest rate ceiling in stages over a six-year period. That was too long a time span to save the thrifts, especially the smaller ones that had very limited access to funding outside their deposit bases. As a result, Congress passed the Depository Institutions Act (DIA) two years later to speed up the process. Eliminating Regulation Q restrictions was only part of the package, however. Another part of the DIA allowed thrifts to purchase corporate bonds, the yields on which exceeded traditional mortgage rates by a sizable margin. Thrifts were now allowed to have more diversified balance sheets, in hopes of lessening their exposure to the real estate market.

The administration of Ronald Reagan proclaimed that deregulation was the best tonic for the failing industry. No one was prepared to argue the point. In 1975, over forty-nine hundred thrifts existed in the country; by 1982 the number had declined to thirty-eight hundred. The large numbers indicated that many of the institutions were small, with limited balance sheets. Yet the danger to the housing industry was stark. The thrifts were the largest providers of residential mortgages in the country. Even the presence of Freddie Mac after 1970 could not shore up the industry in the wake of rising interest rates.

The DIA helped stabilize the industry in the middle 1980s as the thrifts expanded their balance sheet holdings. But one part of investor behavior was not anticipated. Many thrifts took the opportunity to buy the wrong type of corporate bond for a fiduciary institution. They became major buyers of high-yield, or junk, bonds, hoping to cash in on their generous yields at a time when deposit rates were still high in nominal and real terms. Drexel Burnham Lambert was happy to oblige the thrifts by selling them as many bonds as they could purchase legally. The stage was set for a crisis that would be triggered by the next recession.

The situation for junk bonds worsened considerably when the stock market recorded its worst one-day loss in October 1987. Economic conditions worsened quickly, and many of the junk companies fell in value. Many of the bonds subsequently had to be written down or off the thrifts' books. In 1987, 3,175 thrifts still existed. Within a few years, the picture would change dramatically.

The administration of George H. W. Bush and Congress responded by passing the Financial Institutions Recovery, Reconstruction and Enforcement Act (FIRREA) in 1989 to stabilize the industry and to buy the assets of thrifts that could not survive. The new capital requirements of the BIS also were coming into force, affecting all depository institutions in the United States. As a result, a taxpayer bailout of the industry was required. Estimates at the time called for $350 billion in taxpayer funds, but the eventual cost was about $140 billion. Many thrifts were forced to shut or merge with others or with commercial banks, opening the door wider for the banks in residential mortgage lending.

The second round of the industry shakeout was as pronounced as the first. Of the 3,175 thrifts existing in 1987, only 1,670 survived by 1993. Industry assets in 1987 were $1.3 trillion; by 1993 they declined to $775 billion. The inexperience of many of the thrifts' treasurers led them to buy bonds ill suited for their needs as depository institutions, and the results decimated the industry that had been the cornerstone of the housing market. Ironically, new mortgage originations were almost the same in 1993 as the entire industry's assets in 1987. The banks were the beneficiaries of this turnaround. Unlike the thrifts, they were not authorized to buy corporate bonds by the 1982 legislation.

In the wake of the savings and loan crisis, many existing S&Ls changed their charters to become savings banks rather than carry the odious S&L designation. Thrift institutions would rise again to take the lead in the residential housing market, but the process would take time and require access to a wider range of funding than had been the case in the past. But the painful lessons were well remembered. In the next round of mortgage lending, less reliance would be put on deposits as a source of funding and more on securitization. Revolving credit provided by the agencies and by collateralized mortgage obligations (CMOs) would provide the industry with more flexible options to keep itself out of trouble. Only time would tell whether that would be the case.

Mortgage Funding

Until the ABS concept for mortgages was introduced, mortgages were subject to a relatively careful credit review process. The agencies had their individual guidelines for conventional mortgages, and the amounts granted could not exceed a certain limit. But agency intervention aided neither subprime mortgages nor jumbo mortgages, those that exceeded the conventional limit. There were many other mortgages that banks and other originators could securitize beyond the conventionals supported by Fannie Mae or Freddie Mac.

Mortgage funding relied on the bond markets, and the adjustable rate concept already was well received there by institutional investors. The refixings on floating-rate bonds were attractive to many because they provided a hedge against inflation. If the Fed detected inflation, it would allow short-term interest rates to rise. The next refixing on a floating-rate note would reflect that, and the investor would receive higher coupon interest than in the previous period. The interest rate risk was shifted to the bond issuer, which would suffer the consequences unless it swapped the floating risk for fixed rates or had the luxury of passing the rise to its borrowers in turn. The mortgage holder bore the interest rate risk in this case, not the bank lender.

As a result of bond market innovations, mortgages would be more readily available to a wider spectrum of homebuyers than ever before. As the agencies became more popular and influential in the market, mortgage rates began to be linked directly to long-term bond rates, not to the dictates of the FHA or VA. Then financial engineering took over to produce structured investment products out of conventional mortgages and to create appeal to an even broader range of institutional investors.

Beginning in 1983, the mortgage securities market began introducing synthetic securities, better known on Wall Street as CMOs, real estate mortgage investment conduits (REMICS), and many other variations of agency issues. Boiled down to their essential characteristics, synthetics were standard MBSs redesigned by an investment bank to satisfy basic investor needs.[5] If an institutional investor wanted a guaranteed fixed-income payment of (say) seven years with no threat of principal repayment, the bank would split the issue into different parts, selling one investor the guaranteed income stream while selling a stripped bond to another. After slicing and dicing the issue into so-called synthetic parts, the bank created a new class of securities, such as the REMICs, that had never existed before.

The CMO was nothing more than the MBS model applied to the nonagency mortgage market. A securitizer would spin the mortgages off to a trust that would sell a collateralized bond and use the pay-throughs to compensate investors.[6] It extended the MBS concept significantly and allowed banks to offload mortgages that were not eligible for agency intervention. But the whole sector was fraught with technicalities, arcane concepts, and outright confusing language. A CMO was described in 1988 by two bankers working on them as follows: "The basic idea behind the CMO is to sequentially segment the maturity dimension of the underlying collateral by substituting sequential retirement of the bonds for the pro-rata distribution that is the salient feature of pass-through securities." The learning curve of institutional investors would have to increase substantially if they were to keep abreast of this market and others like it. This was a far cry from the standard fixed-income language that dominated the traditional bond market.

Despite the complexity of ABSs in general, the CMOs became popular with both issuers and investors. Revolving credit had come to the residential mortgage market, as it already had in the credit card market. Now both sectors used securitization to fuel growth in lending. Unlike the card industry, however, the mortgage business had a standard set of mortgage rates (for conventionals) established by the agencies against which all other mortgages were priced. Rates for fifteen and thirty years were established, and CMOs using adjustable rates also appeared in the 1980s as well. And unlike credit card balances, mortgage loans were secured by the property collateralizing them. Beyond that, they were nonrecourse loans; if a homeowner defaulted, the mortgage lender could seize the collateral but no other assets of the borrower. Credit card loans usually provided lenders with recourse, an obscure fact that would surface during the credit market crisis after 2007.

As time passed, the distinction between a pass-through and a pay-through became obscured. Originally, pass-throughs were considered the safer of the two because they remained obligations of one of the agencies in the worst-case scenario. Investors could always rely on the agency to make up any shortfall of a mortgage pool should payments be disturbed. Pay-throughs relied solely on the trust pool underlying them, so the only assurances investors had that the pool was investment grade was to rely on the ratings agencies that rated them. Because each pass-through was different from the others, the agencies played a key role in helping persuade investors to buy the securities.

During the 1990s, a variant of the two types of American mortgage-related securities began being noticed. The Pfandbrief, or covered bond, originated in Germany about 200 years ago, and its use spread to most of Western Europe and occasionally to the United States. A covered bond was a CMO that bore the ultimate guarantee of the issuer, unlike a pay-through. Like the MBS, if part of the pool failed, the shortfall would be covered by the issuing bank. In addition, the obligations remained part of the bank's balance sheet, unlike pay-throughs. In American terms, covered bonds closely resembled revenue bonds in the municipal bond market.

Another vehicle developed in the late 1980s also played a part in mortgage and asset funding. Collateralized debt obligations (CDOs) were bonds using loans or other bonds as collateral. Traditionally, CDOs did not use servicers but were retained by the packager of the obligations and were of two types—collateralized loan obligations and collateralized bond obligations. The former was a bond backed by loans, and the latter a bond backed by other bonds.

The most common type of CDO was a balance sheet CDO, by which the issuer specifically desired to clear its balance sheet of assets and transfer the risk to investors buying the collateralized bonds. This instrument served the same purpose as a credit card ABS or a CMO but often was backed by riskier loans used for merger and acquisitions purposes or other bonds. In the bond case, a bond was backed by a bond, making the intricate nature of these obligations obvious. A default by the first bond borrower could lead to problems for the CDO borrower, eventually reaching investors. Although these instruments followed the traditional ABS template, the underlying collateral could prove difficult to unravel. Clearly, no two CDOs were the same, and although that could be said of any securitized bond obligation, others could be more easily traced back to the underlying collateral.

Beyond their basic structure, CDOs were sliced into tranches of cash flows, designed for specific investors based on their taste for, and tolerance of, counterparty risk. These tranches sliced up the risk characteristics and sold them in much the same way that Fannie Mae had been slicing up its own basic bonds into different cash flow packages for investors through REMICS. Limited by the types of bond obligations it could issue to fund mortgages, Fannie adopted REMICs as a way of marketing its debt to investors who may have balked at a more traditional pass-through security. Unfortunately, basic CDOs and REMICs opened other doors of risk that investors may not have been fully aware of.

A more risky type of CDO was based on credit default swaps rather than on other bonds or loans. A bank would enter into swaps with another party, agreeing to provide cash for bonds that it insured against default risk. The payments from these swaps became the cash flows that serviced the bonds. These were known as synthetic CDOs, a far cry from the original synthetics created fifteen years earlier, which seemed simple by comparison. The synthetic element was based on the fact that the bonds' cash flows were from derivative instruments. Many of these instruments would suffer badly during the credit market crisis because the riskier slices were among the first to default or seriously decline in price. More importantly, the credit default swaps (CDSs) used in CDOs were the contemporary financial world's equivalent of a pyramid scheme, using collateral depending on synthetic collateral that would eventually explode in what appeared to be an ordinary security, leaving a trail of ruin that was extremely difficult to trace.

No part of the traditional mortgage or interest rate market was left untouched by financial innovation. In addition to the traditional Libor-based floating-rate concept, the inverse floater was introduced. Instruments based on this concept operated in opposite fashion from the floater.[7] If rates rose, the interest on a reverse floater declined, and vice versa. The concept played a large role in the fiasco in Orange County, California, in 1993 when the county's derivatives portfolio exploded, leaving large losses for it and the other municipal investors who bought part of it as an investment.

On the surface, the reverse floater seems overly fussy as a financial feature attached to bonds. But the idea originated in the interest rate swaps market where it made a greater impression as a hedging concept that could be attached to a swap designed to a particular company's needs. But when this was attached to a residential mortgage as a funding source, the dangers became clear quickly. Would a homeowner recognize the risk these features presented without being well versed in finance and basic risk management techniques? The answer was clearly no, but in a mortgage market designed to offer something for everyone it nevertheless found its way into the homes of the unsuspecting through the back door.

Other parts of financial innovation were used for marketing purposes. A Florida homebuilder offered buyers a $25,000 bond if they bought one of its homes. The catch was that it was a zero-coupon bond, only worth the face value at maturity, so the customer would receive the money but only at the later date. The present value at the time was considerably less. Although the builder kept its promise to provide a bond, the advertising was questionable.

Another questionable practice came from a New York financial firm offering homeowners a chance to significantly reduce the amount paid on their mortgages, for a fee. "If we can save you fifty thousand dollars on the total payments on your mortgage," went the advertising, "will you pay us ten percent of the amount as a fee?" Of course, many customers did not realize they could do the same themselves by simply adding some extra money to their monthly payments as a principal repayment. The great benefit for the firm was that the customer had to pay the fee up front. The benefits would be felt over the shorter life of the mortgage. The present-value fee concept was alive and well. The trick could have been learned from any basic finance book. It is a better known mortgage concept today than it was twenty years ago, and many mortgage holders regularly add extra principal repayments early in the life of the mortgage to reduce costs.

ARM Twisting and the Death of Usury Laws

The wide variety of bond features available in the fixed-income market quickly was translated into mortgage options that could be offered to potential homeowners. In the mid-1980s, homeowners were offered 15- and 30-year fixed mortgages and adjustable rate mortgages tied to a benchmark money market rate. Within 10 years, the same instruments had a wide variety of bells and whistles attached that required serious attention. The features could be valuable to someone aware of the risks that adjustables in particular posed for the homeowner, but they could also be potentially dangerous for those who chose them simply because they offered low payments in the first few years of the life of the loan.

Adjustable mortgages suffered similar problems to credit cards. Complaints began to be heard that they were periodically being fixed incorrectly due to the complicated nature of their features. Many lenders seemed to be confused about the interest rates used for their benchmark pricing. Even when they got the benchmark correct, they were often unsure about whether interest was calculated on a 360- or 365-day basis. Consumer groups naturally pounced on the issue. If customers thought a refixing had been done improperly, they had some recourse. According to the Cranston-Gonzalez Affordable Housing Act of 1990, mortgage lenders providing federally supported adjustable rate mortgages had to acknowledge within twenty days a borrower's written request for information about the math used in a refixing. Within sixty days of the written request for a recalculation, the lender was required to either refund money to the borrower or explain why the lender felt there was no mistake in the new calculations.

Borrowers had good reason to double-check their lenders' math. The Federal Deposit Insurance Corporation found that 20 percent of the banks and thrifts it surveyed made mistakes in calculating ARMs. Additionally, the Office of Thrift Supervision and the Resolution Trust Corporation (both founded during the thrift crisis in 1989) studied the problem and discovered some sort of error in 33 percent of the loans examined. Estimates put the value of the mistake at around $1,500 per residential mortgage. But the problem did not end with homes. Four of every ten businesses were being overcharged on their adjustable rate commercial mortgages, according to one trade group studying the problem. The process became known as "ARM twisting."

Although banks liked adjustable lending because the ARMs shifted risk to the borrower, the mortgages still had their drawbacks. They were considered to have lower servicing profitability in the aftermarket for mortgages and sold for discounts as a result. They also were susceptible to litigation because of the calculation problems at refixings. But customers flocked to them, and by the late 1980s about 60 percent of the mortgages originated were adjustable.

In the 20 years between the market collapse of 1987 and the mortgage bust of 2007, homeowners learned a great deal more about mortgage features than they had in the past. The sheer variety of residential mortgages on offer with a myriad of features did prove daunting to many, but interest rates helped others. After the interest rate rise in

1993, rates moved lower and stayed in a relatively stable curve during the Bill Clinton administrations. Any potential problems posed by adjustables remained in the background, helping the housing market to move higher.

In 1990, a phenomenon that had appeared in the credit card market made its first appearance in mortgages. Several Boston-area banks began offering mortgages to low-income families earning less than $25,000 per household, bowing to pressure from community activist groups demanding better access to credit for lower-income groups. The mortgages were made on fixed- and adjustable-rate bases, although the activist groups complained about the adjustables (to no avail). Part of the pressure came from the groups' complaints heard over the years about a mortgage lending activity known as "redlining." This was practiced in poor minority neighborhoods when banks regularly redlined out whole districts, declaring them off-limits for mortgage lending because of their racial composition or low-income status.

Since 1977, banks had been under federal pressure to provide more effective banking services to low- and moderate-income families in their communities. The Community Reinvestment Act (CRA) was passed that year, requiring the three federal banking regulators to assess a bank's performance in serving its community on a periodic basis. The reporting burden this put on the smaller banks in particular led to an amendment in 1994, entitled the Riegle Community Development and Regulatory Improvement Act, that modified the tests by which a bank was evaluated. In the years after it was passed, the vast majority of banks received scores of satisfactory or outstanding after being monitored. The law did not provide enforcement authority for the regulators, however. The only way they could respond to a noncompliant bank was to consider its performance if it required assistance or wanted further regulatory consideration in the future. After the Gramm-Leach-Bliley Act (Financial Services Modernization Act) was passed in 1999, further amendments were made, allowing less review if an institution scored well. Results were made available publicly so that community groups could monitor a bank's performance.

Conservative critics maintained that this emphasis on lending to lower-income groups led to the mortgage crisis of 2008. The initial move into that sort of lending began in 1995 after the CRA was amended.[8] The Clinton administration fostered the National Homeownership

Strategy, a program spearheaded by housing secretary Henry Cisneros. The intent was to increase the percentage of Americans owning their own home and to aid minority groups at the same time. Operating through the department of Housing and Urban Development (HUD), the program helped people move out of public housing into homes they owned. But the stimulus sought to enlist the private sector, not leave the program to be funded publicly. "The Strategy is not a new government program, it is a unique union of private- and public-sector efforts and commitments to expand opportunities for people and communities too often excluded from the American Dream," Cisneros wrote, defending the strategy. "Rather than requiring new government funds, the Strategy helps the private mortgage market work more effectively to get the money to buy homes to the people who need it."

Unfortunately, enlisting private lenders meant expanding the subprime mortgage market. After leaving his post, Cisneros became a principal in a real estate development firm doing most of its business in Texas in the Latino community and a board member of Countrywide Financial, one of the largest subprime lenders. When the subprime crisis hit, the thrift institution was one of the first to feel the effects. Many of its loans were sold to Fannie Mae, which securitized them in a strategy not in keeping with its mandate.

The drive to increase the percentage of homeowners was a bipartisan effort that carried over to the succeeding George W. Bush administration. The post-2001 phenomenon was caused by another set of similar circumstances. The agencies were called into action by HUD to prepare themselves for more intermediation on behalf of those income groups. Ginnie Mae already served the urban lower-income mortgage market, and Fannie Mae especially was urged to expand its programs to serve those in central cities as well as in rural areas and other overlooked parts of the market. Despite their mobilization, the agencies did not provide any more housing to the target income groups than did private lenders. Subprime lending of that sort was always fraught with risk. Although mortgage delinquency rates in the 2000s averaged about 4.75 percent per year, subprimes averaged about 13 percent. Many of the subprimes also were ARMs, and changing interest rates could have a devastating impact on those customers least likely to understand the process.

As the agencies prepared to take action in 1995, commercial lenders began to announce programs designed to do the same. The Boston banks were joined by others from around the country to make mortgages more available. NationsBank Corporation quickly announced a $500 million affordable housing program that offered 100 percent financing with very liberal underwriting standards when compared with the rest of the industry. At the same time, the depository institutions bore about 28 percent of the overall mortgage risk, the agencies about 17 percent, and private mortgage insurance companies another 17 percent or so. The agencies' share was actually less than it would be 10 years later.

By the mid-1990s, some banks were offering twenty different types of mortgages where they offered only three a decade before. In addition to 15- and 30-year conventional mortgages, there were adjustables, balloons, and hybrids. Negative amortization loans were often attached to the balloons so that, after perhaps five years at a low sweetener rate, the mortgage would require refinancing or payment in full. Any interest accrued during the grace period was added to the outstanding amount when it was refinanced, increasing the homeowners' debt burden. This was known as *negative amortization.*

After the recession of 1991–1992, the mortgage market made up for lost ground. Over $1 trillion worth of mortgages were issued in 1993. The number fell to around $750 billion in the following year, and by 1995 the number had halved to only around $500 billion. Many mortgage lenders were already geared for increased business, so the downturn made them more aggressive in pursuing new business with customers. "There's more competition because everyone wants to get a piece of a shrinking pie," said one California mortgage banker who specialized in hybrids. "I do think lenders are pushing products harder."

Despite all of the bells and whistles that could be attached to mortgages, the most troublesome feature homeowners still had to contend with was the adjustable rate mortgage. These mortgages sounded relatively simple by the late 1990s, but concealed many features that could prove troublesome. The benchmark rates on which the adjustments could be made were dizzying. Over that twenty-year period, mortgage holders had loans adjusted to varying maturities of Libor, Treasury bill rates, commercial paper, prime-based formulas, and other exotic variations containing combinations of them. There were sweetener rates with long grace periods, after which the mortgage would reset to a more conventional form that could prove to be a time bomb for borrowers if they were not aware of the consequences. Assessing adjustable mortgages was akin to playing a game of chess, but unfortunately many borrowers were barely equipped to play checkers.

During the 1990s, many more consumers appeared able to cope with adjustables despite their complexity. The consumer learning curve appeared to have improved substantially. Maximum and minimum rates created a band of risk that consumers could appreciate. If a mortgage was capped at 8 percent and carried a minimum rate of 4 percent, then homeowners knew the range of their risk if not the specific dollar value of the payments.[9] But it was not consumer knowledge alone that prevented foreclosures because of rising interest rates. Lenders adhered to relatively tight standards as they had in the past, requiring down payments in excess of 10 percent and income verification. The standards imposed by the mortgage assistance agencies and the lenders provided some stability to the housing market that would be sorely lacking in the years ahead.

The popularity of ARMs also spelled the death knell for usury laws. Traditionally, the laws had been written to protect the owners of real property from high interest rates, but the language and terms of adjustables defeated those protections. Because adjustables could be reset within a one-year period of the initial setting, they fell in the class of credit card loans rather than that of mortgages. In times of high short-term interest rates, the adjustables could easily violate many states' older usury ceilings, even with caps attached.

Adjustables were purposely created to shift the risk of rising interest rates from lenders to homeowners. This violated the spirit of the original usury laws, although critics contended that they were out-of-date with modern finance. But the resetting periods and collars under which they operate suggest that the original design of the ARMs was meant to circumvent the usury laws on a broad scale. In their absence, many homeowners were left without protection from floating interest rates and the damage they could cause. They passed from the picture in the name of progress but were sorely needed in the post-2007 mortgage crisis.

Home prices continued to rise during the same time period, slowed only by the recession in 1991–1992. The rise in value helped the home equity loan become more popular after 1993 because it became clear that the cash that could be borrowed against the increased value was tax deductible. The term "second mortgage" was no longer used as it had been in the past. Now, home equity loans helped homeowners "unlock" the equity in their homes. The term was more diplomatic than saying homeowners had put themselves further in debt. Leveraged finance had finally arrived at the doorstep of the American consumer. Cannibal consumption now had the second important plank needed to finance the growth that would lead to the bull market of the late 1990s and to the mortgage explosion after 2001. Now homeowners were literally using the primary residence to fuel consumption. As long as property values continued to rise, the warning signs of this trend remained dormant. Only a severe housing downturn could create a problem.

Housing prices never showed signs of slowing except for a brief time during the 1991–1992 recession. And the trillion-dollar boom that followed in 1993 demonstrated that the slowdown was only temporary. The American experience demonstrated that what went up only came down temporarily. This notion became the cornerstone of the housing market.

Borrow Now, Pay Much Later

Little has been said about the causes of the post-2001 mortgage boom. The amount of new loans created dwarfed all previous periods. The complexity of some of those mortgages made the exotics of the 1990s look tame by comparison. At the same time, the percentage of the gross domestic product (GDP) accounted for by consumption actually rose above its traditional two-thirds. Either the United States was in a period of unprecedented growth, or the increased numbers were being produced by the same boom.

Crowd behavior lies at the core of most speculative booms, but the post-2001 one had much legislative and political help. Many existing homes were refinanced, and many new homeowners entered the market. Clearly, many of the latter had no business being there in the first instance. Stories began to emerge of people on welfare in mainly minority neighborhoods being granted mortgages with no earned income and little prospects of finding any soon. Once their houses were repossessed, they could be sold again by unscrupulous lenders at higher prices. The American Dream was being used as a lure for predatory lending.

After the collapse of the dot.com boom and the shock of the September 11 attacks, the mortgage boom began in earnest. Despite the record number of new mortgages created in the 1990s, those created in the new century dwarfed the previous amounts by a substantial margin.

Between 2001 and mid-2008, an estimated $20 trillion in gross new mortgages was created, more than doubling the amount already in existence. The total exceeded the size of the U.S. GDP in 2007, a proportion never seen before.

The new loans created included home equity loans (HELs) and home equity lines of credit (HELOCs). This set off a wave of consumerism that also was unprecedented. By 2004–2005, the percentage of the GDP driven by consumption rose to over 78 percent, demonstrating that much of that money was being used for consumer spending in addition to paying off outstanding credit card balances. The U.S. economy was in a boom driven by consumption on a scale never witnessed before. The home and everything related to it became the driving force behind the economy.

The rationale for much of the refinancing and new loans was not in doubt. The basics underlying the easy money were described simply by Franklin Raines of Fannie Mae when he stated, "Right now we think that rates will stay low, that you'll be able to get a mortgage below seven percent and that's kicked off a refinance boom that's going to put more money in the pockets of consumers." Homeowners took their cue from him and others who shared the sentiment. Borrowing from Peter to pay Paul became the popular personal financing technique. In this case, it was leveraging the home to pay for consumption. The process could be explained away by the mortgage industry claiming that the increase in real estate prices would compensate the homeowner. The reality of additional indebtedness was somehow obscured by the false idea that wealth was increasing.

As with all speculative booms, all strata of American society were involved, not just the traditional homeowners who could afford to make a 20 percent deposit on a home. Those borrowing for purchases within the Fannie Mae or Freddie Mac conventional limit were joined by the poor, who were sold homes on the assumption that values would rise, as well as by those above the conventional limit, borrowing jumbo mortgages. Residential mortgages now were analogous to credit card lines of credit: something for everyone.

The boom naturally fueled a construction boom. New housing developments appeared in states where land was still inexpensive, like Nevada and Florida. Builders offered packages to potential buyers that included financing through related companies. New housing starts showed marked increases each year. In 2001, new residential housing starts registered 1.273 million units, rising to 1.716 million in 2005 before dropping to 1.465 million in 2006 and 1.046 million in 2007. The vast majority were detached homes that were gradually becoming larger each year. In 2001, the average size was 2,310 square feet; by 2007 it was 2,507 square feet.[10]

The major question surrounding the mortgage boom was why it began when it did, in the wake of the dot.com crash that left many investors with serious speculative losses. And what was there about real estate that suddenly became even more appealing? Was there cash left over from the stock market that still needed a home? The confluence of factors triggering the boom included tax breaks, a desire for bigger and better housing, and the usual desire for capital gains. But at its heart, the boom was triggered by politics. Unfortunately, when this combination of politics and the real estate boom met, the results were disastrous.

Ignoring the Signs

The starting date of the boom was not serendipitous. After the September 11 attacks, the economy recovered relatively quickly from its shock and began its recovery. Two years before, the groundwork had been laid for liberal banking and investment banking policies when Congress passed the Gramm-Leach-Bliley Act in late 1999. This law effectively deregulated the banking system, sweeping away the Glass-Steagall protections put in place in 1933.[11]

After intense lobbying from the commercial banks, investment banking and commercial banking could now be combined again after a sixty-seven-year-old divorce that originally was instituted to protect commercial banks from the vagaries and risks of the equities markets. So-called universal banking was now in vogue again in the United States, and most in Congress and the Clinton administration thought the system was now in step with the rest of the world. The universal bank would be able to offer business loans, consumer credit, mortgage loans, investment banking services, and risk trading in an integrated, global marketplace. This clearly was the wave of the future, according to banking reformers.

The deregulated financial environment had a direct and positive effect on the mortgage boom. After 1998, new mortgage originations hit at least $1 trillion every year for the next ten years. In 2003, the amount almost touched $4 trillion before tapering off to around $2.5 trillion per year. In the years immediately prior to the 2008 crisis, about 18 percent of the outstanding amounts were represented by Alternative-A (second-tier quality but above subprime) and subprime mortgages, or about $225 billion each.

Another substantial contribution to the boom came from the mortgage agencies. Over the years, they had come to be thought of as bullet-proof. Because they carried the implicit guarantee of the Treasury and dominated the market, their activities appeared to be taken for granted and their creditworthiness unchallenged. They could make money in good times and bad. Franklin Raines of Fannie Mae touted the firm's resilience to all sorts of economic conditions when he declared, "Fannie Mae produces very strong results for investors when interest rates are high and when interest rates are low, in recession and during booms." Without veering off course, he would have been proved correct. When the agencies became involved in the same sort of shoddy lending that the bank and nonbank originators had engaged in, their fate would prove no better.[12]

The oversight was aided by a laxness in enforcing regulations that clearly existed. The Securities and Exchange Commission (SEC) loos-ened regulatory standards substantially in the spring of 2004 by lifting the capital requirements for the five largest securities firms. The broker-age units of those firms wanted the exemption and were granted it by a somewhat reluctant but willing SEC. The firms then used the excess capital to invest in a wide array of mortgage-related and asset-backed securities and derivatives that leveraged their balance sheets with what would prove to be dubious assets. In many cases, their leverage ratios rose to 40:1. Making matters worse, the agency agreed to rely on those banks' own risk models to monitor the situation, effectively allowing the risk takers to report how much risk they were assuming without oversight.

Four years later, the SEC still appeared to be in the dark concerning the actual state of the investment banks' balance sheets. In March 2008, SEC Chairman Christopher Cox remarked, "We have a good deal of com-fort about the capital cushions at these firms at the moment." Within six months of this statement, all five of the banks in question (Goldman Sachs, Morgan Stanley, Bear Stearns, Lehman Brothers, and Merrill Lynch) were dissolved, merged, or changed their business model to that of a commercial bank. The wheels of securitization had been well lubricated by the banks and the regulators, all under an assumption that self-monitoring markets were preferable to highly regulated ones.

The investment bankers were reacting to the mortgage originations that occurred in 2003, the record year for new residential mortgages. The number reported was $3.81 trillion, up almost $1.5 trillion from the prior year. Numbers on that scale attracted new investors and packagers, and the banks flooded the market with their newfound cash. The following four years were all strong but never approached the 2003 record. They remained remarkably the same, averaging around $2.77 trillion until 2007 when they fell slightly to $2.40 trillion. During those years, the top originating lenders were Washington Mutual Incorporated, Countrywide Financial Corporation, and Wells Fargo, followed closely by JP Morgan Chase, Bank of America, and Citigroup. On average, about $500 billion per year of home mortgages was securitized into private-label residential-mortgage-backed securities (RMBSs). These were the pay-through securities. Fannie Mae and Freddie Mac bought close to 50 percent of residential mortgages during the post-2001 boom. The balance was held on the books of the originating lenders.[13]

The mortgage boom was also aided immeasurably by the tax code. The Taxpayer Relief Act of 1998 increased the exempt amount of capital gain, made when a home was sold, to $250,000 for a single taxpayer and to $500,000 for a married couple. These were the largest tax-exempt amounts ever granted for the sale of primary residences and stipulated that the home had been used as a primary residence for two of the previous five years. The changes from the older law proved to be a tax boon to many individuals, who had held their homes for long periods of time before selling. It also proved an irresistible lure for those who thought they could flip their homes for a profit after two years' time.[14]

Most importantly, the wheels of the mortgage market were lubricated by securitization in the same way that credit cards had been for over twenty years. Collateralized mortgage obligations were created using larger and larger percentages of Alternative-A and subprime loans, mainly to keep yields on the bonds high in order to appeal to investors. Alan Greenspan acknowledged that the demand for many collateralized mortgage securities would have been much lower without the clamor created by the securitizers themselves. When bonds were

THE MORTGAGE CRISIS was exported from the United States to other countries through the bond markets. Investors, including many banks and sovereign wealth funds, bought mortgage-related securities backed by Alt-A or subprime mortgages, only to discover that the securities fell dramatically in price. It was not the first time that foreign investors had been burned by American investments. The *Times* of London wrote, "The science of 'financing' is one which is extensively practiced in the United States, and, as foreign investors know to their sorrow, the American practitioners do not confine their operations solely to citizens of the Great Republic." This appeared in an article published in 1869.

created using them exclusively, the yields proved too tempting for many institutional investors, who spied opportunity in the American mortgage boom. Many foreign banks became avid buyers of the bonds and major victims several years later when the cash flows dried up.

The role that securitization played in the credit market crisis and the financial collapse that followed cannot be underestimated. It is acknowledged now that many of these subprime mortgages should never have been created in the first instance, but securitization still made them possible. How was it possible that people on welfare in Cleveland could have been granted mortgages when they had no income other than a welfare check? Why had lending standards become so lax?

The laxness was created and abetted by securitization. The process had become standard since the early days when teams of financial engineers and bankers had to sit down to hammer together a package of credit card loans into securities. As with credit cards, home loans were being granted and then immediately securitized. The original lenders did not retain them on their books, so their interest was momentary at best. And because they did not keep them, they had little reason to conform to decent lending standards. The loans would be the bondholders' problem, not theirs. Through these substantial cracks in the system, subprime mortgages gained a toehold in the market that later became a foothold. Fifteen years before, $300 billion was the size of all new mortgages created, mostly of a decent quality. Now it was the size of the dubious part of the market alone.

Once the pools of mortgages were assembled to support a bond, the ratings agencies rated them on the basis of the collateral. Many bonds were rewarded with the highest ratings available despite the fact that they were backed by mainly subprime loans. When the credit market crisis began in the late summer of 2007, many of the bonds quickly dropped in value or were severely marked down, presenting investors with losses or illiquid securities. Questions quickly arose concerning the reasons they were assigned such high credit ratings in the first place, but it appeared that the ratings agencies were under the same pressure as the firms that documented the mortgage loans in the securitization process. Too many transactions had forced them to adopt shortcuts to keep up with the volume of business, and the shortcuts overlooked vital information that would have caused the new bonds to be assigned a lower rating. In the great rush to create as many new securities as possible, lack of oversight contributed significantly to the credit market crisis.

Of more concern was the fact that subprime originations during the period increased from less than 5 percent of mortgages made in 2001 to more than 13 percent by 2007. The biggest jump occurred between 2003 and 2004 when the number more than doubled. Alt-A originations showed similar increases. Their numbers almost quadrupled between 2003 and 2005. The originators of subprimes included other banks, not necessarily the same as the general lenders. The major subprime lenders, in addition to Washington Mutual and Countrywide Financial, were New Century Financial Corporation, National City Bank (Ohio), and Ameriquest Mortgage Company.

This record-breaking activity was accompanied by record amounts of mortgage-related bonds issued. Agency bonds were accompanied by CMOs and CDOs, a structured vehicle made up of subprime and Alt-A mortgages and sliced into tranches in much the same fashion as CMOs. A wide range of investors bought them, ranging from the banks themselves to foreign banks eager to earn the marginally higher yield the bonds offered. A major problem was that many mortgage originators also purchased mortgage securities rather than diversify their risk. Many, such as thrift institutions, bought them precisely because they were mortgage related. Although these banks were diversifying their risk, they were not freeing themselves from mortgage-related risk but only counterparty risk. They were still overexposed to the mortgage sector.

Overexposure took an unexpected turn after 2001 when Fannie and Freddie began purchasing and securitizing subprime mortgages. Throughout the previous thirty years, both agencies had followed a relatively conservative model when purchasing mortgages for securitization. But political pressures became more intense after the Gramm-Leach-Bliley bill was passed in late 1999. Both agencies came under pressure from Congress and lobby groups, notably from the mortgage industry, to provide low- and moderate-income mortgages. The decision to do so proved catastrophic for the industry and the markets.

During the 2000s, real income was growing at a low rate of growth but the housing market clearly began to boom. In the wake of the September 11 attacks, the Bush administration asked Americans to spend more money in an effort to keep the economy from slipping. Unfortunately, this was not the type of advice consumers needed. Because wealth was being created in the residential housing sector, expanding mortgages to include a widened array of income groups sounded like sound advice, both economically and politically. Lower-income groups especially were not going to realize a net gain in household wealth in any other manner.

Many of the large lenders began creating subprime and Alt-A mortgages with the express intent of selling them to an agency. Others would securitize them privately. This began a process that started to spiral out of control, beyond oversight. The agencies would enter unknown territory with these loans, and the originators would not check the details of borrowers very closely as a result. And the agencies were being taken advantage of in a way not obvious at the time. Their securitized obligations could be brought to market without registering them with the SEC. Their bonds were exempt.

Investors accustomed to buying agency bonds were aware of the exemption but traditionally came to view the agencies as somewhat prudent lenders. When the agencies departed from the model, investors assumed they did so within permissible guidelines, not simply from political pressure. But the agencies were also under pressure to increase their own profits, and the lower-quality mortgages allowed them to do so. The days of Fannie and Freddie intervening in the market mostly for conventional mortgages ended abruptly.

Getting Darker

The residential mortgage market began suffering problems well before the subprime crisis and the credit market crisis began in August 2007. In June of that year, the Government Accountability Office (GAO) reported that foreclosures were on the rise and had risen significantly since 2005. By mid-2007, over one million mortgages were in default and the number was rising. The culprit was rising interest rates.[15]

The problems were being experienced mostly by homeowners with adjustable rate mortgages. The rise in short-term rates in 2004 and 2005 put pressure on the adjustables and their fixing rates rose, coming as something of a shock to homeowners. The rate rise and the defaults also shed light on many industry practices that went unnoticed. Shoddy lending practices, no income verification, and poor documentation all contributed to the problem, the GAO noted. The agency went on to say that the interest rate situation made more foreclosures likely in late 2007 and 2008, a prediction that came true.

But the role of securitization was central to the problem. As the GAO observed, "data on private label securitized loans show significant increases from 2000 to 2006 in the percentage of mortgages with higher loan to value ratios (the amount of the loan divided by the value of the home), adjustable interest rates, limited or no documentation of borrower income or assets, and deferred payment of principal or interest." But not all originators of subprime mortgages were clearing their balance sheets with private label bonds. Countrywide Financial was one of the major sellers of subprime mortgages and offloaded a great many of them to Fannie Mae, although buying them was clearly beyond the agency's orbit. The agency had undergone an audit in 2006 that had turned up irregularities in its accounting methods for the previous years, and when the review was complete, the bond market assumed that the agency's books were tidier than they were before. That impression collapsed in 2008 when Fannie and Freddie were taken over by the U.S. Treasury.

A major problem that began appearing after 2003 was the widespread use of the alternate mortgage product (AMP). These were mortgages with enticingly low initial interest payments, often deferring principal repayments for several years. The AMPs tended to lull mortgage holders into believing they had been given a low interest rate bargain rather than a mortgage that was due for recalibration at a later date, often with unpleasant consequences. The GAO examined the trend and concluded that "mortgage statistics show that lenders offered AMPs to less creditworthy and less wealthy borrowers than in the past. Some of these recent borrowers may have more difficulty refinancing or selling their homes to avoid higher monthly payments, particularly in an interest-rate environment where interest rates have risen or if the equity in their homes fell because they were making only minimum monthly payments or home values did not increase." Despite the GAO's warnings on these and other types of mortgages, no action was taken on the warnings.[16]

Short-term interest rates rose after 2005, and the change began to affect ARMs within a year. Many of the low sweetener rates began to expire, and the rise caught many holders of ARMs unaware. The damage spread quickly and default rates began to rise. In 2007 and 2008, Fannie Mae had 2.3 million ARMs waiting to be reset. Bank of America had $1.2 trillion of resets coming due, and the International Monetary Fund (IMF) estimated the entire market resets to be $1.3 trillion more. More disturbingly, subprime ARM hybrids had 1.3 million loans waiting to be fixed in 2008. Unlike previous housing slowdowns, the fall in housing prices began to produce negative equity, a situation most American homeowners had never experienced. The complex situation was best summed up by Martin Feldstein, who commented: "Because of the decline in house prices...more than 10 million owners now have mortgages that exceed the values of their house. This is 20 per cent of all homeowners with mortgages. For half of that negative equity group, the debt exceeds the house value by more than 20 per cent. If house prices fall another 15 per cent, negative equity mortgages will rise to 20 million."[17]

Negative equity forced many homeowners to abandon their homes rather than face the financial consequences of paying a mortgage that was worth more than the value of their home. The default rate rose steadily, beginning in 2007, but it was assumed that private mortgage insurance (PMI) would have prevented some defaults. Private mortgage insurance normally was required for homeowners who did not deposit 20 percent equity in their homes upon purchase. Since most subprime mortgages were in that category, it initially was surprising to see how many actually did default, based on the assumption that PMI would prevent it. But on further review, it was discovered that many subprime lenders had wrapped the mortgage with a home equity loan that was used to pay the 20 percent initial equity. The added leverage only hastened the default rate that PMI originally was designed to prevent.

Revolving mortgage credit had a disastrous effect on the market once the mortgages-for-all idea became institutionalized. The contagion spread directly from the questionable creditworthiness of the borrowers to the agencies and securitizers that sold them to bondholders. Many European banks, sovereign wealth funds, and hedge funds held these MBSs, CMOs, and CDOs in their portfolios, originally lured by the higher-than-average bond yields they produced. When the contagion of defaults began to spread, it hit all sectors with equal force. The problem continued because the ARM settings were spread over time, depending on when the mortgages were originally made. This ensured that the subprime crisis would have several years to work its way through the system before subsiding.

The unpleasant result of cannibal consumption became painfully apparent during the credit market crisis when the default rate on homes had more of a significant economic effect than credit card defaults. Why were homeowners willing to default on their homes and abandon them while continuing to maintain their credit card payments? This clearly was a reversal of past behavior when the home was considered worth saving first, not last. Consumers seemed to be unclear about the effects of rising interest rates but certainly seemed to understand how to react to extreme adversity. If a mortgage went into default, the lenders had recourse to the home but not to other assets of the borrower. Not so with credit cards. If a card went into default, the credit card company had recourse to other assets. When push came to shove, consumers apparently knew which resource to preserve while letting the other fail. Once considered the family castle, the home became another casualty of credit cards, a lasting testimony to the power of consumer credit.

Chapter Notes

1. Home ownership statistics are kept by the U.S. Census Bureau in its *Historical Census of Housing Tables*, published periodically.

2. Until 1977, the Treasury was limited in its borrowing to twenty years. Then maturities on long bonds were extended to thirty years maximum.

3. The risk that the government-sponsored enterprises posed to the financial system was examined as early as 1991 in the wake of the savings and loan crisis. See Thomas H. Stanton, *A State of Risk: Will Government Sponsored Enterprises Be the Next Financial Crisis?* (New York: Harper Business, 1991).

4. Pass-through securities provided investors with monthly income but also presented a risk not previously seen. When a mortgage holder in the pool repaid his or her mortgage, that portion of the principal had to be passed through to investors, along with the interest due that month. This added an element of uncertainty for investors because they could never be sure of their monthly income. The securities were said to be *self-liquidating*.

5. Originally, the yields on MBSs were usually found to be about 125 basis points above the thirty-year Treasury yield after that bond became established as the market bellwether. By establishing a default spread, the mortgage rate became more closely linked to the yield on the long Treasury, and the nonmarket guarantee agencies such as the FHA and the VA fell into line because Fannie Mae purchased many of their government-guaranteed mortgages.

6. Pay-through securities allow the bank selling the assets to the specially created trust to retain control over the payments made to investors from the pool. Collection and processing fees are involved as well, so there is still a source of income for the bank even though the mortgages have been pledged to the trust.

7. Features such as inverse floaters were useful in the swap market because they helped institutions manage their variable incomes. For instance, a party receiving inverse floater payments may have been hedging against a previously open position that itself needed to be hedged. Because swaps are not negotiable after becoming operational, the only way to offset a previous swap is to do a new one.

8. The role of agencies and the banks in lending to lower-income groups was evaluated by Glenn B. Canner and Wayne Passmore, "Credit Risk and the Provision of Mortgages to Lower-Income and Minority Homebuyers," *Federal Reserve Bulletin*, Vol. 81, No. 11 (November 1995): 989–1017.

9. The maximum rate, or *cap*, that a homeowner can pay on a mortgage is accompanied by a minimum rate, or a *floor*. These boundaries conform to bond and options features used to create what is known as a *collar*, the difference between them. The collar is the range of uncertainty between interest rates that the lender of the mortgage is immune to. Conversely, it is the range that the mortgage payer is exposed to at the same time.

10. Housing statistics are from the U.S. Census Bureau, *Manufacturing, Mining, and Construction Statistics*, published periodically.

11. A more thorough account of the trend toward abolition of the Glass-Steagall Act and financial deregulation can be found in my *Undue Influence: How the Wall Street Elite Put the Financial System at Risk* (Hoboken, NJ: John Wiley & Sons, 2004).

12. Fannie Mae voluntarily registered its common stock with the Securities and Exchange Commission in March 2003, but its bonds were never required to be

registered because the Securities Act of 1933 exempted agencies of the U.S. government from registering when offering new securities. Freddie Mac did the same in July 2008.

13. Mortgage statistics taken from MortgageDaily.com.

14. Before the Taxpayer Relief Act of 1998, the only way to gain an exemption on the amount of capital gain made on a home sale was to roll over the proceeds into a new residence of equal or greater value than that of the old. That provision of the tax code helped push house prices higher in less expensive areas where retirees from expensive areas tended to move. Price levels in the new areas rose because the new home had to equal the price of the old home or exceed it.

15. The GAO report on the mortgage business is "Information on Recent Default and Foreclosure Trends for Home Mortgages and Associated Economic and Market Developments," GAO-08-78R, October 16, 2007, presented to the House Financial Services Committee.

16. The GAO report on AMPs is found in "Alternative Mortgage Products: Impact on Defaults Remains Unclear, but Disclosure of Risks to Borrowers Could Be Improved," released on September 20, 2006.

17. *Financial Times*, August 26, 2008.

The Politics of Credit

Government is not the solution to our problem. Government is the
problem. —RONALD REAGAN

AFTER MORTGAGE FINANCING became almost as easy as obtaining
a credit card, residential housing became the next great speculative
boom. The terrorist attacks in 2001 helped change the national mood,
and making quick money in housing became as acceptable as having
a dozen credit cards. And the phenomenon was not confined to the
United States. Europeans with a similar predilection for easy consumer
credit also joined the party.

Residential housing boomed worldwide, sometimes in places far
removed from the beaten path. Retail investors began behaving as if
they were hedge funds, moving money around the globe easily, thanks
to easy money policies by the central banks and improved computer
facilities. Low mortgage rates were always available somewhere, in a
currency promising low interest rates. Most central bank policies were
accommodative. Inflation, in everything except property, was considered a relic of the past.

The post–September 11 mood was speculative, and the fever spread
throughout much of the industrialized world. Demographic trends suggested that the U.S. population was aging and that national savings in
some places were not adequate to cover the retirees expected to be
leaving the workforce beginning around 2010. The property market appealed to many as a means of tapping a market protected in the United
States by liberal tax laws, tax deductions, and increasingly lax lending

standards. Fast returns on investment were the order of the day, and housing provided above-average returns if the deals could be timed correctly.

The politics surrounding speculation certainly supported those who tried their hand at property and at the other forms of fast money investments. But as with all get-rich schemes, conditions had to remain stable for these investments to blossom quickly. Any change in interest rates just upsets the apple cart and drives many marginal speculators and homeowners to the brink. Time was of the essence, but the 2000s proved a halcyon period for most investors until it was too late. Interest rates finally did rise slowly, and that spelled the death of the property market, as well as of many currencies and the stock markets.

The contagion spread by the mortgage crisis in 2008 reached most parts of the developed countries in rapid fashion. Much of the disease was spread by the network of banks, investment banks, and insurance companies that created an interdependent network of swaps, monoline insurance, and mortgage-related securities that all began to collapse on each other in a fairly brief time frame. Not all the causes of this epochal phenomenon were financial. Politics played a large part in creating a lax environment in which flimsy financial instruments could flourish.

For decades after World War II, Wall Street and Washington presented American financial markets as the best regulated in the world, with the most stringent financial reporting standards. Much already had been learned from the excesses of the 1920s, leading up to the crash. When the 1930s' securities laws and banking laws were introduced, new generally accepted accounting principles were put in place, and the path to the public securities markets was marked with clear yellow lines. Stock exchanges were regulated, investors were protected, savers' deposits insured, and the public was protected from financial predators who eyed their nest eggs as potential pots of gold. A sheriff was in charge at the corner of Broad and Wall, and his deputies patrolled the intersection of Wall Street and Main Street.

Unfortunately, the sheriff evolved into a traffic cop, and his deputies turned out to be nothing more than meter maids. But only time would prove that assessment correct. In 90 percent of day-to-day financial life, only a traffic cop was necessary, even if the cop's skill levels had to be different and more sophisticated than those of predecessors. And studies began to show that the cop did not have to be on duty full-time.

Over the years, chaos seemed to be proved preferable to order. An Italian study once demonstrated that traffic in Rome was better facilitated and easier to navigate without the ornately dressed police officer in the center trying to direct the city's frantic drivers. By the 1990s, similar studies began to pop up in the financial markets. Transactions were increasing at a frantic pace, but regulators were not considered necessary because markets tended to self-regulate. And it was considered a mistake to stand in the way of prosperity as market volumes climbed and new financial products, many of them computer-driven, appeared and seemed to create a wealth effect where none could be found before. Structured finance was either practicing alchemy or redefining financial and real property assets. For a while, the redefinition worked, but in the end alchemy still remained alchemy.

As in 1929, the economic problems that created havoc in the credit markets beginning in 2007, spilling over into other parts of the financial markets and the real economy, were mainly American in origin but quickly spread to other parts of the world. Globalization proved how quickly a contagion could spread, and a global effort was required to shore up the international financial system against total collapse. And it was the same globalization that had produced some strange quirks in the residential real estate market worldwide. The great irony was that many international investors were taking unhedged risks that could go wrong with the slightest upset to the currency markets or interest rates. Yet it was not until the rise of interest rates in the United States, beginning in 2004, that these risks became felt far and wide.

Similarities in the United Kingdom

The steep rise in real estate values was not just an American phenomenon. Parts of Europe also witnessed dramatic price increases in the value of homes, especially in Britain. The pattern was not coincidental. The United States and the United Kingdom had shared financial practices that made both markets behave in similar fashion.

Residential mortgage statistics in the United Kingdom displayed a similar pattern to that in the States, but the time frame was slightly different. The mortgage explosion in Britain began in 1996 and carried forward to 2007. New mortgage loans exploded to over a million per year in 1997 and remained at over a million until 2007. The peak year was 2002 when 1.396 million were made. The total value of the loans equally exploded, with £60.6 billion created in 1997 and increasing to over £157 billion by 2006. This pales in comparison with the numbers in the United States, which created $20 trillion beginning in 2000, continuing until mid-2008. The United Kingdom created a total of slightly over £1 trillion during that period.[1]

Of the mortgages made, traditionally fixed rates were in the minority until recently. In 1996, only 19 percent were fixed, but by 2007 the percentage had risen to 75 percent. Among the lenders, building societies led the way with six of the top 10 lenders. HBOS (Halifax Bank of Scotland) topped the league tables, followed by Nationwide Building Society and Abbey Building Society Limited in second and third positions. Also included in the top 10 were Northern Rock (5), Alliance & Leicester (9), and Bradford & Bingley (10). By the end of 2008, three of them were either forced to merge with a stronger partner or bailed out by the UK treasury. This was a similar pattern to that in the United States, where three of the top mortgage lenders required assistance from regulators in 2008 and two were thrift institutions (Countrywide and Washington Mutual, in addition to Wachovia Corporation).[2]

The UK market resembled the U.S. market more in broad outline than in function or size. Room for building new residential housing units existed in the States on a much greater scale than in Britain. Housing units were also larger in the United States on average, and they were cheaper per square foot. And Britain went through boom and bust cycles about every fifteen years, in contrast to the States, which had never witnessed a serious bust after World War II. The link between investment banks and commercial banks between the two countries played a large role in making finance more readily available beginning in the 1980s. Traditionally, lending in the United Kingdom was done on an adjustable basis, with fixed-rate mortgages the exception rather than the rule. But securitization still played a large role in funding UK mortgages despite the fact that the corporate bond market in Britain literally had been defunct twenty years before the recent boom began.

When British lenders discovered securitization, they took to it with a vengeance. Mortgage lenders in the United Kingdom made more use of the securitization market than any country other than the United States. Between 2000 and 2007, total European securitization of all sorts of assets stood at 2.440 trillion euros. Of the residential mortgage-backed securities

(RMBS) created, the United Kingdom accounted for about 75 percent. Government agencies like Fannie Mae or Freddie Mac did not exist in Europe, so the securitization market was and is private label. Many of the bonds were covered, however. Barclays led the way as the major investment bank for the bonds. Credit-card-backed ABSs were also much more popular in the United Kingdom than elsewhere in Europe. Over 30 percent of all credit card ABSs originated in the United Kingdom, where credit card use became increasingly popular. Following Britain, Spain and Germany were second and third in using securitization, although their total numbers were much smaller than those in the United Kingdom over the time period.[3] It should be noted that the European version was covered; that is, the bonds had recourse to the original borrower, unlike the private label securitizations in the United States.

Similarities between the U.S. and UK situations with regard to residential mortgages and credit card use invariably focus on the political and social traditions the two have in common, as well as language. But the influence of American investment banks in London is the business and political link that joins the two. New York and London are the two major bond markets in the world; so it is natural that mortgage securitization would be popular in those two places first. Europeans in general are more familiar with the idea of covered bonds (private-label issues that carry the original issuing bank's guarantee should anything go amiss with the pool of collateral backing them). That factor makes the covered bond akin to a Fannie or Freddie obligation, whereas the American private-label RMBS stands alone on the strength of the pool.

The large American investment banks had a major presence in the London financial markets after World War II. Many actively participated in the international (eurobond) market and used many American underwriting techniques there while importing European ones at the same time. Securitized American bond issues had always been popular with foreign investors, and the concept finally began to take hold in Europe as banks realized the risk-management benefits of clearing their books of all sorts of loans. Once European banks became familiar with securitization, the American banks rose to even more preeminent positions as pioneers of the concept.

Despite the ease of entry in the London markets, international banks in general would benefit only when political policies and social inclinations began to favor consumer credit and mortgages. In the United

Kingdom, consumer credit via credit cards was not as popular under the Labour party, preceding the government of Margaret Thatcher. The British household savings ratio also was higher as a result. Once it took hold, however, the boom resembled that following the post-1982 election of Ronald Reagan in the United States. Consumption was acceptable again and affordable, or so it seemed.

The "Revolutions"

As the financial crisis deepened in 2008, it became clear that the U.S. and UK mortgage markets were suffering in similar fashion. Entire communities of newly constructed homes stood empty after foreclosures in places like Fort Myers, Florida, and Las Vegas, and similar instances could be found in northern English communities, which were attempting an economic comeback after years of industrial desolation. Those mortgages also had been financed with subprime securitized bonds that dropped precipitously in value. Clearly, the two phenomena were more than a simple coincidence.

The link between the U.S. and British credit and mortgage markets is much deeper than the financial links between investment banks. Traditionally, Britons and Americans had differing views on indebtedness, based in no small measure on the differences in per-capita income and property values. Britain also came to the game later than the Americans, embracing credit card use and higher levels of mortgage leverage only within the last fifteen years. Data showed that the average Briton was borrowing 3.5 times his or her salary to mortgage a home; not far from the average American level of mortgage indebtedness after 2001. This liberal attitude has common roots extending back almost thirty years.

During the post–World War II years, Britons had a higher household savings ratio and a lower household debt ratio than the average American family. Until the mid-1980s, prosperity there in the American sense was a bit more elusive. Consumer credit was not as easy to obtain, mortgages were granted on the traditional 20 percent down basis, and spending was hardly a national pastime. Britain's first shopping mall opened thirty years after its American counterpart, and old financial habits proved hard to break. By the early 1980s when Americans were already in heavy credit card debt, a common discussion in Britain involved the use of plastic money and its effects on society. In the States, that sort of discussion was rarely heard because credit cards already were considered part and parcel of society.

The factor that changed attitudes in Britain and reinforced them in the United States was the Reagan-Thatcher revolution of the early and mid-1980s. This marked shift in political ideology was responsible for the benign government approach adopted by policy makers on both sides of the Atlantic, but especially in the States, during and after Ronald Reagan's presidency. Adopting Henry David Thoreau's dictum of "that government is best which governs least," the American version of this movement relaxed ideas of indebtedness on the government, corporate, and personal levels, helping to fuel the debt revolution already gaining momentum in the United States. The results were increases in consumption, borrowing, and speculation not seen since the 1920s.

Margaret Thatcher described her social philosophy in simple terms, stating that her vision called for "a man's right to work as he will, to spend what he earns, to have property, to have the state as a servant, and not as a master; these are the British inheritance." Generally, these goals were consistent with the American ones advocated by Reagan and helped the two leaders form a philosophical bond. Their goals were remarkably similar, and the circumstances bringing them about were also similar. Thatcher reacted to the labor and economic strife besetting Britain in the late 1970s and early 1980s, and Reagan and his supporters were dedicated to rolling back many of the New Deal reforms that they maintained created a government intrusion into economic and personal affairs. Whereas Thatcher responded to genuine economic troubles that Conservatives thought were created by years of Labour government's pandering to trade unions, Reagan responded to ideological differences with previous Democratic administrations, which he considered to have caused the problems leading to high interest rates and stagflation.[4] Both looked back further than the immediate administrations preceding them to trace the causes of their problems, and both also proposed solutions that sought root-and-branch change from previous administrations.

Reagan espoused a similar philosophy but left it to others to enunciate it more clearly. The economic and political philosophy of the Republicans was made very clear in a series of volumes published during the 1980s entitled *Mandate for Leadership*. In these volumes, the reorganization of different parts of the executive branch was outlined. Many of the existing laws, such as the Glass-Steagall Act and those governing federal agencies, also were discussed and suggestions made for rolling back their "negative" effects on banks and the markets. The volumes made it clear that smaller government was the goal and that many financial regulations were in the sights of the reformers.[5]

The president was advised by Milton Friedman, whose policies were in vogue during his presidency. Friedman was a member of the President's Economic Policy Advisory Board, a group of experts from outside the government appointed in 1981. A member of the Chicago School, Friedman was well-known in academic and political circles as an advocate of market self-regulation and individual initiative in place of strong central government. The philosophy dovetailed well with the individual contributions made by Chicago School economists and finance experts, many of whom contributed intellectually to the debt revolution. By the mid-1980s, the table already was set for a celebration of hands-off economic policies that would contribute to an historic stock and bond market rally that would set the course of social and economic policy for the next twenty-five years. Free markets were in; highly regulated ones were out.

One of this idea's most ardent supporters was Alan Greenspan. Under his guidance, the Federal Reserve allowed many of the changes embodied in the Gramm-Leach-Bliley 1999 legislation to occur de facto since he first took office in 1987. By the time the law was passed, Citibank had already merged with Travelers Insurance and absorbed Smith Barney and Salomon Brothers, both securities firms; these were amalgams that had once been expressly forbidden. In addition, its CEO, Sanford Weill, sat on the board of the Federal Reserve Bank of New York. Other major financial mergers would soon follow just as the dot.com collapse hit the stock market. The twentieth century distinctly ended on a deregulatory note, and Wall Street braced itself for new challenges and new ways of making money.

The role of the Fed chairman was central to dismantling the older regulations surrounding banking. Few were aware that the Glass-Steagall Act was as much a piece of antitrust regulation as it was banking regulation, but its importance was not lost on Greenspan. By separating banking into commercial banking on the one hand and investment banking on the other, Glass-Steagall effectively kept any one institution from dominating both sides of the financial markets, as J. P. Morgan and his son had done before 1933. Greenspan was acutely aware of the nature of Glass-Steagall. His opposition to antitrust laws in general was noted as early as the 1960s, well before he became Gerald Ford's chair of the Council of Economic Advisers in 1974.

Getting rid of these annoying regulations without congressional approval was a more difficult task, however. Democrats clung to the regulations as part of the social safety net put in place during Franklin D. Roosevelt's first administration and were not receptive to rolling them back to satisfy a free market ideology. But as Fed chairman, Greenspan allowed banks and investment banks to occupy the same space again through some very liberal interpretations of the existing law. Using the language of Glass-Steagall, Greenspan allowed banks and investment banks to engage in activities not specifically proscribed by the law rather than attempt to have it repealed.[6] Because the Fed continually tries to maintain a neutral profile above politics, the changes appeared to be natural, the outcome of some ineluctable force toward deregulation rather than a deliberate policy of undermining Glass-Steagall. Each time a commercial bank wanted to acquire an investment bank before 1999, the mergers were allowed by applying a loose interpretation of activities not specifically prohibited by Glass-Steagall.

Also lending a hand to the deregulation effort was Senator Phil Gramm of Texas, one of the sponsors of the Gramm-Leach-Bliley Act. As chairman of the Senate banking committee, he commented that deregulation was necessary because "the world changes, and Congress and the laws have to change with it." After his term in the Senate was finished, he moved into the private sector. He benefited quickly from the new legislation when he was offered a job with the investment banking unit of UBS as vice chairman in 2002. The job was seen as payback because it was the Gramm-Leach-Bliley Act that allowed UBS to buy securities house Paine Webber for $12 billion in 2000 in a small yet significant result of the new deregulated environment. The *San Francisco Chronicle* commented that it was "glad to see Wall Street is serious about cleaning up its act . . . the man holds a doctorate in economics from the University of Georgia, awarded during the Harding administration." Memories of the Teapot Dome scandal died hard.

From the early 1990s to 1999, the old law effectively had been emasculated to the point where the 1999 Gramm-Leach-Bliley law simply confirmed finally what had already been practiced for at least two years, since Citibank was allowed to merge with Travelers Insurance. Even after the credit market crisis began in 2007, Greenspan acknowledged that he testified for changes in Glass-Steagall many times before it was finally repealed. "Awareness of the detrimental effects of excessive regulation and the need for economic adaptability has advanced substantially in recent years," he wrote in his memoirs, adding, "We dare not go back." The real question becomes whether Glass-Steagall was excessive regulation. During its lifespan, no major economic crisis created by banks had occurred. Within ten years of its passing, several major crises quickly occurred: the Enron and WorldCom scandals and the financial collapse of 2008.

Lobbying efforts also helped to create a lax financial environment. Over $100 million was spent by Citigroup alone to ensure that the Glass-Steagall Act was overturned by Gramm-Leach-Bliley in 1999. Credit card companies, the government-sponsored enterprises (GSEs), and the investment banks spent enormous sums just since 2000 to ensure that their industries were allowed to benefit from as little government interference as possible. A traditional Wall Street practice has been to donate equal amounts of money to campaigns of presidential candidates as a hedge against the unexpected candidate winning. Efforts by the credit card industry would seem to have been the most effective over the years because the payment companies have suffered no serious interruption in their activities.

The commercial banks were the main beneficiaries of this new deregulated environment. Investment banks were less keen to merge with their larger banking cousins but few could resist the forces converging on them. Universal banking had come to the United States and its advocates thought the country now was in step with the rest of the developed world. The financial marketplace concept from the 1920s was finally a reality and new products and services would add to banks' future profitability. It was not a coincidence that Citibank was the major force behind the changes. Since the 1920s, it had actively sought to expand banking beyond its traditional boundaries. Unfortunately, the results in the near future would be the same as they were in the 1920s.

Most observers on both sides of the political spectrum acknowledged that regulations governing banking and the securities markets were a patchwork of laws cobbled together over the years. The United States had no fewer than three bank regulators on the national level, in addition to the states' banking laws. The securities markets had the Securities and Exchange Commission (SEC), always somewhat underfunded and short of staff to cope with the expanding markets. The futures markets had the Commodity Futures Trading Commission (CFTC), but the agency had no jurisdiction over the derivatives markets that would cause the economic woes brought about by the credit market crisis.

Both federal agencies experienced problems in the post-1999 deregulatory period. The CFTC was not allowed jurisdiction over the derivatives and swaps markets in Gramm-Leach-Bliley after lobbyists convinced legislators not to expand its power. The agency had its share of problems in the past obtaining jurisdiction over new futures products, but the omission of swaps and related derivatives would prove a costly mistake.[7]

While the CFTC had its hands tied, the SEC adopted a hands-off policy under Christopher Cox, a Republican appointee who previously had served in Congress. The decision to allow the investment banks to self-regulate their own activities in 2004 was its most crucial decision, although the decision to allow naked short selling of stocks and abolishing the uptick rule for selling short also contributed significantly to market volatility as the credit market crisis unraveled.

Although this patchwork worked reasonably well during specific crises, it clearly was less able to respond to the systemic crisis brought about by the freezing of the credit markets and the mortgage market crisis. Contrary to the popular belief, markets were not able to self-adjust and desperately needed assistance, especially after the government bailout of Fannie Mae and Freddie Mac. By late 2008, no one was claiming that the best government is that which governs least, at least not in public.

The Baby-Boomer Generation

These ideological changes were caused by a significant demographic phenomenon emerging after World War II. The debt revolution, the ideological shift to the right on economic issues, and the increased number of financial transactions in society could be traced to the baby boom following the war. A powerful generation had been created whose financial demands and tastes were responsible for the consumer trends beginning in the 1980s.

Increased consumer demand for credit and housing easily traced their origins to the baby boomers, the first generation to be raised with the buy-now-pay-later mentality. The generation preceding them was the product of the Great Depression and witnessed the problems that consumer credit could cause when it collided with severe economic contraction. Bank failures made average citizens aware that highly optimistic projections about the future came with certain risks that might be realized only occasionally yet still had the potential to cause economic ruin.

Meeting the needs of baby boomers became crucial to ensure success in financial services and all other sorts of marketing. The demographic group included anyone born between the mid-1940s and the early 1960s. The oversized tennis racket, commonly used today, was originally marketed to them beginning in the 1980s as an easier way to hit a ball as one became older and slower. Catering to their needs was vital in marketing any good or service. Boomers became the main target group for sellers of all sorts. The same trend was not seen as clearly in European societies, including Britain, because World War II had taken a much higher toll on their young male populations. This in part explains why Britons took to credit cards later than did Americans; the post-boomer generation was the first to embrace them. In the United Kingdom, cards gained a wider acceptance only in the later 1980s and early 1990s.

But it was in the United States that politicians and marketers understood the financial power of this demographic group. As baby boomers began to reach their thirties, pension laws were written and rewritten, the tax code revised, and a wide array of products were offered for sale, catering to their tastes. This group caused financial transactions in particular to explode exponentially within a twenty-year period. In 1979, the record New York Stock Exchange volume was 65 million shares in one day. Twenty years later, volume increased to an average of around 400 million shares, and within five years it topped 1 billion. In 1979, the oldest boomer was around thirty-three years old and twenty years later he was fifty-three, an age when demand for stocks for retirement plans or ordinary investing was at peak demand.

Robert Rubin, treasury secretary under President Bill Clinton, recognized the economic importance of dealing with the baby-boomer generation. When the Clinton administration was able to reduce the budget deficit that had plagued the government for the previous 20 years and finally achieve a surplus, he noted that "after 2010, the huge baby-boomer generation will begin retiring which will put increased pressure on Social Security and it was on that basis that we reached the conclusion that nothing should be done with these surpluses until that problem is addressed." The surplus soon disappeared, but the demographic problem remained the same.

Changes in the laws surrounding retirement in the latter 1980s made demand for equities higher than ever before as the baby boomers began setting money aside for retirement and also speculated with their disposable income. The Employee Retirement Income Security Act (ERISA) first created individual retirement accounts (IRAs). They were created in part by fear that the Social Security system would not be able to cover all of the retiring baby boomers within thirty years. As birth rates declined nationally, there would be more beneficiaries of Social Security than there were workers to pay into the fund's coffers. With the introduction of the 401(k) plan in the 1978 Revenue Act, employees now were able to invest their own funds in the market and equities were the main beneficiaries. It would take several years before the Tax Reform Act of 1986 made its effects felt in regard to these individual plans, but the Reagan bull market made equities attractive and a long stock market rally began, lasting five years before the market collapse in 1987. After the collapse, the market indices again rose, temporarily ending with the dot.com bust in 2000.

But after the market lost value during that bust, investors already had turned to what were considered to be safer investments with more tax advantages. Real estate again entered the picture after 2000, especially because real wages were not rising more than 1 percent per year for a large majority of the population. As already seen, they were urged to dabble in real estate because an ownership society was being encouraged. What could not be earned the old-fashioned way could be compensated for by speculating in the housing market. For several frenzied

THE CONNECTION BETWEEN speculation and real estate certainly is not new and has been noted before. George Bernard Shaw once noted that "Gambling promises the poor what property performs for the rich, something for nothing." Even the invention of the Internet and online trading has not changed that basic fact, but only reinforced it.

years, the formula worked, before the bottom fell out. When it did, it was the first time that negative consequences were felt financially because of the baby-boomer generation.

Housing Wealth

The major problem confronting the Bush administration after 2000 was the low level of growth in real wages. In the wake of tax cuts widely criticized for benefiting those in higher income brackets, the administration was faced with the additional criticism of not doing enough to aid the average working family. But real estate could prove a boost to those in the lower income brackets because it would provide a way of increasing household wealth when the average paycheck was not increasing. The president had gone on the record stating that he wanted to preside over a homeowners' society. The best way to achieve that goal was to allow the mortgage boom to continue.

The increase in house prices and the heightened use of credit cards were accompanied by low growth in real wages, as had been the case for two decades. To achieve the American Dream, average American families were going into more debt given the low growth in incomes, factoring in inflation. The revised tax breaks for capital gains on homes sold also played a large part. An example of the income problem can be found in the following remark made by Robert Reich, secretary of labor in the Clinton administration, before the National Press Club in 1995: "Since 1979, household incomes have swelled by $826 billion, in 1993 dollars. But about 98 percent of the increase has gone to the top fifth. Everyone else—80 percent of American households—has shared just 2 percent of the income gains. The typical American family is living on less than it did fifteen years ago, adjusted for inflation." What is more remarkable about the statement was that inflation and interest rates were very low during the period following the 1990–1991 recession.

In 2007, the labor secretary in the Bush administration, Elaine Chao, in a presentation to the National Center for Policy Analysis, confirmed the same message in less direct terms: "Since January 2001, real after-tax personal income has risen 11.9 percent." Using simple division, the message was the same. For a six-year period, that amounted to less than 2 percent per year, not substantially different from the previous twenty years. The statement that middle- and lower-middle-income families were suffering while the top 20 percent of wage earners were prospering was not just anecdotal; the middle class was being pressed economically. In response, it had been using credit cards and home equity loans to keep abreast of the purchasing power of the lost income. But the price was proving high. Card indebtedness grew and personal bankruptcies were at historic highs before 2005. Real estate speculation appeared a viable way out of the income trap for middle- and low-income groups.

This is where regulation was sorely missed in the real estate market. The market was never regulated because it existed on a local level and was considered the market least needing regulation, at least until securitization appeared. Then real estate mortgage providers began granting mortgages when real wages did not support the high leverage ratios being given to the average mortgage applicant. In traditional terms, any ratio of home price to annual income in excess of 2.5:1 placed great strain on the borrower. Since real wages increased only about 1 percent during the boom for the lower 80 percent of the population, ratios in excess of the standard were totally unrealistic. While it may have been more realistic to grant the upper band of wage earners ratios that could have been met by future earnings, the average wage earner clearly could not afford them.

The mortgage boom was not confined to the United States, Britain, and parts of Western Europe. It extended far and wide, from Romania and the Czech Republic to Patagonia. Securitization did not play a part in these other booms but a trick learned from international finance did. Once it was applied to the retail level, the boom was off and running. Real estate speculation quickly jumped borders and pushed up property prices in some unlikely places. Much of it was caused by developments in the currency markets, not usually associated with residential real estate.

For years, Wall Street and the City of London had known and practiced what became known as the "carry trade." The surfeit of cheap money produced by many central banks after 2001 made this type of investing particularly easy. Money could be borrowed with low-interest-rate loans and used to purchase higher-yielding assets, with the buyer pocketing the difference. An investor could borrow at 3 percent and buy an asset with a 7 percent yield. The 4 percent difference would be profitable if the trade was done on a large scale. The profit on a $100,000 borrowing paled in comparison to a $1 billion borrowing; in any event,

DURING THE HEIGHT OF the property boom, investors and speculators went far afield in search of undervalued property, which offered something different for the discriminating buyer. The *Financial Times* regularly ran ads for exotic real estate in Patagonia in southern Argentina, among other places. In 2003, an article described the local real estate market: "The trouble is that in the past year alone, the cost of land has soared by 70 to 80 per cent. Foreign demand for ranches is so fierce, says [a local land broker], that helicopters often fly potential buyers in to view a property as he is showing other clients around. 'It feels a little like a gold rush,' he says." Ranches in the area started at around $1 million.

either the $4,000 profit or the $40 million profit certainly was better than working for a living.

Obviously the larger the spread between borrowed money and the asset yield, the greater the profit would be. Borrowing and investing in the same currency were usually the norm in this carry trade, but when hedge funds entered the picture in the early 2000s the game plan began to change. If a low-interest-rate currency could be borrowed, sold, and reinvested in another currency area promising a higher return, the carry trade would easily be exported. In the post-2001 boom, it was clear that Icelandic bonds yielded almost 9 percent while other hard currencies could be borrowed at around 3 percent. But why settle for 6 percent carry when the Japanese yen could be borrowed for 1 percent? That would increase the carry to 8 full percent, a decent margin for doing nothing more than transferring funds from one locale to another.

The only risk involved was currency risk. The spread was appetizing but could be devoured if the currency values changed. But at returns double the average Treasury bond, the trade was considered worth the risk. Hedge funds began borrowing yen in order to sell it for Icelandic krona with which they would buy Icelandic government bonds. If done in large sizes, the trades paid off handsomely. The Japanese authorities were not inclined to intercede because the yen were borrowed outside Japan, providing little incentive to intervene.

The strategy worked well for a while but began to unravel during the subprime crisis. Carry trades by hedge funds helped bring Iceland to its financial knees in 2008 as the country teetered on the verge of bankruptcy. Once the yen began to appreciate and the krona weakened, money was transferred out of Iceland as it had arrived—quickly. The key ingredient in the carry trade was that the currency borrowed remained at the same exchange rate or moved lower in value. But the credit market crisis helped push the yen to all-time highs against other major currencies and the krona. Once it became apparent that currency risk threatened once profitable carry trades, money began to flee. Government bond prices slumped, and so too did the investments made in Icelandic banks and industry, all of which began to totter on the brink of bankruptcy as carry trade money was sold for yen and left the country. A loan was granted by the International Monetary Fund to help the country overcome its problems, the origins of which did not go unnoticed by its citizens. Acknowledging that the government had pursued American and British economic policies for too long, one Icelandic bank depositor noted, "There's so much anger in the society now because of what has happened, we're witnessing the death of Reaganism-Thatcherism. We have to go back to our older values. The free market is not doing what it's supposed to be doing." Ironically, it was just over thirty years before, under a Labour government, that Britain was the last major industrialized country to apply for IMF assistance.

The carry trade concept was appealing to individual investors trying to keep costs down in an attempt to buy second homes or simply speculate. Real estate companies in places such as Romania and other locales in Eastern Europe realized that property in their countries would be more appealing to foreign investors if it was linked to a low-interest-rate currency. They began offering mortgages based on yen interest rates, much lower than the rates in many less developed countries. The trick worked and real estate values began to rise, although the currency risk side was always present. The new homeowners were certainly welcomed warmly. The mayor of Bucharest told a conference of real estate investors that "Bucharest's only alternative is foreign direct investments," not the greatest advertisement for his city. But real estate buyers in Britain and Israel, among other countries, took advantage of the low rates and incentives offered by municipal councils and began buying second homes in places that were not necessarily within commuting distance, such as

Bucharest, Patagonia, and the Gulf Emirates. Another trick of the institutional investing market had filtered down to retail investors, crossing borders in the process.

Americans also participated in the overseas home quest, often looking for inexpensive places to retire. They too were drawn to some of the more exotic places that lured Europeans. London's *Spectator*, with tongue in cheek, posed the ultimate property question to them: "Why not take the ultimate contrarian investment of all—real estate in Baghdad? Those who bought property in London during the Second World War certainly didn't do themselves any harm." Suggestions included an apartment complex with a four-bedroom flat and its own private security force.

An even more unusual by-product of the speculative 2000s was found in the proliferation of online currency trading services, offering the small investor or speculator the opportunity to trade foreign exchange at institutional spreads. This helped make the once exotic world of currency trading less formidable. For bid-offer spreads as small as 3 or 5 pips of a point, small speculators depositing only $500 or $1,000 could leverage up to fifty times to trade the hard currencies. The services were offered by many futures market brokers as well as international brokers, many of whom recognized the opportunity for retail business in a market traditionally dominated by corporate trading. The trading would have gone unnoticed except that it became contagious in some places, with some unpleasant consequences.

The risks and rewards of the highly leveraged trading were apparent. A small trader could gain substantially from currency movements, but the opposite was also true, more often than not. In Japan, a housewife known as Mrs. Watanabe managed to lose over $1 million playing the market, lured by the prospects of huge gains. Investors and speculators appeared to understand the mechanics of foreign exchange trading if not the risks of high leverage. Taking full advantage of her predicament after her loss, she started an investment club and wrote a book about her experiences.

The episode was not a joke and certainly was not isolated. Until the credit crisis in 2007, the value of foreign currencies traded online by private Japanese citizens averaged $9.1 billion a day—almost a fifth of all foreign exchange trading during trading hours in Tokyo.[8] Other losses by women of $100,000 equivalents were not uncommon. Real estate speculation was more difficult in Japan because of the already high prices for property, and so other leveraged forms of speculation became popular. Retail investors had discovered highly leveraged foreign exchange trading, much to their dismay. But a similarity with the United States still existed. Many Japanese, suffering from over a decade of low growth, low wage growth, and deflation, took to speculation to fuel their purchasing power. Technology and the growth in information helped make foreign exchange trading possible. But the irony was that the activity was not actually foreign exchange trading in the traditional sense, only exposure to a currency's price changes. It allowed the small speculator to bet on currency movements but did not actually provide any real currency. To sell yen for dollars, the investor still needed the services of a bank.

This link between currency rates and residential property did not exist prior to the post–September 11, 2001 period. A September 11 effect appears to have occurred, encouraging a new, widespread use of leverage. A similar outburst of speculation had followed most wars, beginning with the Civil War. September 11 inspired a carpe diem attitude among millions who decided to speculate in order to fund their lifestyles in the shadow of terrorism when wages were lagging. The general trend is indicative of how global the markets have become worldwide, due to the improvements in computer technology and the ease with which funds can be moved across national boundaries. At the same time, it also is indicative of how fragile these links are because they tend to make leverage available to anyone with a computer, enabling individuals to execute trades or real estate deals that may be above their financial capabilities. When the property downturn began, what began as a domestic problem quickly spilled over borders and became an international one. The larger problems created by excessive securitization, poor lending procedures, and a fee-driven mortgage lending system were exacerbated by these smaller problems. They also help underline the problem that regulators will face when attempting to cope with them in the future.

In real estate, the widespread use of personal leverage needed more help than simply a computer and access to an online broker. Revolving mortgage credit was at the heart of the phenomenon. One of the more successful American exports of the last fifteen years has been securitization. Because of its influence, banks abroad have entered the credit card business, engaged in lending for mergers and acquisitions, and extended themselves in subprime real estate lending.

But international investors have had a different reaction to foreign securitization than they have had to the American or British types. Over the last several years, businesses in all of the developed European countries have entered the securitization market. In addition to the major members of the European Union, borrowers in Russia, Turkey, the Czech Republic, Ukraine, and Kazakhstan have all issued securitized bonds in varying degrees.[9] Russia is the largest issuer in this group. The major securitized borrowing area for European and non-European countries has been residential real estate, followed by CDO issues and commercial real estate. Ukraine and Brazil both began studying or using securitization on a small scale with the hopes of further developing their residential real estate markets.

But it was the desire to participate in the mortgage boom that led many foreign banks and other institutional investors to buy subprime CMOs in great quantities. Late entrants from outside the European Union have issued moderate or small amounts of securitized bonds. Collateral from outside the European markets, where the legal systems are less familiar to investors, will be treated more gingerly than the more familiar American or British collateral. The idea that the American regulatory system, led by the SEC, and the ratings provided by the credit-rating agencies would protect investors from fraud or excess proved to be incorrect, however, and the benefits that securitization could bring to less developed economies suffered a setback. Since the bond defaults of the 1920s, investors have been wary of collateral that they could not assess properly. The shadow of Ivar Krueger still looms over the fixed-income markets.

Internationally, securitization also made advances in areas not previously associated with it, such as wind assets, intellectual property, carbon trading, and life insurance. Technically, any asset or receivable considered acceptable by investors is eligible for the method. But investor reception is the key ingredient for success. After the subprime crisis began, securitization in the United States dwindled substantially. It did remain relatively strong in the international bond market for about a year before investors began to shy away from it as a way of participating in temporary booms.

The Transaction Society

All of these developments in the securities markets and real estate occurred at a dizzying pace after the mid-1980s. Transaction volume grew exponentially in all areas of the financial service industry and in other sectors touched by it, including legal services and property services. What once would have been considered far-fetched ideas, such as buying Romanian real estate with yen or depositing money in Icelandic banks, became a reality much sooner than imagined. The use of securitized bonds increased exponentially before investor interest finally cooled. Financial transactions of all sorts were increasing exponentially. The causes were manifold and hazy at the same time.

In addition to being a significant demographic group and a sizable market in their own right, the baby-boomer generation was better educated than its predecessors. It had a higher percentage of college graduates than ever and that distinction was not confined to the United States. Most countries in the developed world shared the same educational characteristics and aspirations of the large middle class. At the same time, the trend toward providing more services through service industries at the expense of manufacturing made financial ideas like leverage and property speculation more appealing because the new generation understood the concepts better than their predecessors. And use of the personal computer gave this large middle class access to information on a grand scale.

Computer scientist Gordon Moore, a cofounder of Intel, made a prediction in 1965 that embodied the nature of developed societies for two generations to come. He made a prediction that came to be known as Moore's Law: The number of transistors on a microprocessor chip would double every two years into the foreseeable future. Intel proved that prediction correct. In the mid-1980s, the largest microchip had about one hundred thousand transistors on it. One million was reached by the late 1980s, 10 million by the late 1990s, and 25 million by 2001. Then the numbers became truly astounding, reaching 220 million by late 2002, 600 million by 2004, one billion by early 2005, and 2 billion in 2008. It appeared Moore had proven the modern answer to the ageless medieval question: How many angels can fit on the head of a pin? The contemporary answer appeared to be an almost infinite number.

The financial markets saw their own version of this in transaction volume. The New York Stock Exchange, which recorded a record daily

IN THE 1920S, Charles Mitchell, the president of the National City Bank in New York (today Citibank) presided over the stock market boom and the good times it brought until the crash occurred. He later described the process of bringing new securities to market, something the bank's securities subsidiary was particularly adept at doing, as "manufacturing securities." Many of the bonds underwritten were for companies and foreign political entities almost bankrupt at the time although the bank had no problem selling them. The use of the term "manufacturing" and the record of Wall Street in general in the years leading to the crash eventually cost him his job at National City although he did return to Wall Street as the head of a securities house.

volume in 1979 of 65 million shares, hit its first billion-share day in 1997 and then 2 billion shares in 2001. In 2005, it recorded 3 billion shares, 4 billion in 2006, almost 6 billion in 2007, and over 8 billion in 2008. Share volume actually outpaced the number of transistors on a chip, a phenomenon that would have been totally unexpected ten years before. The NYSE seemed to be the perfect example of Moore's Law. And it was not alone.

Similar numbers were found in Britain. As the *Financial Times* noted, in 1965 equity market turnover was 9.7 percent of GDP. By 1995, it was 88 percent and by 2007 it was 296 percent. The numbers also showed the contributions that finance had made to the economy as a whole. GDP rose from £36 billion to £1.40 trillion within that time period, but financial transactions were growing disproportionately.[10] London constantly kept pace with New York as a major financial center because of this astonishing growth, and the UK mortgage market grew exponentially as a result.

The growth in computing power was accompanied by the application of new, powerful financial software that could now be run much more quickly than in the past. Compounding the problem was the information surrounding many of these instruments. In the 1990s, many securities houses began developing new financial products in debt and derivatives instruments, which they protected by patent. The designer instruments were made for clients with particular needs and were known only to the client and its investment bankers. The problem was that these instruments were opaque, not transparent as the postwar trend in finance seemed to suggest. If something were to go wrong with one of them, the consequences would not be clear to regulators or even to the parties themselves.

Powerful computing also led to the introduction of algorithm trading (algo trading), where traders developed their own trading programs and executed them by computer. This led to an increase in proprietary trading (prop trading) by traders on behalf of their securities firms and for the firms' own accounts. This trading was not confined to the stock markets but was found in all other sectors of the markets, including derivatives, foreign exchange, and fixed income. Volume in other markets soared as well. In 2004, foreign exchange trading volume averaged about $1.80 trillion equivalents per day; by 2007 it exceeded $3 trillion.

The same phenomenon could be found in the fixed-income market. In the 1980s, corporate bond issuance totaled about $250 billion in the United States in a good year. In 2007, the amount of new issues was $2.30 trillion. New commercial paper totaled almost $2 trillion in 2006; only seven years before it had been $1.4 trillion. The original securitization performed by Fannie Mae, Ginnie Mae, and Freddie Mac would not have been possible without the aid of faster computers. The pass-through process (as well as the pay-through process) relied on a homeowner's making a monthly payment, the agency's receiving that payment, and the agency's passing it through to the bondholders in a quick process that would not tolerate delay. The only way to monitor the payments sequence was to use increasingly fast computers because the number of securitizations of all sorts kept increasing from the 1980s.

The growing number of transactions at all levels of the financial services business made abuse of any one process more likely. During the credit market crisis, a company responsible for documenting the mortgages in the collateral pool for pay-throughs admitted that it was able to verify only some of the mortgages pooled and had to rely on statistical inference to make judgments about the rest. They were only able to verify that 15–20 percent of the mortgages fit the criteria of the securitized bond. The rest were assumed to follow in step. Anyone familiar with that process could then easily include mortgages in the pool above the appropriate threshold of risk. Equally important, as the number of transactions swelled, regulators began to rely more and more on the expertise of outsourcing companies, such as bond ratings companies, to perform some of the work usually associated with regulators themselves. Contracting regulatory work may sound efficient in boom markets, but the potential for abuse also needs to be taken into account.

The sheer complexity of many financial transactions also made market transparency difficult. The increased speed with which transactions could be done only complicated the problem. Since the Enron scandal five years before the mortgage crisis, it was apparent that many vehicles created by structured finance, such as special-purpose vehicles (SPVs), could easily be used to perpetrate fraud on investors and accountants because of their complexity. There were other precedents. As they were sorting out the derivatives scandal in Orange County, California, in 1993, forensic accountants found swaps in its portfolio tied to German interest rates. No one could explain how they got there, but the damage they and other inappropriate derivatives did to that large multibillion-dollar portfolio was clear to see. Finance was becoming too complicated for the average investment manager or investor to cope with.

The ability to create private-label ABSs, CMOs, and CDOs is a testament to the sophistication of the financial community. The ingenuity to take a bundle of CDOs or bonds and use it as collateral for a new bond is a good risk-mitigation technique. But the application of these sorts of techniques on a large scale led to serious problems in the marketplace because of their ability to generate underwriting fees and obscure the quality of the underlying collateral. But it also demonstrated the ability to manufacture profits, a product of financial engineering that no one criticized for obvious reasons over the last 10 years.

During the dot.com boom of the late 1990s, it was widely assumed that the use of the Internet had eliminated the costs of dealing with intermediaries when doing business because customers were able to deal with suppliers directly. This in turn led to low inflation because costs were reduced and would not be passed on to customers. This new economy was different from its predecessor and was creating new types of wealth, signaling a major turning point in economic history. It has become clear that this phenomenon was aided immeasurably by financial engineering and structured finance, which were doing the same thing in consumer credit and mortgage credit. Gordon Moore almost proved that an infinite number of transistors could be placed on the head of a pin. Wall Street almost proved that one could create profits out of nothing.

Chapter Notes

1. UK mortgage statistics are from the Council of Mortgage Lenders (CML).

2. Northern Rock became the first official casualty of the subprime crisis on either side of the Atlantic and had to be bailed out by the UK treasury several months before any of its American counterparts were given assistance by the U.S. Treasury and the Federal Reserve.

3. European securitization statistics are from the European Securitisation Forum.

4. Thatcher's original emphasis on home ownership was somewhat different from that in the United States because she initially was interested in having people who lived in state-subsidized council housing buy the dwellings and become owners rather than subsidized renters. This idea later surfaced in the States under the homeowner initiative during the Clinton administration, spearheaded by Henry Cisneros.

5. The original *Mandate for Leadership* dealt primarily with reforming and reorganizing government departments. In the section concerning the Securities and Exchange Commission (SEC), it advocated allowing banks to underwrite certain types of municipal revenue bonds, which they were not allowed to do at the time. It admitted that the action would probably result in many of the smaller brokers and securities houses going out of business, in the name of greater competition. See Robert Knabel, "Securities & Exchange Commission," in Charles L. Heatherly, ed., *Mandate for Leadership: Policy Management in a Conservative Administration* (Washington, DC: Heritage Foundation, 1981), pp. 808–811. In *Mandate for Leadership III*, published in 1989, the repeal of Glass-Steagall was again advocated, along with some of the insider trading laws, in the name of market efficiency. See Charles L. Heatherly and Burton Yale Pines, ed., *Mandate for Leadership III: Policy Strategies for the 1990s* (Washington, DC: Heritage Foundation, 1989).

6. The language of the Glass-Steagall Act required that no more than 10 percent of a bank's earnings could be generated from securities operations. This was known as the *principally engaged rule* (Section 20 of the act). Using the Fed powers through the Bank Holding Company Act, Greenspan allowed banks to acquire securities operations, with the caveat that they earn no more than 10 percent from them. As time passed, the percentage was increased to the point where banks, and especially Citibank, were effectively in the corporate securities business de facto until Gramm-Leach-Bliley was passed in 1999.

7. The original Commodity Futures Trading Act, passed in 1936, defined futures trading as confined to agricultural futures; when a new product appeared in the futures market, the CFTC had to battle for jurisdiction after the fact.

8. *New York Times*, September 16, 2007, p. 14.

9. The statistics for Asian securitizations are not as well recorded as those for the American and European ABSs and CMOs.

10. *Financial Times*, November 22, 2008.

7

Policy Implications

Credit is a system whereby a person who can not pay gets another person who can not pay to guarantee that he can pay. —CHARLES DICKENS

ALTHOUGH THE CRISIS in the housing market and credit markets that spilled over into the economy presented the most substantial threat since the Great Depression, its extensive nature made it clear that it was a policy failure on a systemic level. Banking and securities regulators failed to detect the intrinsic risks presented by easy credit and a hands-off policy adopted throughout government. Everyone was too busy making money or congratulating themselves on the good times to apply the regulatory brakes.

Nine years before the crisis began, Alan Greenspan attended a party at the Capitol, drinking champagne to celebrate the demise of Glass-Steagall when Gramm-Leach-Bliley was passed in 1999. Champagne flowed in other places as well. The banking and securities CEOs attending the annual World Economic Forum at Davos, Switzerland, during the 2000s took no heed of those policy makers and academics daring to raise questions about the mortgage boom and the prosperity it created on Wall Street. The financial services industry had no time for naysayers. They were not the true risk takers. Wealth was not created by asking questions.

Responses to the crisis used many of the powers given to the Federal Reserve over the years and added a few new wrinkles. The Fed had to intervene directly in the money market by buying new commercial paper, stepping into unknown territory. It also provided emergency repurchase (repo) facilities with investment banks, also a departure from previous policy. The Treasury ultimately abandoned any idea of a truly American solution to the problem and began quickly cooperating with other industrialized nations to work on a common solution to the global crisis. Confusion reigned in other quarters as well. Politicians appeared in public explaining why the bailouts of the banks and mortgage-assistance agencies were not socialistic after all, only weeks after they swore fealty to the principles of free markets. Karl Marx would have rolled over in his grave. Perhaps capitalism did bear the seeds of its own destruction after all.

The extent of the financial and economic crisis can be gauged by the debate it has sparked about the role of the state in modern life. Such debates had not been heard since the 1930s when long breadlines convinced many that a hands-off social policy advocated by the Old Guard on Wall Street and in corporate America would bring the United States to its knees. Statist intervention was necessary to preserve the social order, not simply to become an inconvenience for the hard-line Wall Street contingent who still thought wealth could be manufactured in the securities markets.

Yet there was much to celebrate even after the Ronald Reagan presidency ended. In the wake of the collapse of Soviet communism, it appeared that capitalism had emerged triumphant. Ultimately, it seemed obvious to many that the main power in the United States was financial, not political. Wall Street was creating prosperity in the 1990s, and politicians benefited from it. The budget deficit, once a major policy issue during the Reagan and George H. W. Bush years, had been converted to a surplus by the late 1990s, thanks to increased tax revenues brought about by the boom. Even after the Enron and WorldCom debacles, many conservatives believed that the transparency reforms introduced by the Sarbanes-Oxley Act (2002) were unnecessary and only added to the expense of doing business. Borrowing a page from the Greenspan-led Federal Reserve System, they countered that regulation only impeded economic growth. The less regulation there is, the more growth there will be, went the argument. Despite being compelling, this was arguable, and supporting statistics were hard to find. The one precedent for the mess was the period leading up to the Crash of 1929, and many scholars had been working on the premise that the market collapse did not cause the Great

Depression that followed so quickly. The only cloud on the 1990s horizon was that low rate of real income growth.

Before the recent financial collapse, politics was becoming less relevant and finance more important to the lives of ordinary citizens. Extra money was easy to find, and the implications of being in debt seemed not to matter. The height of that sentiment led the George W. Bush administration to suggest that a portion of Social Security funds could be directed by taxpayers into equity investments. The growth rate in stocks would help bail out a government faced with serious future Social Security funding problems once the baby-boomer generation began retiring in large numbers. The adverse public reaction against that proposal helped save the financial system from what would be serious trouble within several years. But the role of the state had still been relegated to the role of a traffic cop on the corner. Will Rogers once remarked that the original Securities and Exchange Commission kept a shotgun behind the front door in case of trouble. Within seventy years, it had been mounted over the fireplace as a relic of the past.

The reaction was peculiar. Thirty years of denigrating the state in the name of politics had become embedded in the psyche and would be difficult to dislodge in the future, although the depth of the financial crisis helped speed the process. Outside the United States, especially in the places where Reaganism-Thatcherism had not been embraced, a more flexible interpretation of the role of the state prevailed. During the early stages of the 2008 economic crisis, a member of the French parliament took exception to Reagan's remark about the state being part of the problem rather than the solution. The idea was inconceivable in France. "The state is a form of life insurance," he remarked. At that stage, no one argued the point.

Coordinating Policy

The collapse of the residential housing market and the crisis in consumer credit underlined the need for effective regulation in both of those critical areas if economic recovery was to prove long lasting. Without proper oversight, the same problems would reappear in the future, obviating any economic progress made since a previous recovery. This obviously is much easier said than done. The systemic nature of the crisis defied easy remedies.

In the early stages of the subprime crisis, the differences between the policies of the Fed and the European Central Bank (ECB) became obvious as the two institutions attempted to solve the tensions in the money markets. American and European monetary policies had different primary aims, requiring different policy implementations. When the Americans lowered interest rates to help free the paralysis in the money markets, the Europeans seemed content to stay the course, leaving rates unchanged. How was it possible that the Europeans initially seemed so oblivious to the crisis in the markets?

Even within Europe, policies differed over banking basics. In the wake of the bank capital crisis, the Swiss National Bank imposed maximum leverage ratios on its banks after UBS reported its enormous losses. Other national banking authorities with the European Union were slow to react in similar fashion, believing in part that the ratios would prove too conservative, not allowing their banks to continue growing. However, it soon became obvious that growth was no longer the issue.

The answer depends on the policy goals of a central bank, at least in more normal periods. Over the last seventy years, the goals of the Fed and (originally) the Deutsche Bundesbank differed. When the ECB was created, it followed the Bundesbank model for Europe. Given the German experiences with inflation in the Weimar Republic, the Bundesbank was created primarily to fight inflation, the bête noir of economic progress in postwar Europe. That inflation led to World War II and the unrest created—an experience not to be repeated again.

Federal Reserve governor Henry Wallich, an emigrant from Germany in his boyhood, once recalled the personal effects of Weimar inflation. While the family was living above a bakery, his mother gave him a few pfennigs to buy a loaf of bread. He dutifully went down the stairs, only to be told that the price of bread was rising and that the money she had given him was not enough. He went up and down the stairs several times before it became obvious that the trips were futile. Prices were doubling with every trip. This sort of exponentially rising inflation was never experienced in the United States, and it never became the primary focus of Federal Reserve policy.

The goal of the Fed is somewhat different. In the United States, the defining economic moment of the twentieth century was the Great

Depression. High unemployment rates, lack of capital investment, and a collapse of the financial markets prompted the Fed to concentrate on economic growth in the future, not on inflation. The American experience did not include serious price inflation, and therefore the emphasis shifted to growth. Making liquidity available for lending by banks, in order to spark growth, was the avowed aim of the Fed. In 1930s terms, the lyrics of "Hey Buddy Can You Spare a Dime?" recalling the hobos' lament were the equivalent of Wallich's story about his trips up and down the staircase.

At the same time, the differences in regulations in the European Union, Britain, and the United States also seemed to be in sharp contrast. The Europeans in general used a principles-based regulatory system, whereas the Americans used a rules-based system. It was the rules-based system in the States that had come under attack from conservative quarters since the Reagan presidency. Break the banking or securities rules and prosecution could follow. It should be noted that little, if any, of the prosecutions were criminal; most were civil prosecutions that brought not-so-harsh penalties against banks or securities houses. And under the system, remedies could come only after a rule had been broken. By that time, it was already too late to redress a problem, other than to demand accountability. Prevention had given way to possible prosecution only.

Over the last thirty years, the softened regulatory climate gave way to calls for a principles-based system in the United States. That shift already was well under way when the subprime crisis hit, as already noted. The principles-based system is not known for prosecutions as much as it is for prevention, most of it on a voluntary basis. The crisis put that myth on the shelf. The only way to ensure that the financial system is not attacked from within by its own excesses is strong legislation to stop malfeasance and to punish it if necessary. If criminal prosecutions were threatened against banks or securities houses, many market excesses would quickly disappear.

Practically, the state of American regulation will make that a difficult task. At first glance, it would seem that the Fed has only limited powers in the creation and control of consumer and mortgage credit and that it has a very spotty record in exercising them. It has the power to preside over consumer credit lending policies through Regulation Z but has not been particularly active in this respect. Mortgage lending is even more

WHAT IS THE MAXIMUM rate of interest? The question is not asked frequently anymore, but it was a burning question in the past. As early as 450 BC, the Romans determined that it was 8.33 percent, and it remained at that level for almost 800 years. In the Middle Ages, the Church publicly did not tolerate interest but recognized privately that a rate of 4 percent or under would not harm a borrower. Lenders to Edward III of England were not as generous, however, and the king paid rates of around 50 percent for loans when he could find someone to lend him money. In 1571, the English parliament established 10 percent as the legal rate after equivocating for a number of years. The dispute was not about the actual rate but whether interest should be tolerated publicly at all. Anyone charging more than the maximum rate was liable for triple damages.

remote because, like consumer credit, it is created by nonbanks as well as by banks. Without a blanket mandate, any policy implemented among the banks can be circumvented by the nonbanks to their advantage. For the last thirty years, the question has been whether it is preferable to have a partial policy or none at all.

The recent ruling by the Fed concerning rates of interest charged on credit cards follows this tradition. It also implicitly acknowledges the Fed's allegiance to its bank constituents. In December 2008, the Fed ruled that credit card companies could not take advantage of consumers by raising rates arbitrarily without a clear explanation and advanced notice. Many lenders were raising interest rates on business loans or cutting back credit lines to customers, making an economic rebound more difficult, and the measures were ostensibly aimed at protecting consumers. They were described by Ben Bernanke as "the most comprehensive and sweeping reforms ever adopted by the Board for credit card accounts." On the surface, this appeared to be a move in the right direction, although the Fed said that the new regulation would not take effect until July 2010, more than enough time for the lenders to raise their rates without fear of reprisal.

During the credit crisis, this question has become largely irrelevant as a bailout has taken preference over policymaking. Both mortgage and consumer credit need regulation to foster economic recovery. Economic growth again will be the primary focus of the Fed although this goal needs to be mixed with the new order of the day—stability. A combined effort by the Fed and the Treasury, acting together as they have in the financial crisis to ensure that monetary and fiscal policy are both set on a similar course, should replace growth as the goal of the central bank. If stability can be achieved, future growth is not a problem. If it is not achieved, any future growth will be prone to evaporate in another future crisis. At the time of writing, the jury is still out.

The American tradition is not to implement heavy-handed centralized regulation but to devise regulation that sets a clear path under a set of defined rules. The recent trend toward principles-based regulation, as seen in the Basel II bank regulations of the Bank for International Settlements (BIS) and in the voluntary capitulation of the SEC to the investment bank capital requirements, must be swept aside in favor of a strengthened set of rules and proper policing procedures. Banks have proven they are incapable of policing themselves in the name of unrestricted markets. The crisis of 2008 and the 1929 Crash and Depression both have that same common trait, and it should not be ignored in the future.

The best way to implement this policy change is from the top. The Fed and the Treasury will need to coordinate monetary and fiscal policy, especially when it involves consumer credit and mortgage credit. If the Treasury recognizes that Fannie Mae and Freddie Mac are indeed instrumentalities of the government, then their activities should not run counter to Fed monetary policy. If the Fed decides to tighten monetary policy in the face of an inflationary threat, then Fannie and Freddie's activities should be adjusted by the Treasury accordingly. There is little point in the right hand not knowing what the left hand is doing until it opens a newspaper.

Fannie and Freddie need to be controlled by the Treasury and treated like public utilities. Their shareholders (if they remain publicly owned institutions) will need to expect decent dividends and bond yields but not large capital gains generated by participation in another mortgage boom. The Tennessee Valley Authority, the most demure of the federal agencies, could serve as their model in this respect, and some of the changes and regulatory apparatus could be paid for by not allowing them to lobby anymore.

Before the credit market crisis, this argument would have required a significant change in the prevailing ideology about free markets and small government. But the crisis has shown that free markets bear the seeds of their own destruction and that government is not small and never has been. In the months before the bailout of Fannie and Freddie, an argument could have been made for a part-time nanny state where government serves as a supervisor of financial markets. In short fashion, the tenor of the debate has changed substantially.

Originally, Fannie Mae and Ginnie Mae were thought of as instruments of fiscal policy. Recently, they have been seen mainly as facilitators for the residential housing market without the policy implications. By the time they were joined by Freddie Mac in the 1970s, securitization was becoming embedded in their activities and so-called intermediation alchemy became dominant. Off-balance-sheet financing won the day, and the agencies began to develop distinct personalities of their own. Another forgotten characteristic of the government-sponsored enterprises (GSEs) is that Congress did not build in a sunset clause to them when they were created.[1] As a result, they are not subject to renewal as other federal agencies are and were, including the Federal Reserve. They have been permanent since their inception and have often behaved as if they were accountable to no one.

Ideally, if government decided to tighten the housing market, it could instruct the agencies to tighten their own lending requirements. Requiring a larger down payment or requiring stronger borrower coverage ratios usually would be sufficient to slow the agencies' intermediation because new borrowers would be discouraged unless they could meet the tougher requirements. But doing so might have a dampening effect on a mortgage boom, and few politicians have been content to be the party crasher during good times created by real estate. Usually the opposite has been true.

Being instrumentalities of the federal government means that the agencies, especially Freddie and Fannie, still are subject to this sort of control from the top, but control has rarely been exercised. As both agencies have gradually been freed from their original models, politicians of both stripes have been happy to criticize them without admitting that they can be constrained or encouraged to create mortgage credit, instead leaving them to swim the political waters on their own. What is more difficult to admit is that the water level can be controlled.

The more complicated the agency intermediation process becomes, the more difficult it is to see the forest for the trees. Both agencies have spent considerable sums recently lobbying Congress, usually to keep a distance from their activities. By analogy, a mortgage-assistance agency lobbying Congress is similar to a chief financial officer of a company taking his board of directors out for dinner and charging it to his expense account. It might have been a good dinner, but any member of the board would have to ask what the purpose was. Kent Cooper, the founder of CQMoneyLine, told *The Washington Post*, "You've got a public trust-type function going on, and yet they're spending money for lobbying the legislature that, in essence, created them. You would think organizations created by Congress wouldn't need to lobby Congress."[2]

Fannie and Freddie were two of the top ten spenders among American corporations after 2001 in fees paid to lobbyists. Their motives were fairly transparent. Congress was considering creating a new regulator for them, and both resisted strenuously. The money spent, approaching $10 million each in some years, was almost the largest sum spent by any company and clearly was a deliberate strategy. Speaking at a Congressional hearing, Representative Christopher Shays (Republican from Connecticut) remarked, "I am tempted to ask how many people in this room are on the payroll of Fannie Mae, because what they do is they basically hire every lobbyist they can possibly hire—they hire some people to lobby and they hire some people not to lobby so that the opposition can't hire them."

Ralph Nader noted that the two mortgage agencies spent too much on frivolities, based on their protected status as private corporations under the government umbrella:

> With these valuable ties to the government, the GSEs in effect enjoy a government subsidy, which the Congressional Budget Office estimates at about $20 billion annually. Only part of the subsidy goes to lower costs for homebuyers. The remainder—$6.3 billion—is pocketed by Fannie and Freddie. It helps finance their political operations, lobbying, and public relations as well as the grandiose compensation of their executives.[3]

Fannie's CEO Franklin Raines received compensation worth $90 million between 1998 and 2003. But critics realized it was not compensation of that sort that was the problem; the organization needed to be redesigned. Nader's intent was to return them to their original status as government corporations and end their behavior as powerful political forces in their own right. Others wanted to end the government link entirely.

The subsidy mentioned by most commentators was not a direct cash payment to the agencies but their low cost of borrowing. Because most in the bond market assumed that they would never default because of their GSE status, the agencies were able to borrow at very low rates of interest, historically below even that paid by AAA corporate borrowers. The amount they saved is considered the subsidy. Although the subsidy obviously is beneficial for the homeowners, it was also particularly useful for the lobbyists they hired and for the executives who received huge compensation packages while employed by them.

Overcomplexity

The American debt model has been broken and is in need of serious repair. It has become clear that as a nation of spenders rather than savers, many American families now are at the brink of economic ruin because of the profligate spending habits aided and abetted by the consumer credit companies and mortgage lenders. The problem is so large that it requires a targeted response aimed at lenders and borrowers.

IN THE ISLAMIC WORLD, practicing usury still is forbidden, although recent developments in finance have made debt financing possible. Traditionally, banks did not make mortgages because receiving interest was proscribed by the Koran. Recently, however, mortgages are being offered using a different process from the one familiar in the West. A buyer finds a home he would like to purchase, contacts a bank, and arranges a mortgage. The bank buys the home from the seller and then sells it at a higher price to the buyer, who then will be compensating the bank as profit rather than paying interest. No interest is shown on the statements, only the profit the bank made by buying and then reselling. Profit is not contrary to Islamic law, only interest. A large bond market for Islamic borrowers is also growing, using the same principle.

The first obvious response is to change the tax law regarding capital gains on housing. The exempt amount homeowners gain on the sale of a primary residence should be limited to perhaps a few occurrences within a fixed time period. This restriction would discourage home speculation and reduce the demand for mortgages. Subprime lending and similar activities appear during the white-hot phase of a property boom, and if that stage is never reached, then what lending remains should be kept within reasonable bounds.

Second, the same credit card company computers that have been programmed with neural networks should be put to a more positive use. Such networks should be able to access an individual consumer's total credit card and other revolving debt, and then the amount of credit offered to the consumer should be limited, perhaps to 10–15 percent of gross income. Minimum credit scores also need to be raised, especially by mortgage lenders. The current average eligibility credit score of 693 (Experian) should be raised by at least 10 points or more for a mortgage loan.[4] To shut the back door, home equity loans should also be limited to no more than 20 percent of the equity in a home, based on a third-party evaluation, not one provided by a bank lender. This is the same sort of simple coordination that the Fed and Treasury should engage in, to ensure that one gap closed does not leave another open.

An antipredatory law has been proposed in the House in response to the mortgage crisis in fall 2007. The bill is known as H.R. 3915, the Mortgage Reform and Anti-Predatory Lending Act, which passed the House by 291 votes to 127 in November of that year. The bill proposed minimum regulatory standards for lenders to follow, similar to those required of real estate agents. Antipredatory lending laws have met with limited success to date, however. Some states have passed laws banning credit card companies from soliciting students but only on the campuses of state-funded universities. These sorts of laws need to be passed generally under the let-the-seller-beware banner. As with banking and securities violations, lenders who prey on the poor or lower middle class with promises of easy money should be required to pay the price through criminal prosecution if the loans go bad because of difficult or misleading terms.

American politicians have been famous for declaring war on socially undesirable practices as a method of highlighting their intentions. The War on Poverty of the 1960s and the War on Drugs of the 1980s are two

ALTHOUGH IT IS CUSTOMARY to think of mortgages as a means of financing real estate, the term "mortgage" has been used with other sorts of property as well. Most notable is the chattel mortgage, a mortgage on property not tied to real estate. The term once was more popular than it is today, although it is still in use. Currently, the term "collateral" or "security" is used instead of chattel, in part because chattel slavery was a widely used term before the Civil War. Today, it is the sort of mortgage associated with property not related to land. The financing provided on mobile homes is a good example: a home not valued with the land underneath it.

examples. It would not be inappropriate to declare a new War on Predatory Lending as a means of highlighting the current problem and the intent to deal with predators harshly. But as former wars have shown, it is not possible to declare war on human nature and hope to succeed. Wagers of the War on Predatory Lending must realize that financial literacy has not been achieved in the population ranks, although some progress has been made. Potential homeowners will continue to borrow amounts they cannot afford, and that kind of borrowing may lead them into financial difficulties. But the easy money era must not return, and it must not be left to an assumption that it cannot because of the crisis. Banks that securitize shoddy mortgages and ratings agencies that give them a clean bill of health must bear the financial responsibility for putting them right. If that were the case, lending could resume on a healthier path than in the immediate past.

Fixing Finance

Many of the proposed solutions to the lending crisis will be industry-based, affecting both the credit card and mortgage lending industries. But policy should also be aimed at Wall Street and at the finance industry that created the many products responsible for the chaotic economic conditions that followed. In addition to securitization, the whole issue of complexity in financial design needs to be addressed because that sort of complexity has produced much confusion among legislators and laymen seeking a remedy to the problem.

Most importantly, the securitization process is in need of immediate repair. It has been shown that it allows lenders to create questionable loans and then proceed to offload them to investors via bonds. The best way to prevent this is to require all securitized bonds to be covered; that is, to allow the investors to have recourse to the bond issuer if interest or principal repayments from the collateral pool fail. Fannie Mae and Freddie Mac successfully employed the concept for decades before being caught in inappropriate lending activities, but that part of their model remains viable for the future. European securitization also employs the coverage concept with much more success than the American uncovered, private-label type. Being responsible for the underlying pool of assets on a bond would immediately make lenders more prudent in their original lending activities because they will not be free of liability if the pool fails. If American securitizers had employed this method, it is doubtful whether the financial crisis would have been as wide or would have spread internationally.

Much of the financial crisis can be laid at the doorstep of a finance specialty known as *structured finance*. This esoteric area of the discipline allows financial engineers to design instruments specifically for clients' needs. In many cases, they are one-off designs, not replicated anywhere else. In other cases, structured finance has taken securitization to new heights, most notably in the creation of collateralized debt obligations (CDOs) based on other bonds or risky loans. The techniques used are ingenious but the confusion caused by their failure is monumental. Banks will continue to apply stress tests to their models, but this current crisis must be part of the test. Any future what-if scenario must include a breakdown of the financial system in all its possibilities and assign it a larger probability than in the past.

The confusion caused by the complexity of many synthetic securities and complicated derivatives products requires that they be simplified. Unfortunately, there is no practical way of doing so without impeding progress in finance. The only practical method is to regulate the amount of synthetics or derivatives a company can create based on its balance sheet strength. Swaps in particular can be created by banks ad infinitum, a process that must be stopped. The amount of contingent liabilities an institution can incur must be subject to limits. It is estimated that the amount of credit default swaps (CDSs) in existence presently totals around $50 trillion. That represents the GDP of the Group of Seven. What exactly is being hedged in such large numbers? Or is most of that volume attributable to speculation?

The credit default swap is a case in point. An institutional investor wants protection against a portfolio holding of bonds and enters into a CDS with a financial institution. Its $10 million holding can be guaranteed by the financial institution, which will receive payments from the investor at the appropriate swap rate for the time period involved. If the bonds default or suffer serious price erosion for credit reasons, the financial institution will pay the investor the original swap price for the bonds and receive them in return. The investor gets the protection originally needed, and the swapper incurs the risk of the bonds. Most financial institution swappers claim that the risk of default is so small that it is worth their risk in return for the payments paid by the investor. In most cases, those payments were the reason the financial institutions entered into swaps in the first place.

What the investor did in this example was swap one counterparty risk for another. As the financial crisis continued, many of the swappers—banks, investment banks, and insurance companies—proved to be less creditworthy than the companies they insured. "Insurance" became the operable term. The swappers were helping clients guarantee against financial liability the same way that property, casualty, and life insurers were. The major difference was that they did not need an insurance license to do so. When insurers got into the act of creating CDSs with investors, they only compounded their own problems because they were doubling their insurance exposures without having to identify the risk as insurance risks. This was a classic case of an unregulated part of finance attracting many participants precisely because the field was unregulated.

All forms of derivatives need limits applied to their creation.[5] Otherwise, they create an endless bog of financial obligations that are difficult to sort out when a crisis occurs. The newest wrinkle in swaps, the longevity swap, is one example. Designed for life insurance companies and pension funds, these swaps allow an institution exposed to longevity to hedge its risks associated with the products it offers the public. But the risk that more swap products raise is also obvious. The U.S. pension system overall is strained because of the baby-boomer generation.

Allowing a fiduciary to speculate against those risks will not help the situation. For every hedger there is a speculator willing to assume large risks for potentially large rewards. If that market proceeds without intervention by regulators, the problems will become clear within a short time.

If derivatives of this nature can be defined and regulated effectively, their use might revert to being of sound economic use rather than a simple means of generating fee income without regard for the consequences. The regulation must have some teeth; in this case, the teeth must be the ability and willingness of the regulator to use criminal prosecution if necessary for any institution found violating its limits or causing financial hardship. That includes closing institutions that repeatedly violate regulations.[6] The history of Wall Street and banking is full of instances where institutions violated the law and received only civil penalties or slaps on the wrist in the form of insignificant amounts of money. Regulators long ago subscribed to the notion that risk takers require kid-glove treatment, except in very high-profile cases when the public becomes aware of the violations.

The focus of regulation has been badly skewed in the deregulatory era. Prevailing wisdom has held that the presence of a regulator is all that is necessary to prevent fraud or bad behavior on the part of a financial institution. Therefore, many institutions have fled to the secrecy afforded by opacity rather than embrace the transparency that the official party line of the markets has subscribed to over the last 15 years. After several years of heated discussion, the New York Stock Exchange and the Nasdaq (National Association of Securities Dealers Automated Quotations) both moved to stock price quotes in decimals in the earlier part of this decade. That was accompanied by more demands from investors for immediate execution for stock market trades with instant reporting. It would have appeared that transparency finally had created an efficient, clean marketplace for equities.

At the same time, many securities houses have invested in creating platforms for so-called dark pools of investment money for investors who do not want to be seen trading in public. Trades may be crossed between buyers and sellers without reporting a price so that the transactions occur parallel to trading on the stock markets. This was done clearly to accommodate hedge funds, which value the privacy involved at the expense of transparency. The dark pools emerged at the same time that other financial "reforms" were being introduced. The same was true of naked short selling and the abolition of the uptick rule. These developments could not have occurred without the implicit sanction of the SEC, which flew in the face of its own policing the markets over its seventy-year history. The regulator was in place but was content to watch rather than to regulate.

The Safety Net

Discussions swirling around the financial crisis partially obscure the fact that the legacy of the Reagan era helped remove the safety net constructed since the New Deal. But calling the problem a lack of regulatory control is too general when discussing the policy problem that Gramm-Leach-Bliley has created. This dismantling has come to be accepted and needs to be reassessed to prevent future problems.

Traditionally, the safety net included the Social Security system plus banking and securities laws designed to protect society from predatory behavior that could destroy wealth. As Social Security has come under attack for being incapable of meeting future annuity payments, supplementary legislation was passed creating individual retirement accounts and tax-deferred savings plans. Although not providing sufficient income for most to retire, the additions did provide additional layers of income that would provide supplementary income in retirement.

The banking laws since Glass-Steagall provided complementary coverage. Deposit insurance, decried as socialist in the 1930s by conservatives, was designed both to protect savers' funds and keep banks from becoming illiquid at the same time. Without it, the United States and most other developed countries engulfed by the financial crisis would have been swept up in chaos. This protection has become so ingrained as a basic financial right that to violate it would be political suicide, not to mention the social disorder it would create. But that has not stopped some conservatives from arguing for its repeal over the years.

Most of these objections were based on the premium the banks had to pay to the Federal Deposit Insurance Corporation (FDIC) as part of the insurance. Almost as soon as the deposit fund began, the major New York banks threatened to withdraw from the plan in a dispute over the premiums, a move that would have threatened the Fed's control over the banking system because all federally chartered banks were required to participate in the fund. Battles of that nature should never have occurred because the Fed and FDIC were being blackmailed by the banks they were designed to regulate. The battle has been fought many times since then.

More recently, the issue of increasing deposit insurance again has become topical, with many bankers actually supporting an increase in the insured amounts. Before the financial crisis, the limits were last increased from $40,000 to $100,000 per account by the Depository Institutions Deregulation and Monetary Control Act (DIDMCA) in 1980. Opposing any deposit insurance increase in 2002 were Republican Texas Senator Phil Gramm, Federal Reserve Chairman Alan Greenspan, and Treasury Secretary Paul O'Neill. Gramm repeatedly told Texas bankers that he would roll back coverage to $40,000 or even to zero. His argument invoked moral hazard. Depositors are not interested in evaluating the condition of their banks because deposit insurance protects them from the bank risk and shifts the risk to the FDIC.

Even a banking publication from Gramm's home state took exception to that logic. It commented:

> Frankly speaking, these arguments have the integrity of Swiss cheese. Small savers are not in a good position to critique banks. If the world's most sophisticated analysts couldn't spot Enron's chicanery, how can we expect Grandma, Uncle Buddy and 22-year-old, tragically widowed Cousin Suzy with a $150,000 insurance check to decipher a call report?[7]

Even common sense criticism could not stem the tide of free market thinking, regardless of the level of sophistication.

Gramm's influence was even more directly felt when the Commodity Futures Trading Commission (CFTC) had to be renewed in 2000. The result was the Commodity Futures Modernization Act, given a name similar to the Financial Services Modernization Act. During the 1990s, most sitting on the commission militated for stronger regulation of the swaps market but to no avail. Gramm and Greenspan were in favor of as little regulation as possible. When the act was renewed, there literally was no provision made for oversight of the swaps market, and it escaped unregulated. When the credit market crisis began and many CDSs, including those of Lehman Brothers, had to be unwound, the lack of oversight became obvious. Later, he commented on the financial crisis caused by the lack of oversight: "There is this idea afloat that if you had more regulation you would have fewer mistakes," Gramm said. "I don't see any evidence in our history or anybody else's to substantiate it." He added, "The markets have worked better than you might have thought."[8]

Alan Greenspan made similar comments about deposit insurance. Absent from the remarks are any indication that ordinary bank depositors care or understand how to check their bank's credit rating or risk category. The fact that that sort of credit check is routinely done by large, institutional investors who clearly have more than $100,000 on deposit at a bank is not reason to assume that small investors do the same. If a moral hazard exists at all at the retail level, the blame is not on the depositors but on those who lend their funds, knowing that the small customer is not well versed in banking practices. As Greenspan stated, "If a bank's loan portfolio or its employees are suspect, depositors disappear, often very quickly. But when deposits are insured in some way, a run is less likely."[9] Not a run by small customers, however.

The dismantling of the banking safety net was accompanied by a similar one in securities, although the task was more difficult. In the public view, banks were supposed to provide safe havens for their money as well as a source of loans. But Wall Street was always viewed with some suspicion. Trading practices and finance terms were difficult to decipher and left most casual observers glassy-eyed. While it was not difficult to imagine the reaction if securities laws were rolled back wholesale, the same approach could be taken with them as was taken with the banking laws: Roll them back gradually. The free market would take care of the rest.

The liberalization of the securities markets came after 2001. In the 1990s, a law had been passed making it difficult for shareholders to sue publicly traded companies because of poor financial results, in part a reaction of Republican lawmakers to tort lawyers, many of whom they claimed were Democrats. On a daily basis, however, the task would be easier and more market friendly if existing rules simply were allowed to lapse. The public probably never heard of naked short selling in any event.

That assessment proved only partially correct. In the summer of 2008, many financial stocks came under intense selling pressure, and the SEC halted naked shorting more than once to reinstate some stability to that sector. By the late summer, the shares of Fannie and Freddie, along with those of Wachovia and some smaller banks, had been forced down to historically low levels. Market participants argued that short selling was not primarily to blame, although the slide in prices was reminiscent of the bear raid in 1932 that forced many companies into bankruptcy at the start of the Great Depression. The short selling debate had been engaged many times since the early 1930s, and the rules put in place by the SEC years before should have put an end to the debate. Yet it reappeared in full force in 2008.

In the primary market, the path to the new issues market for securitized bonds became too congested during the mortgage boom to allow regulators and the ratings agencies a good look at the securities in the pipeline. The only viable way to keep an eye on the process is to hire more staff for the SEC. The ratings agencies need to do the same. But that alternative may prove impractical financially. An older form of market regulation may prove a viable solution.

Until the 1980s, when the U.S. securities regulation process was streamlined, many European regulators used what was known as a "queuing system" to direct traffic on the way to the new issues market.[10] New bond issues would be given a place in the queue to market, and investors knew when the issue would be launched. If market conditions turned negative, the issue could be postponed or cancelled without having to be launched quickly, as it is today. Although the system certainly had its drawbacks, making the entry to the primary market very mechanical, it also had its benefits because it was very predictable and stable.

If controlling the securitization process does not slow the path to market for new issues in the future, a queuing system could be used to prevent congestion and the slipshod oversight that accompanies it. The rapid process by which new securitized issues came to market during the mortgage boom needs to be slowed down in the future so that a sensible alternative can be found. Due diligence of new issues has become obsolete in the quest to bring more and more product to investors. Slowing down will also give the ratings agencies more room to breathe because they equally are culpable in this rush to the market.

Contracting Quality

The reliance on credit-rating agencies in the investment community is much deeper than any one sector of the market may suggest. Prudent investor behavior is based on the agencies' ratings of bonds and equities; the term "investment grade" is their invention. The types of money market paper that can be purchased by money market mutual funds depends on those ratings, as does the traditional definition of a junk bond. The entire notion of the sorts of investments that fiduciaries may invest in and the foundations of the ERISA are also directly tied to the agencies. These are just a few examples of their influence in the markets. It has been difficult to live without them since the 1950s.

The assembly line process used for manufacturing securitized bonds was aided and abetted by the ratings agencies. Investors relied on these supposedly impartial ratings to determine the investment quality of securitized bonds backed by mortgages, credit cards, and other receivables. In the case of mortgages, their decision was relatively easy. Most of the bonds were rated AAA. Similar to equity analysts' ratings in the 1990s' bull market, few criticisms were heard of asset-backed security (ABS) or collateralized mortgage obligation (CMO) issuers.

The ratings agencies are not part of the safety net but always have been considered one of its closely associated links. Ever since Lewis Tappan founded the Mercantile Agency in New York in 1841, the ratings agencies gradually evolved into what became the credit ratings process. John Moody established his manual of industrial companies in 1900, and the Poor's Publishing Company began rating companies in 1916. Fitch's was founded in 1913. They all evolved into credit-rating agencies rather than credit reporting agencies and began to compete with each other. But it was never assumed that their ratings necessarily would be identical. Neither was it assumed that they might simply copy one another to save time and effort.

It is easy to see how the ratings agencies, as the SEC, were overwhelmed with a steady stream of new issues coming to market. Originally, the oversight was thought to have been created by a heavy workload. But it soon came to light that the agencies did realize that the process they used in the ratings was flawed. They often piggybacked each other's ratings rather than produce their own. Once the credit market crisis began and many of the bonds began defaulting, the process grew and questions began to be asked about how the bonds, some issued only months before the crisis, could default so quickly. The responsibility of the ratings services to investors had been breached.

Once the defaults began and the problem came to light, criticism was not far behind. "I view the ratings agencies as one of the key culprits," said Joseph Stiglitz, the Nobel Prize–winning economist. "They were the party that performed that alchemy that converted the securities from F-rated to A-rated. The banks could not have done what they did without the complicity of the ratings agencies." And the problem was not one of modest proportion. Driven by the desire for fees, between 2002 and 2007 the New York–based companies cranked out top ratings for debt pools that included $3.2 trillion of loans to homebuyers with bad credit and undocumented incomes.[11] Poor oversight and venality had combined with a loose regulatory environment and a political desire for widespread home ownership to create the worst debt default crisis in U.S. history.

While it is easy to accuse the agencies of derogation of duty in the quest for ratings fees, evidence suggests that their oversight may have been more deliberate than previously thought. According to the new capital requirements for banks set out in the Basel II accords by the Bank for International Settlements, the amount of capital required of a bank is determined by a value-at-risk approach (VaR). Basically, the amount is determined by the amount of risk a bank incurs daily as it trades in the market. It also depends on the quality of the assets at risk. When determining the riskiness of a particular asset, the BIS accord gave the banks considerable leeway in determining it for themselves. In a transaction society, that may be a reasonable assumption theoretically but bad judgment practically. Banks will always tend to minimize their exposure in the market in order to use as little capital as possible.

This is another case of using a principles-based system of regulation rather than one based on rules. It has led to considerable confusion during the credit market crisis because many of the securities that banks traded in the market or held on their books seriously eroded in value to the point where the banks required capital infusions by their governments or outside investors. Little of this was mentioned in the reporting surrounding the crisis even though it was a substantial factor. And in the quest for flexibility in determining capital, the Basel II accords may have been slightly naïve.

For instance, if bonds trading in the market have been rated differently by two of the ratings agencies, the capital risk standard is lowered if a third ratings agency gives it a higher rating.[12] Two out of three does not seem to form the majority in this case. What this means is that if two agencies rated a CMO or a CDO traded by a bank as A and AA respectively, a third agency rating it AAA would dictate a lower capital requirement in that instance. The majority view for a higher standard would not apply. Similarly, if two of the agencies realized that the third would possibly give an issue a lower rating as it may have in the past, they might set similar ratings to offset it. The Basel II standard relied on outsourcing for setting capital standards, not necessarily a foolproof method of determining bank capital.

The poor performance of the ratings agencies raises additional policy questions that investors need answered. Their reputations are vital to their continued presence in the marketplace; without a blemish-free past, their role in the investment process is questionable. Considering that their function is a fiduciary one, the ratings agencies are completely without public accountability for their actions. If not regulated or held accountable for their actions, their future functions will be rendered useless.

Privatizing the Payments System

The current crisis has demonstrated structural and functional weakness in many parts of the financial system. One of the least visible parts is the payments system, where purchases of goods and services are settled between financial institutions. But ideology has crept into the vast system where several trillion dollars of transactions are settled per day. That same ideology has helped credit card companies immeasurably.

Because credit cards have become a vital part of consumers' finances, the card companies have been in fierce competition with one another. Of the four major card brands—Visa, MasterCard, American Express, and Discover—Visa and MasterCard typically controlled 75 percent of the market. When they began offering debit cards, the competition became even more fierce, and violations of antitrust law were alleged for both companies. Merchants filed suit against the two in 1996 over their honor-all-cards policy, meaning that accepting a credit card meant accepting a debit card as well. In 1998, the charges were expanded and formalized when the Justice Department charged them both with violations of the antitrust laws, alleging that the associations required banks to offer a particular card to the exclusion of others. Two years later, the presiding judge certified the case as a class action case, allowing many millions of merchants to join the suit.

According to the suit, the banks required merchants to accept their "branded" debit cards at the same time, and this was the source of disagreement. Credit cards and debit cards had different sorts of fees attached to them, and retailers felt they should be able to refuse the branded debit cards bearing higher fees than regular debit cards. But the banks that ran both associations disagreed. At the time, neither Visa nor MasterCard was a public company but rather associations run by the banks offering their cards.[13] The directors at both boards of directors were the same interlocking group. The requirement to accept the debit cards was considered "tying-in," a violation of antitrust law.

The problem was complicated by the types of credit and debit cards on offer. American credit cards used a signature-based system in which the cardholder's name was signed on the reverse side of the card. Ordinary debit cards used the same technology, and any charges were deducted from the cardholder's checking account when the card was used. Signature-based cards require a signature and are processed offline after the transaction is complete. Pin-based debit cards, on the other hand, require the user to enter a personal identification number at the time of purchase and are processed online. As a result, they are cheaper to process and carry lower transaction fees than the signature-based types.[14]

The differing transaction fees angered merchants. During the antitrust proceedings against the payments companies, it was alleged that Wal-Mart Stores, used a training video instructing cashiers on how to identify and process different types of cards, and to distinguish the ordinary pin-based cards from the branded signature cards. The ordinary debit cards were preferred because each transaction cost the company 10 to 15 cents to process versus 75 cents for a credit card; the video did not specify this but claimed that pin-based cards represented a significant cost savings for the company. MasterCard alleged that Wal-Mart instructed cashiers to suggest that customers pay with a pin-based card. For its part, Wal-Mart did not deny the accusation and saw little wrong with the practice.

The potential stakes were enormous. The retailers, led by Wal-Mart, Sears, Roebuck, and Safeway, claimed $13 billion in damages, an amount they reckoned to have lost by being forced into accepting all cards. If the case had been successful, the total bill for the card companies would have been $39 billion because antitrust cases typically involve triple damages. Both card issuers fought fiercely to protect their positions, often accusing American Express of being the instigator of their troubles. Lost in the long legal wrangling was the nature of the debit card part of the industry and the effect it was having on the American payments system.

By the early 2000s, debit card use had overtaken credit card use slightly, so the battle was a real one in every sense of the word. In 2002, 6 billion card transactions took place in the United States, and 3.04 billion involved debit cards. From a credit point of view, this was a positive trend because it did not involve consumer indebtedness, but it foreshadowed an even larger looming problem with potential ramifications far beyond the credit card industry. If debit cards were cheaper to process than credit cards, what was so appealing about the card companies' offering them in the first place?

Payments industry projections for future debit card use are very high, demonstrating that they are considered the future of the industry. That projection comes with implications for the payments system provided traditionally by the Federal Reserve, the ultimate clearer of checks. As more and more consumer credit transactions take place by card, the role of the Federal Reserve is diminished in this respect. The ultimate question becomes whether the payments system should be in the hands of the major credit/debit card companies. Or is it there already?

The answer is a bit of both. Payments system transactions are cleared by the Fed currently through the Fedwire, a system designed to settle claims between financial institutions. The system has been in use since 1918 when a wire transfer system based on Morse code was introduced so that financial institutions would not have to settle claims on each other in gold or cash. The growing number of transactions during World War I made that old system obsolete. In addition to the Fedwire, the Fed operates the National Settlement Service, with over 70 participants, including credit card processors, allowing "participants in private-sector clearing arrangements to exchange and settle transactions on a net basis through reserve or clearing account balances," according to the Fed.[15] Started in 1999, the system is open to depository institutions that have an account with the Fed.

The increasing number of debit card transactions, the ability of customers to pay directly from their checking accounts, and the ability of consumers to pay credit card bills through direct online banking all have reduced the number of checks written. Check clearing is a Fed function, although, because of these other arrangements, that function is declining in volume. The number of checks paid in the United States has fallen from 42 billion in 2001, to 37 billion in 2003, and to 30 billion in 2006.[16]

This reduction in transactions is a natural result of the payments industry but also signals a partial privatization at the same time. Those in favor of the settlements system being in private hands also pointed to the success of the Clearing House Interbank Payments System (CHIPS). Founded in 1970, the system originally processed $540 million worth of transactions. By 2007, it cleared $485 billion, and the number of institutions participating had increased from an original 9 to 45. The more transactions that take place, the more natural it is for regulators to rely on outsourcing of some functions in the clearing process that otherwise would overwhelm the Fed or any other regulator. But once the contracting firms recognize this and their vital role, there is more room for abuse. The more debit cards that are used in the future, the more the function will shift to the private sector. As the number of transactions increases in the transaction society, some of this is to be expected, but it signals a shift that is being made bureaucratically. Has this been a natural shift or another subtle shift designed to get the government out of the clearing business for securities, checks, and other sorts of financial transactions?

Alan Greenspan wrote that "I had always thought the payment system should be wholly private but I found that Fedwire, the electronic funds-transfer system operated by the Federal Reserve, does offer something no private bank can: riskless fund settlements."[17] That remark sheds considerable light on the extent to which the entire regulatory and settlements apparatus was thought to require less attention than in the past. The entire banking system suffered serious shocks in the financial crisis, but the idea of the actual payments system being in partially private hands was never publicly discussed. Creeping privatization was reaching the payments system, as it had the securities regulations and banking sectors. The matter of control over the money supply basically was, and is, at stake. The credit card companies demonstrated that they were interested in filling that void, and the Fed seemed willing to concede. To contradict the basic Reagan premise, there are some areas the state cannot concede to the private sector in the name of ideology. The control of the money supply is perhaps the most important.

These policy matters have been caused by growing market volume and increasingly heavy demand for financial transactions of all sorts. As a result, the patchwork American regulatory framework has fallen into the hands of the private sector, which it was originally intended to regulate in the first place. The financial crisis is a direct result of this broad neglect and is sufficient proof that the regulatory system needs serious overhaul. Consumer credit needs to be included in this overhaul. If it is not, the old saying about those ignorant of their own history will become true again in the future.

Mortgage credit should be included in the category of consumer credit because the links between them are too interconnected to ignore. Traditionally, they have been considered separate topics, but that no longer is the case. Cannibal consumption has proved that consumers were willing to sacrifice their homes to consume in the fashion to which they thought they had become accustomed. That alone requires the two types of credit to be considered one and the same. When these types of collateral damaged the entire financial system, the distinctions became much less important.

Chapter Notes

1. See Thomas H. Stanton, "The Life Cycle of the Government-Sponsored Enterprise: Lessons for Design and Accountability," *Public Administration Review*, Vol. 67, No. 5 (September–October 2007): 837–845.

2. Lobbying by companies is tracked and statistics are compiled by CQ MoneyLine, a publication of *Congressional Quarterly*.

3. Ralph Nader, "Don't Privatize the GSEs—Federalize," *American Banker*, Vol. 170, No. 48 (March 11, 2005): 10.

4. The average credit score is reported by MortgageDaily.com. The range for Experian scores is A: 901–990 (Super Prime), B: 801–900 (Prime Plus), C: 701–800 (Prime), D: 601–700 (Non-Prime), F: 501–600 (High Risk). This puts the average score for mortgage holders in the subprime category.

5. When call and put options were first introduced on the Chicago Board Options Exchange in the early 1970s, one of the main problems they presented was the quantity that could potentially be created. If traded in large enough quantities, they could actually exceed the number of stocks outstanding for a particular company. While remotely possible, the problem did surface before being remedied. The old financial problem of how many derivatives can fit on the head of a pin clearly resurfaces when discussing swaps in particular because no one is quite sure of the amount of any particular swap outstanding at a point in time or who the major traders of it are.

6. The case of Salomon Brothers in 1990 is an example. Despite violating the limits of a Fed auction of new notes for the Treasury, the firm was given a slap on the wrist rather than being expelled from the ranks of primary dealers, the select group of money market dealers through which the Fed conducts monetary policy. The SEC was more harsh with Drexel Burnham Lambert, however, closing the firm after violations in the junk bond market.

7. Ann Graham, "Deposit Insurance Reform: What's on the Table and What Will It Cost?" *Texas Banking*, Vol. 91, No. 5 (May 2002): 48–49.

8. *New York Times*, November 16, 2008.

9. Alan Greenspan, *The Age of Turbulence: Adventures in a New World* (New York: Penguin Books, 2008), p. 374.

10. The primary market was streamlined by the SEC in 1982, when it introduced Rule 415, the shelf registration rule. Companies were allowed to preregister their securities and then bring them to market quickly, when conditions were favorable. The rule replaced the old 21-day cooling-off period for new securities.

11. Eliot Blair Smith, "Bringing Down Wall Street as Ratings Let Loose Subprime Scourge," *Bloomberg* (www.Bloomberg.com), September 24, 2008.

12. Mark J. Flannery, "Supervising Bank Safety and Soundness: Some Open Issues," *Economic Review* (Federal Reserve Bank of Atlanta), Vol. 92, No. 1/2 (First quarter 2007): 83–101.

13. MasterCard went public in 2007 with an initial public offering, and Visa followed in 2008.

14. Smart cards are a combination of debit and credit technologies that contain security information about the cardholder embedded in a chip on the card, and they use a hologram etched on the front to prevent fraud. Smart cards are more popular outside the United States than they are within.

15. Board of Governors of the Federal Reserve System, www.federalreserve.gov/paymentsystems.

16. Federal Reserve, *Press Release*, by Financial Services Policy Committee, November 6, 2008.

17. Greenspan, *Age of Turbulence*, p. 374 fn.

CHAPTER

8

Prescription and Outlook

Complexity is the mother of confusion. —Anonymous

One of the major myths about American society is that it is a nation of savers who only recently went astray during the mortgage boom of the 2000s. In reality, Americans have always been accustomed to heavy levels of personal indebtedness, especially since banks and finance companies developed to provide the credit necessary to attain the American Dream.

This is not to say that savings and prudent banking have not played a vast role in the development of the United States over the last one hundred years. Without them, the American high standard of living could not have been attained. But the high standard also produced a complacency that led to an unsustainable mortgage and consumer credit boom ending in financial disaster for all involved. Any prescription for the future must recognize these facts. If it does not, the same problems will be created again, although they may not appear for some time because of the depth of the current crisis.

Confusing the goal of consumers with the means to attain it has always been a central problem in consumer life. The *American Dream*, a term first coined by writer James Truslow Adams in the early 1930s and used effectively by Theodore Dreiser among others, always suggested owning a home and having two cars in the driveway. Debt has been the means of attaining it. As a result, borrowing by the ever growing middle class became embedded as a democratic concept. The genuine problem appeared when it became accepted as a political principle, not simply a goal. Everyone should be able to attain it, even if they do not have the means. In the past, that meant living within one's means. Beginning in the 1980s, it meant discounting one's future earnings to have it now.

The politics of the current crisis have not yet been subdued. Conservatives maintain that the financial crisis was not caused by the ideology of an ownership society and the deregulation of free markets but by their poor application. John Major, Margaret Thatcher's Tory successor, blamed most of the problem on Gordon Brown, who was chancellor of the exchequer in Tony Blair's Labour government succeeding him. "Who ignored the debt spiral as it built up? Who weakened regulation and allowed Northern Rock to offer 125 per cent mortgages? Who diminished Bank of England control over our banking system?" he asked, leveling a blanket criticism against the Labour governments that replaced the Conservatives.[1] Thatcherism was not to blame. Labour's applications of it were, causing the crisis. There was some truth to the charge, but the origins of the crisis were firmly in the Conservative quarter.

The same attitude could be found in the United States. Speaking shortly after the presidential election in 2008, George W. Bush warned the new Democratic Congress not to throw the baby out with the financial bathwater when it took office. Addressing a Wall Street audience, he extolled the virtues of unfettered capitalism, saying that "the crisis was not a failure of the free-market system, and the answer is not to try to reinvent that system," he said in a speech at Federal Hall in downtown Manhattan. "Free-market capitalism is far more than an economic theory. It is the engine of social mobility, the highway to the American Dream."[2]

The stark fact was that the American Dream was born and baptized in the 1930s but may have seen its last days in the 2000s. Prior to its official naming, the markets were indeed unfettered, but, also typical of the 1930s, the highway mostly was unpaved. The result was a crash of disastrous proportions. The same problem occurred in 2007–2008 after the road signs were removed from the rebuilt highway, like all parts of the American infrastructure needing repair. Capitalism itself was in danger; it had survived crises before, but its road signs and the pavement were at the point of structural dissolution.

The idea of a stricter form of market capitalism frightened even hardened market participants. Similar remarks to those of Bush came from George Soros, usually on the other side of the political spectrum from conservatives. Speaking before the House Oversight Committee about the influence of hedge funds on the markets, Soros cautioned against "going overboard with regulation." He added:

> Excessive deregulation has inflicted enormous losses on the general public and there is a real danger that the pendulum will swing too far the other way. The bubble has now burst and hedge funds will be decimated. It would be a grave mistake to add to the forced liquidation currently dislocating markets by ill-considered or punitive regulations.[3]

Similar remarks could be heard from other conservative architects of the deregulated markets, as well as fund managers and investment bankers who had a great deal to lose if new regulations were enacted. Many emphasized a return to prudent lending practices for the future after not having spoken out for them initially. Calls for less securitization and the need to deemphasize synthetics could also be heard from reformers, but none accepted that growth might have to be deemphasized in favor of economic stability and a steady, evenhanded public policy. No one was willing to decouple ideology from the American Dream, restoring the notion to its place as an ideal rather than as a political blueprint requiring high levels of indebtedness.

The advanced state of the financial markets and the trend toward deregulation of banking and of the securities markets both militate against strong regulation in the future. Possible remedies against future financial fiascoes would have to include enhanced powers for regulators, centralization of the regulatory functions, much stronger penalties for rule breakers, and a clear demarcation of the political and financial sectors so that politicians cannot create a deregulated structure that will embrace them with open arms when they leave office. Those may be easy policy choices compared with the greater problems that finance has presented.

Levels of Reform

Traditionally, financial reforms have been passed after a crisis has occurred. Sometimes the damage is assessed before acting, as in the case of the original 1933 and 1934 banking and securities laws, and sometimes not, as in the wake of Enron. Usually, the reforms have been one dimensional or more precisely targeted against a specific type of abuse. Rarely have they been systemic.

The latter type of reform is crucial now but even more difficult to develop without a broad political consensus. Financial instruments need to be simplified so that the dangers they cause are more obvious and less opaque. The only way to achieve this goal without impeding useful developments in finance requires a strong supervisory system that can stop the creation of liabilities by using derivatives in much the same way that circuit breakers do in the futures markets and equities markets. Fifty trillion dollars worth of outstanding credit-default swaps is an impressive number, but it needs to be compared with the actual amount of securities being hedged. It would be a great irony if a major corporation failed and all of its outstanding debt was discovered to have been hedged, laying the risk off on private insurers and financial institutions. In theory, derivatives hedging is capable of running amuck in such a manner.

Attempts to reform the financial system need to be aimed at different levels of intermediation. Consumer advocates and specialists in retail consumer finance have concentrated on consumers and their vulnerability to exotic financial products. The more complicated the mortgage or consumer product, the more protection consumers need to avoid predators. One suggestion was a Financial Products Safety Commission similar to the Consumer Products Safety Commission, urged as a remedy for the sorts of complex products offered to investors. This is based on the fact that consumer products have fairly strong regulations in place to protect consumers against faulty design or fraudulent advertising. "Why are consumers safe when they purchase tangible consumer products with cash, but when they sign up for routine financial products like mortgages and credit cards they are left at the mercy of their creditors?" asked Elizabeth Warren, a longtime advocate of reform in the consumer finance sector, in 2007.[4] Purchases of consumer goods are protected by law, whereas those big-ticket items such as houses have surprisingly little protective legislation surrounding mortgages. The question is legitimate, but the emphasis at the retail level is not enough to protect consumers and society from another financial debacle with the strength to create systemic risk, destroying the housing industry in the process.

A consumer credit protection agency needs to be coupled with a similar idea aimed at prevention at the wholesale (i.e., Wall Street) level. The Group of 20 (G-20) came close to this when it suggested establishing a college for regulators in the G-20 countries aimed at educating regulators in recent developments in finance. The better that regulators are educated in structured finance and financial engineering, the better able they will be to detect fraud or faulty design that could lead to further problems.

That suggestion needs to be taken one step further. Ironically, Wall Street itself provided part of the answer fifteen years ago when some of the securities houses began patenting financial products with the U.S. Patent Office. A similar agency function is needed to review new and existing financial products with an eye to sanctioning them or suggesting modification. This has been the role of the Securities and Exchange Commission (SEC), but the financial crisis has proven that an agency needs to have this power before problems occur, not after the fact. Before the crisis, the SEC allowed many questionable practices in those areas in which it could have exercised its authority to restrain Wall Street. And this is not only a matter for securities regulators. Since derivatives and synthetics can simulate the behavior of securities, this preemptive power needs to be given to a regulator that oversees both sectors, not just securities or derivatives separately. This was at the heart of the Treasury recommendations made in March 2008 when the financial crisis had just begun.

If added to the protections afforded by a consumer-style agency, such a wholesale-level prevention agency should be able to stop most if not all problems before they reach the consumer level. Any problem areas that still trickle through to the consumer area could then be detected and ferreted out more easily. The financial crisis was a product of structured finance, and participants in this activity need to be restrained from preying on consumers and investors in the future. Financial developments can occur with dizzying speed, and such speed can turn into a stampede of bad products and misrepresentations, as the relatively short period after 2001 demonstrated.

Another problem is broader still. Finance has grown to be what Aristotle once called the "master science." For two thousand years, politics occupied that pivotal role in human affairs, until the early 1980s when finance took over. The disproportionate influence of finance cannot be overstated. George Soros observed that "the size of the financial sector is out of proportion to the rest of the economy. It has been growing excessively... ending in this super-bubble of the last twenty-five years." The complex network created within finance between structured products, derivatives, and traditional debt securities needs to be simplified and demystified. Without it, no consumer protection agency will be able to protect the public from financial excess and complexity.

Within structured finance, securitization needs to be reformed if it is to continue the many positive benefits provided in the past. The post-2001 experience has demonstrated that some forms of collateral ultimately are unacceptable backing for bonds. In this category are derivatives producing synthetic collateralized debt obligations (CDOs), subprime mortgages, and marginal credit card receivables. The number of these CDOs created in the two years preceding the credit market crisis was astounding. JP Morgan Chase estimated that there were $757 billion outstanding of synthetic CDO tranches based solely on corporate debt derivatives. Most of these were created and sold during the boom between 2006 and 2007, in addition to the credit card asset-backed securities (ABSs) and subprime collateralized debt obligations (CMOs).[5] At the end of 2008, the default rate on the synthetics was about 10 percent and rising, casting a long shadow over the potential for the economy to recover in the years immediately following.

One of the other drawbacks of securitization is that it obscures the true owners of debt. It is difficult to renegotiate a loan if the borrower or lender is not sure who the true owner is. If the securitized loan is in a pool, it may be impossible to extract it from the pool without substantial trouble and cost. Securitization has many virtues for risk mitigation, but it also presents substantial problems for extracting poorly performing loans and identifying their owners, making debt renegotiation and stable economic conditions more difficult.

Ultimately, Wall Street needs to be reminded that debt and debt financing have been responsible for most of its ills over the past hundred years. The crash of 1929 was caused in large part by worthless new issues of debt and large amounts of margin money lent to investors. Consumer credit also was popular at the time, stretching consumers to their personal limits in the quest for the American Dream. Despite the long hiatus, the current crisis is remarkably similar to conditions existing before and after the 1929 crash. Debt financing still dwarfs new equity financing by a considerable multiple each year and remains the institutional investors' favorite financial instrument. It was part of the debt financings that went wrong, creating a crisis of confidence that seriously eroded capital spending because long-term financing dried up. Wall Street complained then, as now, that risk takers were being judged unfairly. Then, as now, it was apparent that they had risked too much and ultimately lost their bets.

All of this is overshadowed by an even larger demographic problem. The baby-boomer generation is on the verge of retirement, which will deprive the stock market of its familiar source of funds that it has enjoyed for the last twenty-five years. While the boomers may understand stock market leverage better than their predecessors, they did not apply it to housing finance. The bear market beginning in 2007–2008 destroyed much of the accumulated wealth in private pension plans and will be extremely difficult to recoup. This brings to an end the bull market conditions the baby boomers created from the mid-1980s. One commentator noted that the stock market bust alone in late 2008 wiped eleven years of value off the market indexes within a period of months. The greatest period of prosperity ended in a financial crisis with the potential to last for decades after the fact.

Bring Back the Usury Laws

It is no coincidence that many of the financial innovations that have caused so much trouble have developed during the same period that the usury laws were dismantled. This has been a matter of political ideology as much as it has been a disregard for the lessons of the past. Usury laws have been under attack since the late 1920s in the United States, but it was the advent of the credit card and (later) of adjustable rate mortgages that signaled their death knell. The major problem over the years—over the centuries for that matter—was that they were not flexible. They need to be reinstated, with flexibility built in.

A newer version of the usury laws could state a maximum rate of interest for mortgages but still offer flexibility in the ranges below the cap. The derivatives markets already offer methods for lenders to hedge risk by establishing caps and floors for loans, and they must be required to assume more risk on their lending activities than they have in the last twenty years. Banks need to begin acting like banks again, not as hedge funds. Only then will they pay more attention to the creditworthiness of the potential borrowers rather than simply being content to securitize their lending risks.

Although it may be argued that usury laws have no useful place in contemporary society, the more powerful argument against them is quite different. The only real criticism of them has been their arbitrary nature. The various states in the United States have used different maximum rates to define how much can be charged on chattel loans and unsecured personal loans. But no one argued with the ceilings when applied to mortgage rates. Those limits have faded out of sight only because of the popularity of the adjustable rate mortgage, which, because of its one-year reset feature, usually falls outside the traditional ceilings that were designed for fixed-rate mortgages over the long term. And it should be noted that most of the prohibitions against criminal usury have been left in place even when the other laws have been allowed to fall by the wayside. Most states still prohibit predatory behavior, but it has become more difficult to define.

The current state of interest rates is a mess at the consumer level. Within recent years, even some securitizations that were discounted in the secondary market came under the scrutiny of state usury laws. The fact that this has not been the case at the consumer level is troubling. Lobbying by the payments industry must not be allowed to block future consideration of new usury laws and a reexamination of Regulation Z at the Fed. The Fed has been interested only in ensuring that lenders are clear concerning the rates they charge consumers, not whether the rates themselves are fair. The old 1920s argument for allowing any interest the market will bear on consumer credit does not carry much weight anymore in light of the financial crisis. Allowing consumer interest rates to rise because loan sharks were at work charging even higher rates was not a good argument for allowing credit companies to charge high rates to counter them. Allowing consumer credit companies to act as loan sharks in the name of deregulation is not a compelling argument either. The presence of predators requires a game warden, not just an observer.

The disingenuous argument that imprudent lending, not mortgage rates, helped destroy the mortgage market is not a valid argument either. One of the reasons that so many bells and whistles were attached to exotic mortgages was to raise the effective rate of interest above the low teaser rates initially offered borrowers. Those adjustable rate mortgages (ARMs) with low rates at 2.50 or 3.00 percent for the first five years were still accruing interest that was added to the outstanding principal amount after the grace period was over. When features are added to disguise another more important factor such as the effective rate of interest, that factor needs to be reformed. The bells and whistles then disappear under their own weight.

Abuses of interest rates by lenders of all sorts require a new national usury law. The old laws at the state level were ineffective because banks sought out states with soft laws or with state legislatures willing to roll back existing laws in favor of tax revenues or employment prospects. The new laws need to be aimed at both consumer interest *and* mortgage rates because of the link between consumer interest and home equity loans. To protect against further abuses, alternatives to the menu need to be confined. Home equity loans cannot be so easily available that consumers can go on a spending spree without fear of consequences, especially individuals who cannot afford a down payment but who are lent the money anyway. The good collateral damaged by violating this simple banking truism is inestimable.

Another way of arguing for a national usury ceiling is to limit the amount of time that consumers take to pay off their debts. If a consumer pays only the minimum on balances over a prolonged period of time, that law should require mandatory debt counseling and a new, reasonable repayment schedule so that the debt does not become perpetual. Although no statistics currently exist on this delicate topic, there is a general unease that many consumers effectively may be in perpetual debt because of their previous spending habits and their use of credit cards as a source of working capital. That working capital too often is converted into unfunded long-term debt.

The American political system has an admirable combination of checks and balances working to ensure that legislation, the execution of the laws, and their interpretation all provide the necessary counterbalancing forces to achieve equity within society. The same cannot be said of the powerful financial system, which has supplanted politics over the last thirty years. The checks and balances have been removed in favor of market efficiency, ideology, and a belief that markets regulate themselves. Finance has proved itself to be a shadow form of government, attempting to provide the greatest good for the greatest number.

It requires the same sort of checks on its power that constrain the traditional branches of government. Until thirty years ago, Wall Street was the fifth estate in American society. Its position has risen since to a much higher level.

Within the last thirty years, a considerable amount of time and money has been spent reinterpreting history in favor of the new market ideology. The pragmatic tenets of the New Deal, especially those associated with the financial safety net, have been turned upside down in favor of a free market ideology that was more appropriate for textbooks than it was as a blueprint for reasonable growth. Human nature was left out of the discussion, with disastrous consequences. As long as consumers chase the American Dream with high levels of personal leverage and lenders are more than willing to overlook their financial inadequacies in favor of fee-producing business, the cycle cannot be broken. It will take considerable bipartisan effort to clear away the ideological trappings of the anti–New Deal rhetoric and install a pragmatic market system designed to encourage financial innovation while protecting savings and retirement plans from predatory behavior.

Chapter Notes

1. *The Times*, November 13, 2008.

2. *New York Times*, November 14, 2008.

3. *The Times*, November 14, 2008.

4. Elizabeth Warren, "Unsafe at Any Rate," *Democracy*, No. 5 (Summer 2007): 1–4.

5. *Financial Times*, November 18, 2008.

Statistical Appendixes

THE FOLLOWING SIX APPENDIXES provide the numbers behind the consumer credit and mortgage phenomena, especially over the last four decades. As the numbers demonstrate, consumerism and home buying increased at unprecedented rates until the recent financial crisis set in.

Appendix 1 shows the growth, and contraction, in consumer credit between 1929 and 1939. The numbers are easy to decipher since they represent a simpler time when a billion was still an amount worth considering carefully. The Great Depression was accompanied by (or caused) the sharp fall in consumer credit after 1929.

Appendix 2 shows the number of bankruptcy filings in the early 2000s, a controversial period for the number of personal or nonbusiness bankruptcies in particular. Appendixes 3 and 4 show the amount of consumer debt outstanding at banks and finance companies (nonbanks) since revolving credit was introduced. The detail is necessary to illustrate two trends. The first is the constant growth in consumer credit, especially after 2001, in both sectors. The second is the seasonal nature of consumer borrowing, which tends to rise in the months preceding Christmas and to fall thereafter, providing a simple yet effective way of predicting the course of the economy for the year ahead.

Appendix 5 shows the number of residential mortgages outstanding, the growth of which has been phenomenal since 2001. Appendix 6 shows the number of mortgage originations, numbers that will not necessarily coincide with Appendix 5 because of mortgage retirements. Together they demonstrate the breadth and depth of the mortgage boom and the crisis that followed.

Appendix 1

Consumer Credit 1929–1939

(millions of dollars)

Year	Total	Installment	Other
1929	6,444	3,151	3,293
1930	5,767	2,687	3,080
1931	4,760	2,207	2,553
1932	3,567	1,521	2,046
1933	3,482	1,588	1,894
1934	3,904	1,871	2,033
1935	4,911	2,694	2,217
1936	6,135	3,623	2,512
1937	6,689	4,015	2,674
1938	6,338	3,691	2,647
1939	7,222	4,503	2,719

Source: U.S. Bureau of the Census, Historical Statistics of the United States: Colonial Times to 1957 (Washington, DC: 1960)

Appendix 2

Bankruptcy Filings

Bankruptcy Filings	2008	2007	2006	2005	2004
Consumer bankruptcy filings	1,064,927	822,590	573,203	N/A	N/A
Nonbusiness bankruptcy filings	1,074,225	822,590	597,965	2,039,214	1,563,145
Chapter 7 filings	744,424	519,364	360,890	1,659,017	1,137,958
Chapter 11 filings	10,160	6,353	5,163	6,800	10,132
Chapter 13 filings	362,762	324,771	251,179	412,130	449,129

N/A = not available
Source: MortgageDaily.com

Appendix 3

Consumer Credit Made by Banks

(millions of dollars)

Month, year	Total	Revolving	Nonrevolving
Jan 68	51,193.00	1,401.00	49,792.00
Feb 68	51,488.00	1,418.00	50,070.00
Mar 68	51,962.00	1,439.00	50,523.00
Apr 68	52,849.00	1,494.00	51,355.00
May 68	53,554.00	1,536.00	52,018.00
Jun 68	54,327.00	1,598.00	52,729.00
Jul 68	55,075.00	1,649.00	53,426.00
Aug 68	55,962.00	1,719.00	54,243.00
Sep 68	56,550.00	1,788.00	54,762.00
Oct 68	57,309.00	1,881.00	55,428.00
Nov 68	57,770.00	1,922.00	55,848.00
Dec 68	58,464.00	2,105.00	56,359.00
Jan 69	58,331.00	2,271.00	56,060.00
Feb 69	58,588.00	2,310.00	56,278.00
Mar 69	59,197.00	2,349.00	56,848.00
Apr 69	60,208.00	2,462.00	57,746.00
May 69	60,855.00	2,586.00	58,269.00
Jun 69	61,695.00	2,698.00	58,997.00
Jul 69	62,021.00	2,803.00	59,218.00
Aug 69	62,323.00	2,919.00	59,404.00
Sep 69	62,703.00	3,081.00	59,622.00
Oct 69	62,951.00	3,210.00	59,741.00

(continued)

Month, year	Total	Revolving	Nonrevolving
Nov 69	62,993.00	3,343.00	59,650.00
Dec 69	63,395.00	3,720.00	59,675.00
Jan 70	62,827.00	3,907.00	58,920.00
Feb 70	62,595.00	3,948.00	58,647.00
Mar 70	62,526.00	3,965.00	58,561.00
Apr 70	62,954.00	4,055.00	58,899.00
May 70	63,324.00	4,112.00	59,212.00
Jun 70	64,022.00	4,227.00	59,795.00
Jul 70	64,892.00	4,334.00	60,558.00
Aug 70	65,225.00	4,445.00	60,780.00
Sep 70	65,434.00	4,601.00	60,833.00
Oct 70	65,405.00	4,684.00	60,721.00
Nov 70	65,137.00	4,765.00	60,372.00
Dec 70	65,625.00	5,128.00	60,497.00
Jan 71	65,428.00	5,142.00	60,286.00
Feb 71	65,479.00	5,093.00	60,386.00
Mar 71	65,927.00	5,037.00	60,890.00
Apr 71	66,974.00	5,124.00	61,850.00
May 71	67,854.00	5,168.00	62,686.00
Jun 71	68,903.00	5,253.00	63,650.00
Jul 71	69,697.00	5,315.00	64,382.00
Aug 71	70,854.00	5,408.00	65,446.00
Sep 71	71,740.00	5,512.00	66,228.00
Oct 71	72,372.00	5,505.00	66,867.00
Nov 71	73,222.00	5,564.00	67,658.00
Dec 71	74,325.00	5,951.00	68,374.00
Jan 72	74,435.00	5,915.00	68,520.00
Feb 72	74,807.00	5,860.00	68,947.00
Mar 72	75,646.00	5,833.00	69,813.00
Apr 72	76,840.00	5,920.00	70,920.00
May 72	78,281.00	6,007.00	72,274.00
Jun 72	80,008.00	6,142.00	73,866.00
Jul 72	80,964.00	6,219.00	74,745.00
Aug 72	82,432.00	6,378.00	76,054.00
Sep 72	83,393.00	6,536.00	76,857.00

Month, year	Total	Revolving	Nonrevolving
Oct 72	84,441.00	6,588.00	77,853.00
Nov 72	85,439.00	6,702.00	78,737.00
Dec 72	87,001.00	7,183.00	79,818.00
Jan 73	87,362.00	7,260.00	80,102.00
Feb 73	88,164.00	7,260.00	80,904.00
Mar 73	89,240.00	7,226.00	82,014.00
Apr 73	90,737.00	7,290.00	83,447.00
May 73	92,352.00	7,408.00	84,944.00
Jun 73	94,107.00	7,615.00	86,492.00
Jul 73	95,217.00	7,752.00	87,465.00
Aug 73	97,010.00	8,001.00	89,009.00
Sep 73	97,529.00	8,177.00	89,352.00
Oct 73	98,397.00	8,306.00	90,091.00
Nov 73	99,045.00	8,525.00	90,520.00
Dec 73	99,620.00	9,092.00	90,528.00
Jan 74	99,382.00	9,274.00	90,108.00
Feb 74	99,229.00	9,194.00	90,035.00
Mar 74	99,294.00	9,049.00	90,245.00
Apr 74	100,366.00	9,134.00	91,232.00
May 74	101,222.00	9,257.00	91,965.00
Jun 74	102,221.00	9,458.00	92,763.00
Jul 74	102,915.00	9,683.00	93,232.00
Aug 74	103,965.00	10,039.00	93,926.00
Sep 74	104,123.00	10,265.00	93,858.00
Oct 74	103,847.00	10,449.00	93,398.00
Nov 74	103,309.00	10,572.00	92,737.00
Dec 74	102,989.00	11,077.00	91,912.00
Jan 75	101,921.00	11,204.00	90,717.00
Feb 75	101,298.00	11,038.00	90,260.00
Mar 75	100,425.00	10,741.00	89,684.00
Apr 75	100,679.00	10,779.00	89,900.00
May 75	100,812.00	10,760.00	90,052.00
Jun 75	101,549.00	10,834.00	90,715.00
Jul 75	102,135.00	10,973.00	91,162.00

(continued)

Month, year	Total	Revolving	Nonrevolving
Aug 75	103,187.00	11,217.00	91,970.00
Sep 75	104,026.00	11,449.00	92,577.00
Oct 75	104,638.00	11,535.00	93,103.00
Nov 75	104,899.00	11,616.00	93,283.00
Dec 75	106,055.00	12,313.00	93,742.00
Jan 76	105,770.00	12,382.00	93,388.00
Feb 76	105,379.00	12,181.00	93,198.00
Mar 76	105,611.00	11,926.00	93,685.00
Apr 76	107,314.00	12,032.00	95,282.00
May 76	108,405.00	12,067.00	96,338.00
Jun 76	110,077.00	12,195.00	97,882.00
Jul 76	111,657.00	12,479.00	99,178.00
Aug 76	113,202.00	12,767.00	100,435.00
Sep 76	114,633.00	13,112.00	101,521.00
Oct 76	115,524.00	13,281.00	102,243.00
Nov 76	116,109.00	13,458.00	102,651.00
Dec 76	118,043.00	14,359.00	103,684.00
Jan 77	117,827.00	14,328.00	103,499.00
Feb 77	118,423.00	14,188.00	104,235.00
Mar 77	119,842.00	14,095.00	105,747.00
Apr 77	122,455.00	14,352.00	108,103.00
May 77	124,703.00	14,528.00	110,175.00
Jun 77	127,616.00	14,933.00	112,683.00
Jul 77	129,569.00	15,203.00	114,366.00
Aug 77	132,408.00	15,809.00	116,599.00
Sep 77	134,369.00	16,347.00	118,022.00
Oct 77	135,842.00	16,629.00	119,213.00
Nov 77	137,392.00	17,004.00	120,388.00
Dec 77	140,302.00	18,374.00	121,928.00
Jan 78	140,724.00	18,644.00	122,080.00
Feb 78	141,193.00	18,601.00	122,592.00
Mar 78	143,291.00	18,705.00	124,586.00
Apr 78	146,693.00	19,055.00	127,638.00
May 78	149,962.00	19,378.00	130,584.00
Jun 78	154,140.00	20,009.00	134,131.00

Month, year	Total	Revolving	Nonrevolving
Jul 78	156,648.00	20,566.00	136,082.00
Aug 78	159,770.00	21,314.00	138,456.00
Sep 78	161,619.00	21,935.00	139,684.00
Oct 78	162,870.00	22,126.00	140,744.00
Nov 78	164,193.00	22,653.00	141,540.00
Dec 78	166,512.00	24,341.00	142,171.00
Jan 79	167,148.00	24,746.00	142,402.00
Feb 79	167,623.00	24,648.00	142,975.00
Mar 79	168,703.00	24,666.00	144,037.00
Apr 79	171,379.00	24,993.00	146,386.00
May 79	173,941.00	25,279.00	148,662.00
Jun 79	176,177.00	25,817.00	150,360.00
Jul 79	177,750.00	26,090.00	151,660.00
Aug 79	180,739.00	26,881.00	153,858.00
Sep 79	182,530.00	27,475.00	155,055.00
Oct 79	183,876.00	27,919.00	155,957.00
Nov 79	184,489.00	28,432.00	156,057.00
Dec 79	185,725.00	29,862.00	155,863.00
Jan 80	185,458.00	29,801.00	155,657.00
Feb 80	184,753.00	29,641.00	155,112.00
Mar 80	183,415.00	29,177.00	154,238.00
Apr 80	181,628.00	28,987.00	152,641.00
May 80	179,552.00	28,617.00	150,935.00
Jun 80	177,822.00	28,280.00	149,542.00
Jul 80	177,658.00	28,088.00	149,570.00
Aug 80	178,822.00	28,337.00	150,485.00
Sep 80	179,789.00	28,451.00	151,338.00
Oct 80	179,734.00	28,288.00	151,446.00
Nov 80	179,216.00	28,226.00	150,990.00
Dec 80	180,215.00	29,765.00	150,450.00
Jan 81	178,158.00	29,705.00	148,453.00
Feb 81	176,335.00	29,148.00	147,187.00
Mar 81	176,465.00	28,776.00	147,689.00
Apr 81	176,975.00	28,880.00	148,095.00

(continued)

Month, year	Total	Revolving	Nonrevolving
May 81	177,343.00	28,871.00	148,472.00
Jun 81	179,065.00	29,523.00	149,542.00
Jul 81	179,944.00	29,290.00	150,654.00
Aug 81	181,201.00	29,779.00	151,422.00
Sep 81	182,849.00	30,687.00	152,162.00
Oct 81	182,116.00	30,696.00	151,420.00
Nov 81	182,353.00	30,742.00	151,611.00
Dec 81	184,193.00	32,880.00	151,313.00
Jan 82	183,683.00	32,542.00	151,141.00
Feb 82	182,932.00	31,948.00	150,984.00
Mar 82	182,922.00	31,687.00	151,235.00
Apr 82	183,682.00	31,937.00	151,745.00
May 82	183,897.00	32,083.00	151,814.00
Jun 82	185,223.00	32,618.00	152,605.00
Jul 82	185,450.00	32,937.00	152,513.00
Aug 82	186,557.00	33,509.00	153,048.00
Sep 82	188,072.00	34,017.00	154,055.00
Oct 82	187,513.00	34,104.00	153,409.00
Nov 82	187,241.00	34,218.00	153,023.00
Dec 82	190,932.00	36,666.00	154,266.00
Jan 83	188,756.00	36,313.00	152,443.00
Feb 83	186,259.00	35,541.00	150,718.00
Mar 83	186,947.00	35,625.00	151,322.00
Apr 83	187,581.00	35,773.00	151,808.00
May 83	187,973.00	35,687.00	152,286.00
Jun 83	190,915.00	36,697.00	154,218.00
Jul 83	193,784.00	37,358.00	156,426.00
Aug 83	197,482.00	38,162.00	159,320.00
Sep 83	200,673.00	39,041.00	161,632.00
Oct 83	203,203.00	39,774.00	163,429.00
Nov 83	206,285.00	40,774.00	165,511.00
Dec 83	213,663.00	44,184.00	169,479.00
Jan 84	213,461.00	43,118.00	170,343.00
Feb 84	217,589.00	43,506.00	174,083.00
Mar 84	219,840.00	45,235.00	174,605.00

Month, year	Total	Revolving	Nonrevolving
Apr 84	223,588.00	46,149.00	177,439.00
May 84	229,961.00	47,936.00	182,025.00
Jun 84	236,045.00	49,734.00	186,311.00
Jul 84	239,880.00	50,358.00	189,522.00
Aug 84	245,373.00	52,313.00	193,060.00
Sep 84	248,051.00	54,258.00	193,793.00
Oct 84	250,706.00	55,276.00	195,430.00
Nov 84	252,654.00	56,641.00	196,013.00
Dec 84	258,844.00	60,549.00	198,295.00
Jan 85	260,285.00	61,445.00	198,840.00
Feb 85	262,680.00	62,137.00	200,543.00
Mar 85	267,381.00	63,758.00	203,623.00
Apr 85	271,745.00	65,338.00	206,407.00
May 85	273,572.00	65,205.00	208,367.00
Jun 85	276,513.00	66,052.00	210,461.00
Jul 85	279,497.00	67,105.00	212,392.00
Aug 85	282,757.00	68,433.00	214,324.00
Sep 85	286,728.00	70,824.00	215,904.00
Oct 85	287,981.00	72,009.00	215,972.00
Nov 85	290,736.00	74,142.00	216,594.00
Dec 85	297,227.00	78,850.00	218,377.00
Jan 86	297,500.00	79,308.00	218,192.00
Feb 86	296,259.00	79,103.00	217,156.00
Mar 86	296,270.00	79,397.00	216,873.00
Apr 86	299,869.00	81,018.00	218,851.00
May 86	301,951.00	81,369.00	220,582.00
Jun 86	304,100.00	82,056.00	222,044.00
Jul 86	306,303.00	82,701.00	223,602.00
Aug 86	308,352.00	83,604.00	224,748.00
Sep 86	311,443.00	84,012.00	227,431.00
Oct 86	314,178.00	85,069.00	229,109.00
Nov 86	314,969.00	86,415.00	228,554.00
Dec 86	320,187.00	90,686.00	229,501.00
Jan 87	316,103.00	87,800.00	228,303.00

(continued)

Month, year	Total	Revolving	Nonrevolving
Feb 87	313,062.00	86,836.00	226,226.00
Mar 87	309,795.00	85,998.00	223,797.00
Apr 87	313,583.00	87,717.00	225,866.00
May 87	315,096.00	88,374.00	226,722.00
Jun 87	316,822.00	90,555.00	226,267.00
Jul 87	319,011.00	92,421.00	226,590.00
Aug 87	322,671.00	93,695.00	228,976.00
Sep 87	325,602.00	96,173.00	229,429.00
Oct 87	326,917.00	96,705.00	230,212.00
Nov 87	328,850.00	96,827.00	232,023.00
Dec 87	334,090.00	103,350.00	230,740.00
Jan 88	333,390.00	103,981.00	229,409.00
Feb 88	333,075.00	103,323.00	229,752.00
Mar 88	333,855.00	103,253.00	230,602.00
Apr 88	338,430.00	104,792.00	233,638.00
May 88	340,195.00	105,675.00	234,520.00
Jun 88	341,529.00	107,857.00	233,672.00
Jul 88	343,669.00	108,571.00	235,098.00
Aug 88	348,768.00	110,499.00	238,269.00
Sep 88	351,421.00	112,460.00	238,961.00
Oct 88	352,273.00	113,653.00	238,620.00
Nov 88	354,935.00	117,327.00	237,608.00
Dec 88	360,816.00	123,020.00	237,796.00
Jan 89	353,344.00	114,143.00	239,201.00
Feb 89	353,025.00	112,734.00	240,291.00
Mar 89	355,578.00	112,088.00	243,490.00
Apr 89	359,803.00	114,262.00	245,541.00
May 89	361,528.00	115,018.00	246,510.00
Jun 89	363,704.00	115,580.00	248,124.00
Jul 89	365,107.00	116,214.00	248,893.00
Aug 89	368,832.00	118,083.00	250,749.00
Sep 89	371,715.00	119,413.00	252,302.00
Oct 89	373,483.00	120,410.00	253,073.00
Nov 89	376,021.00	122,527.00	253,494.00
Dec 89	383,309.00	130,811.00	252,498.00

Month, year	Total	Revolving	Nonrevolving
Jan 90	382,385.00	128,481.00	253,904.00
Feb 90	377,311.00	125,151.00	252,160.00
Mar 90	372,789.00	122,322.00	250,467.00
Apr 90	374,395.00	124,262.00	250,133.00
May 90	373,770.00	125,619.00	248,151.00
Jun 90	372,319.00	122,516.00	249,803.00
Jul 90	373,236.00	125,248.00	247,988.00
Aug 90	377,272.00	126,683.00	250,589.00
Sep 90	379,467.00	127,415.00	252,052.00
Oct 90	380,625.00	127,425.00	253,200.00
Nov 90	380,586.00	129,752.00	250,834.00
Dec 90	381,982.00	133,385.00	248,597.00
Jan 91	376,400.00	127,083.00	249,317.00
Feb 91	374,255.00	127,259.00	246,996.00
Mar 91	370,499.00	126,523.00	243,976.00
Apr 91	371,625.00	128,230.00	243,395.00
May 91	370,112.00	128,585.00	241,527.00
Jun 91	368,385.00	126,961.00	241,424.00
Jul 91	368,452.00	127,818.00	240,634.00
Aug 91	368,426.00	129,277.00	239,149.00
Sep 91	366,312.00	129,331.00	236,981.00
Oct 91	364,599.00	131,299.00	233,300.00
Nov 91	364,185.00	130,455.00	233,730.00
Dec 91	370,176.00	138,005.00	232,171.00
Jan 92	366,160.00	133,939.00	232,221.00
Feb 92	360,708.00	130,738.00	229,970.00
Mar 92	357,166.00	128,419.00	228,747.00
Apr 92	357,471.00	128,389.00	229,082.00
May 92	356,312.00	127,838.00	228,474.00
Jun 92	355,981.00	127,700.00	228,281.00
Jul 92	357,018.00	127,574.00	229,444.00
Aug 92	357,719.00	127,063.00	230,656.00
Sep 92	357,300.00	126,971.00	230,329.00
Oct 92	356,412.00	127,120.00	229,292.00

(continued)

Month, year	Total	Revolving	Nonrevolving
Nov 92	357,412.00	127,737.00	229,675.00
Dec 92	362,901.00	132,966.00	229,935.00
Jan 93	362,312.00	130,079.00	232,233.00
Feb 93	359,813.00	128,517.00	231,296.00
Mar 93	358,900.00	128,847.00	230,053.00
Apr 93	362,295.00	130,446.00	231,849.00
May 93	365,102.00	131,895.00	233,207.00
Jun 93	366,632.00	131,073.00	235,559.00
Jul 93	371,137.00	135,544.00	235,593.00
Aug 93	375,059.00	136,874.00	238,185.00
Sep 93	379,364.00	138,262.00	241,102.00
Oct 93	381,660.00	138,816.00	242,844.00
Nov 93	387,621.00	143,615.00	244,006.00
Dec 93	395,704.00	149,920.00	245,784.00
Jan 94	394,842.00	146,196.00	248,646.00
Feb 94	394,867.00	144,928.00	249,939.00
Mar 94	397,802.00	146,486.00	251,316.00
Apr 94	404,865.00	150,181.00	254,684.00
May 94	407,966.00	151,019.00	256,947.00
Jun 94	413,413.00	154,210.00	259,203.00
Jul 94	419,979.00	158,248.00	261,731.00
Aug 94	428,924.00	162,856.00	266,068.00
Sep 94	434,560.00	166,294.00	268,266.00
Oct 94	439,238.00	164,840.00	274,398.00
Nov 94	445,114.00	172,321.00	272,793.00
Dec 94	458,777.00	182,021.00	276,756.00
Jan 95	457,033.00	178,655.00	278,378.00
Feb 95	455,749.00	178,966.00	276,783.00
Mar 95	459,689.00	180,888.00	278,801.00
Apr 95	466,365.00	182,054.00	284,311.00
May 95	469,628.00	185,897.00	283,731.00
Jun 95	471,591.00	187,286.00	284,305.00
Jul 95	475,250.00	187,375.00	287,875.00
Aug 95	484,446.00	195,423.00	289,023.00
Sep 95	485,920.00	194,962.00	290,958.00

Month, year	Total	Revolving	Nonrevolving
Oct 95	485,565.00	195,898.00	289,667.00
Nov 95	490,368.11	197,437.11	292,931.00
Dec 95	502,327.91	210,662.91	291,665.00
Jan 96	493,573.79	200,462.79	293,111.00
Feb 96	490,790.43	199,291.43	291,499.00
Mar 96	490,807.02	197,266.02	293,541.00
Apr 96	498,613.01	201,604.01	297,009.00
May 96	498,794.55	203,933.55	294,861.00
Jun 96	503,766.24	204,536.24	299,230.00
Jul 96	507,883.89	207,782.89	300,101.00
Aug 96	513,914.99	210,251.99	303,663.00
Sep 96	513,906.45	211,681.45	302,225.00
Oct 96	518,430.40	215,546.40	302,884.00
Nov 96	520,592.72	218,546.72	302,046.00
Dec 96	527,462.61	229,308.61	298,154.00
Jan 97	522,153.52	223,944.52	298,209.00
Feb 97	513,753.26	216,593.26	297,160.00
Mar 97	505,158.47	208,129.47	297,029.00
Apr 97	511,279.65	210,247.65	301,032.00
May 97	512,703.82	213,895.82	298,808.00
Jun 97	512,016.61	214,653.61	297,363.00
Jul 97	516,038.02	220,548.02	295,490.00
Aug 97	518,003.27	219,293.27	298,710.00
Sep 97	509,663.26	211,383.26	298,280.00
Oct 97	508,540.72	211,793.72	296,747.00
Nov 97	508,850.90	215,079.90	293,771.00
Dec 97	515,064.04	222,327.04	292,737.00
Jan 98	500,985.99	210,390.99	290,595.00
Feb 98	494,213.05	206,234.05	287,979.00
Mar 98	493,846.32	203,025.32	290,821.00
Apr 98	501,913.87	210,975.87	290,938.00
May 98	499,216.07	209,267.07	289,949.00
Jun 98	493,316.89	202,852.89	290,464.00
Jul 98	493,306.15	199,538.15	293,768.00

(continued)

Month, year	Total	Revolving	Nonrevolving
Aug 98	500,030.60	202,276.60	297,754.00
Sep 98	499,624.21	199,369.21	300,255.00
Oct 98	504,273.86	203,066.86	301,207.00
Nov 98	501,555.20	199,640.20	301,915.00
Dec 98	512,006.76	213,420.76	298,586.00
Jan 99	512,401.53	208,540.53	303,861.00
Feb 99	504,946.46	202,140.46	302,806.00
Mar 99	499,257.83	195,246.83	304,011.00
Apr 99	500,393.79	197,025.79	303,368.00
May 99	499,066.36	196,430.36	302,636.00
Jun 99	484,471.01	184,728.01	299,743.00
Jul 99	485,049.28	183,069.28	301,980.00
Aug 99	483,987.64	177,698.64	306,289.00
Sep 99	480,406.24	176,764.24	303,642.00
Oct 99	481,921.72	175,348.72	306,573.00
Nov 99	488,641.68	180,223.68	308,418.00
Dec 99	507,763.28	197,357.28	310,406.00
Jan 00	506,793.20	193,655.20	313,138.00
Feb 00	507,529.85	194,760.85	312,769.00
Mar 00	505,672.96	193,453.96	312,219.00
Apr 00	508,317.63	197,312.63	311,005.00
May 00	510,675.69	200,997.69	309,678.00
Jun 00	514,963.54	203,511.54	311,452.00
Jul 00	515,101.53	203,337.36	311,764.17
Aug 00	529,474.27	213,047.21	316,427.06
Sep 00	531,032.48	211,609.93	319,422.55
Oct 00	530,133.70	209,868.47	320,265.23
Nov 00	537,424.68	215,605.36	321,819.32
Dec 00	551,074.41	227,667.61	323,406.80
Jan 01	549,331.26	220,274.67	329,056.59
Feb 01	544,583.96	218,573.62	326,010.33
Mar 01	542,799.31	217,165.31	325,634.00
Apr 01	550,755.14	224,698.14	326,057.00
May 01	552,844.05	226,064.15	326,779.90
Jun 01	550,373.66	222,607.66	327,766.00

Month, year	Total	Revolving	Nonrevolving
Jul 01	545,661.59	218,988.09	326,673.50
Aug 01	548,029.51	216,450.81	331,578.70
Sep 01	546,508.64	213,184.64	333,324.00
Oct 01	550,854.00	220,053.80	330,800.20
Nov 01	560,472.69	229,955.59	330,517.10
Dec 01	568,437.42	234,894.42	333,543.00
Jan 02	567,381.49	229,169.95	338,211.54
Feb 02	562,399.43	226,472.93	335,926.50
Mar 02	561,547.61	226,964.61	334,583.00
Apr 02	567,072.17	232,300.06	334,772.12
May 02	568,929.83	229,777.25	339,152.58
Jun 02	566,783.04	227,684.04	339,099.00
Jul 02	569,686.88	226,493.69	343,193.19
Aug 02	585,363.02	237,615.22	347,747.79
Sep 02	589,192.34	239,655.34	349,537.00
Oct 02	591,440.71	238,820.25	352,620.47
Nov 02	594,839.01	240,511.98	354,327.03
Dec 02	602,569.76	246,394.76	356,175.00
Jan 03	598,345.72	236,822.62	361,523.10
Feb 03	598,672.16	236,015.56	362,656.60
Mar 03	593,231.42	230,408.42	362,823.00
Apr 03	595,529.68	231,703.81	363,825.87
May 03	601,381.83	236,734.70	364,647.13
Jun 03	603,683.84	236,963.84	366,720.00
Jul 03	603,381.99	234,818.39	368,563.60
Aug 03	610,809.74	236,891.54	373,918.20
Sep 03	614,123.82	236,011.82	378,112.00
Oct 03	608,947.23	231,315.53	377,631.70
Nov 03	639,767.74	264,437.64	375,330.10
Dec 03	669,385.77	285,014.77	384,371.00
Jan 04	669,762.97	277,003.77	392,759.20
Feb 04	661,742.51	273,148.11	388,594.40
Mar 04	658,035.76	268,612.76	389,423.00
Apr 04	661,040.03	270,748.43	390,291.60

(continued)

Month, year	Total	Revolving	Nonrevolving
May 04	667,047.60	278,034.70	389,012.90
Jun 04	660,571.18	275,482.18	385,089.00
Jul 04	664,144.00	278,453.90	385,690.10
Aug 04	673,769.45	286,046.05	387,723.40
Sep 04	676,318.61	286,200.61	390,118.00
Oct 04	676,956.83	285,384.13	391,572.70
Nov 04	674,507.61	284,847.01	389,660.60
Dec 04	704,269.88	314,648.88	389,621.00
Jan 05	698,236.99	303,883.32	394,353.67
Feb 05	691,784.58	297,070.74	394,713.83
Mar 05	683,112.01	287,979.01	395,133.00
Apr 05	690,490.05	295,968.45	394,521.60
May 05	685,201.41	292,529.81	392,671.60
Jun 05	683,951.01	293,725.01	390,226.00
Jul 05	694,674.02	296,834.55	397,839.47
Aug 05	705,420.87	298,039.44	407,381.43
Sep 05	708,229.99	300,550.99	407,679.00
Oct 05	701,905.08	294,521.11	407,383.97
Nov 05	697,083.92	299,808.39	397,275.53
Dec 05	707,038.98	311,203.98	395,835.00
Jan 06	706,577.49	301,626.43	404,951.07
Feb 06	696,350.14	289,423.80	406,926.33
Mar 06	697,479.99	281,127.99	416,352.00
Apr 06	704,648.31	287,983.81	416,664.50
May 06	713,087.05	292,857.85	420,229.20
Jun 06	694,749.00	291,029.00	403,720.00
Jul 06	701,261.40	295,830.33	405,431.07
Aug 06	715,117.22	301,163.69	413,953.53
Sep 06	710,501.99	298,859.99	411,642.00
Oct 06	712,209.31	298,167.85	414,041.47
Nov 06	725,238.90	310,221.67	415,017.23
Dec 06	741,200.00	327,302.00	413,898.00
Jan 07	742,420.05	316,767.02	425,653.03
Feb 07	725,922.53	302,588.66	423,333.87
Mar 07	723,277.99	299,158.99	424,119.00

Month, year	Total	Revolving	Nonrevolving
Apr 07	729,133.24	304,693.64	424,439.60
May 07	735,749.29	307,934.62	427,814.67
Jun 07	737,869.01	311,006.01	426,863.00
Jul 07	748,568.09	312,597.96	435,970.13
Aug 07	763,851.60	319,481.73	444,369.87
Sep 07	771,518.01	322,419.01	449,099.00
Oct 07	771,267.23	321,144.50	450,122.73
Nov 07	788,004.77	336,176.40	451,828.37
Dec 07	804,096.02	353,446.02	450,650.00
Jan 08	808,705.53	338,286.66	470,418.87
Feb 08	800,045.66	330,183.63	469,862.03
Mar 08	796,317.00	322,463.00	473,854.00
Apr 08	807,442.28	327,109.92	480,332.37
May 08	807,859.47	325,991.93	481,867.53
Jun 08	812,984.00	328,882.00	484,102.00
Jul 08	820,314.74	335,636.31	484,678.43
Aug 08	832,940.03	343,748.56	489,191.47
Sep 08	844,087.01	356,334.01	487,753.00
Oct 08	850,623.34	365,486.60	485,136.73
Nov 08	863,094.91	376,827.85	486,267.06
Dec 08	878,494.01	390,551.01	487,942.99
Jan 09	895,108.62	390,020.98	505,087.64
Feb 09	882,024.40	382,006.53	500,017.87

Source: Federal Reserve Board

Appendix 4

Consumer Credit Made by Finance Companies
(millions of dollars)

Month, year	Total	Revolving	Nonrevolving
Jan 68	24,328.00	NA	24,328.00
Feb 68	24,273.00	NA	24,273.00
Mar 68	24,283.00	NA	24,283.00
Apr 68	24,386.00	NA	24,386.00
May 68	24,503.00	NA	24,503.00
Jun 68	24,816.00	NA	24,816.00
Jul 68	25,070.00	NA	25,070.00
Aug 68	25,330.00	NA	25,330.00
Sep 68	25,322.00	NA	25,322.00
Oct 68	25,480.00	NA	25,480.00
Nov 68	25,642.00	NA	25,642.00
Dec 68	26,074.00	NA	26,074.00
Jan 69	25,953.00	NA	25,953.00
Feb 69	25,959.00	NA	25,959.00
Mar 69	25,971.00	NA	25,971.00
Apr 69	26,159.00	NA	26,159.00
May 69	26,408.00	NA	26,408.00
Jun 69	26,769.00	NA	26,769.00
Jul 69	27,021.00	NA	27,021.00

(continued)

Month, year	Total	Revolving	Nonrevolving
Aug 69	27,246.00	NA	27,246.00
Sep 69	27,304.00	NA	27,304.00
Oct 69	27,441.00	NA	27,441.00
Nov 69	27,575.00	NA	27,575.00
Dec 69	27,846.00	NA	27,846.00
Jan 70	27,612.00	NA	27,612.00
Feb 70	27,508.00	NA	27,508.00
Mar 70	27,330.00	NA	27,330.00
Apr 70	27,361.00	NA	27,361.00
May 70	27,348.00	NA	27,348.00
Jun 70	27,543.00	NA	27,543.00
Jul 70	27,237.00	NA	27,237.00
Aug 70	27,452.00	NA	27,452.00
Sep 70	27,525.00	NA	27,525.00
Oct 70	27,540.00	NA	27,540.00
Nov 70	27,464.00	NA	27,464.00
Dec 70	27,580.00	NA	27,580.00
Jan 71	27,369.00	NA	27,369.00
Feb 71	27,286.00	NA	27,286.00
Mar 71	27,218.00	NA	27,218.00
Apr 71	27,330.00	NA	27,330.00
May 71	27,437.00	NA	27,437.00
Jun 71	27,600.00	NA	27,600.00
Jul 71	27,947.00	NA	27,947.00
Aug 71	28,188.00	NA	28,188.00
Sep 71	28,252.00	NA	28,252.00
Oct 71	28,443.00	NA	28,443.00
Nov 71	28,763.00	NA	28,763.00
Dec 71	29,224.00	NA	29,224.00
Jan 72	29,092.00	NA	29,092.00
Feb 72	29,103.00	NA	29,103.00
Mar 72	29,184.00	NA	29,184.00
Apr 72	29,440.00	NA	29,440.00
May 72	29,823.00	NA	29,823.00
Jun 72	30,273.00	NA	30,273.00

Month, year	Total	Revolving	Nonrevolving
Jul 72	30,582.00	NA	30,582.00
Aug 72	30,936.00	NA	30,936.00
Sep 72	31,007.00	NA	31,007.00
Oct 72	31,104.00	NA	31,104.00
Nov 72	31,407.00	NA	31,407.00
Dec 72	31,893.00	NA	31,893.00
Jan 73	31,783.00	NA	31,783.00
Feb 73	31,877.00	NA	31,877.00
Mar 73	31,947.00	NA	31,947.00
Apr 73	32,170.00	NA	32,170.00
May 73	32,673.00	NA	32,673.00
Jun 73	33,139.00	NA	33,139.00
Jul 73	33,625.00	NA	33,625.00
Aug 73	34,120.00	NA	34,120.00
Sep 73	34,356.00	NA	34,356.00
Oct 73	34,708.00	NA	34,708.00
Nov 73	35,050.00	NA	35,050.00
Dec 73	35,359.00	NA	35,359.00
Jan 74	35,148.00	NA	35,148.00
Feb 74	35,110.00	NA	35,110.00
Mar 74	34,860.00	NA	34,860.00
Apr 74	35,032.00	NA	35,032.00
May 74	35,388.00	NA	35,388.00
Jun 74	35,723.00	NA	35,723.00
Jul 74	35,971.00	NA	35,971.00
Aug 74	36,340.00	NA	36,340.00
Sep 74	36,301.00	NA	36,301.00
Oct 74	36,190.00	NA	36,190.00
Nov 74	36,059.00	NA	36,059.00
Dec 74	36,087.00	NA	36,087.00
Jan 75	35,598.00	NA	35,598.00
Feb 75	35,442.00	NA	35,442.00
Mar 75	34,997.00	NA	34,997.00
Apr 75	34,824.00	NA	34,824.00

(continued)

Month, year	Total	Revolving	Nonrevolving
May 75	34,790.00	NA	34,790.00
Jun 75	32,197.00	NA	32,197.00
Jul 75	32,440.00	NA	32,440.00
Aug 75	32,478.00	NA	32,478.00
Sep 75	32,358.00	NA	32,358.00
Oct 75	32,298.00	NA	32,298.00
Nov 75	32,403.00	NA	32,403.00
Dec 75	32,570.00	NA	32,570.00
Jan 76	32,261.00	NA	32,261.00
Feb 76	32,061.00	NA	32,061.00
Mar 76	31,935.00	NA	31,935.00
Apr 76	32,117.00	NA	32,117.00
May 76	32,268.00	NA	32,268.00
Jun 76	32,625.00	NA	32,625.00
Jul 76	32,908.00	NA	32,908.00
Aug 76	33,120.00	NA	33,120.00
Sep 76	33,136.00	NA	33,136.00
Oct 76	34,020.00	NA	34,020.00
Nov 76	34,208.00	NA	34,208.00
Dec 76	33,704.00	NA	33,704.00
Jan 77	33,769.00	NA	33,769.00
Feb 77	33,717.00	NA	33,717.00
Mar 77	33,902.00	NA	33,902.00
Apr 77	34,142.00	NA	34,142.00
May 77	34,576.00	NA	34,576.00
Jun 77	35,026.00	NA	35,026.00
Jul 77	35,574.00	NA	35,574.00
Aug 77	36,030.00	NA	36,030.00
Sep 77	36,241.00	NA	36,241.00
Oct 77	37,965.00	NA	37,965.00
Nov 77	38,553.00	NA	38,553.00
Dec 77	37,314.00	NA	37,314.00
Jan 78	37,341.00	NA	37,341.00
Feb 78	37,346.00	NA	37,346.00
Mar 78	37,600.00	NA	37,600.00

Month, year	Total	Revolving	Nonrevolving
Apr 78	38,156.00	NA	38,156.00
May 78	38,954.00	NA	38,954.00
Jun 78	39,858.00	NA	39,858.00
Jul 78	40,533.00	NA	40,533.00
Aug 78	41,405.00	NA	41,405.00
Sep 78	41,952.00	NA	41,952.00
Oct 78	42,489.00	NA	42,489.00
Nov 78	43,415.00	NA	43,415.00
Dec 78	44,448.00	NA	44,448.00
Jan 79	44,977.00	NA	44,977.00
Feb 79	45,472.00	NA	45,472.00
Mar 79	46,420.00	NA	46,420.00
Apr 79	47,547.00	NA	47,547.00
May 79	48,551.00	NA	48,551.00
Jun 79	49,743.00	NA	49,743.00
Jul 79	50,911.00	NA	50,911.00
Aug 79	51,512.00	NA	51,512.00
Sep 79	52,697.00	NA	52,697.00
Oct 79	53,311.00	NA	53,311.00
Nov 79	54,551.00	NA	54,551.00
Dec 79	55,445.00	NA	55,445.00
Jan 80	56,865.00	NA	56,865.00
Feb 80	57,461.00	NA	57,461.00
Mar 80	58,074.00	NA	58,074.00
Apr 80	58,906.00	NA	58,906.00
May 80	59,211.00	NA	59,211.00
Jun 80	61,353.00	NA	61,353.00
Jul 80	61,799.00	NA	61,799.00
Aug 80	61,854.00	NA	61,854.00
Sep 80	61,949.00	NA	61,949.00
Oct 80	62,063.00	NA	62,063.00
Nov 80	61,754.00	NA	61,754.00
Dec 80	62,248.00	NA	62,248.00
Jan 81	62,328.00	NA	62,328.00

(continued)

Month, year	Total	Revolving	Nonrevolving
Feb 81	62,516.00	NA	62,516.00
Mar 81	63,411.00	NA	63,411.00
Apr 81	63,916.00	NA	63,916.00
May 81	64,353.00	NA	64,353.00
Jun 81	64,827.00	NA	64,827.00
Jul 81	65,508.00	NA	65,508.00
Aug 81	66,007.00	NA	66,007.00
Sep 81	69,096.00	NA	69,096.00
Oct 81	69,526.00	NA	69,526.00
Nov 81	70,122.00	NA	70,122.00
Dec 81	70,070.00	NA	70,070.00
Jan 82	71,181.00	NA	71,181.00
Feb 82	70,869.00	NA	70,869.00
Mar 82	71,072.00	NA	71,072.00
Apr 82	71,905.00	NA	71,905.00
May 82	73,297.00	NA	73,297.00
Jun 82	74,050.00	NA	74,050.00
Jul 82	73,862.00	NA	73,862.00
Aug 82	73,874.00	NA	73,874.00
Sep 82	73,942.00	NA	73,942.00
Oct 82	73,501.00	NA	73,501.00
Nov 82	74,410.00	NA	74,410.00
Dec 82	75,271.00	NA	75,271.00
Jan 83	75,556.00	NA	75,556.00
Feb 83	75,542.00	NA	75,542.00
Mar 83	77,087.00	NA	77,087.00
Apr 83	77,638.00	NA	77,638.00
May 83	78,348.00	NA	78,348.00
Jun 83	79,871.00	NA	79,871.00
Jul 83	80,688.00	NA	80,688.00
Aug 83	81,534.00	NA	81,534.00
Sep 83	81,777.00	NA	81,777.00
Oct 83	82,426.00	NA	82,426.00
Nov 83	83,081.00	NA	83,081.00
Dec 83	83,310.00	NA	83,310.00

Month, year	Total	Revolving	Nonrevolving
Jan 84	82,958.00	NA	82,958.00
Feb 84	82,704.00	NA	82,704.00
Mar 84	82,939.00	NA	82,939.00
Apr 84	83,378.00	NA	83,378.00
May 84	84,413.00	NA	84,413.00
Jun 84	85,743.00	NA	85,743.00
Jul 84	86,915.00	NA	86,915.00
Aug 84	87,970.00	NA	87,970.00
Sep 84	88,337.00	NA	88,337.00
Oct 84	88,931.00	NA	88,931.00
Nov 84	89,418.00	NA	89,418.00
Dec 84	89,883.00	80.00	89,803.00
Jan 85	89,714.00	295.00	89,419.00
Feb 85	90,026.00	510.00	89,516.00
Mar 85	91,715.00	725.00	90,990.00
Apr 85	93,961.00	940.00	93,021.00
May 85	96,740.00	1,155.00	95,585.00
Jun 85	97,935.00	1,370.00	96,565.00
Jul 85	99,967.00	1,585.00	98,382.00
Aug 85	102,257.00	1,800.00	100,457.00
Sep 85	108,503.00	2,015.00	106,488.00
Oct 85	111,031.00	2,230.00	108,801.00
Nov 85	111,182.00	2,445.00	108,737.00
Dec 85	111,656.00	2,660.00	108,996.00
Jan 86	113,183.00	2,875.00	110,308.00
Feb 86	114,150.00	3,090.00	111,060.00
Mar 86	115,207.00	3,305.00	111,902.00
Apr 86	116,809.00	3,520.00	113,289.00
May 86	119,679.00	3,735.00	115,944.00
Jun 86	122,950.00	3,950.00	119,000.00
Jul 86	126,043.00	4,165.00	121,878.00
Aug 86	128,119.00	4,380.00	123,739.00
Sep 86	134,756.00	4,595.00	130,161.00
Oct 86	137,500.00	4,810.00	132,690.00

(continued)

Month, year	Total	Revolving	Nonrevolving
Nov 86	135,680.00	5,025.00	130,655.00
Dec 86	134,002.00	5,240.00	128,762.00
Jan 87	131,676.00	5,455.00	126,221.00
Feb 87	130,410.00	5,670.00	124,740.00
Mar 87	130,339.00	5,885.00	124,454.00
Apr 87	131,490.00	6,100.00	125,390.00
May 87	131,803.00	6,315.00	125,488.00
Jun 87	133,862.00	6,530.00	127,332.00
Jul 87	135,949.00	6,745.00	129,204.00
Aug 87	138,098.00	6,960.00	131,138.00
Sep 87	140,570.00	7,175.00	133,395.00
Oct 87	141,315.00	7,390.00	133,925.00
Nov 87	140,462.00	7,605.00	132,857.00
Dec 87	140,025.00	7,820.00	132,205.00
Jan 88	139,906.00	8,035.00	131,871.00
Feb 88	139,765.00	8,250.00	131,515.00
Mar 88	140,268.00	8,465.00	131,803.00
Apr 88	141,136.00	8,680.00	132,456.00
May 88	141,783.00	8,895.00	132,888.00
Jun 88	143,070.00	9,110.00	133,960.00
Jul 88	143,503.00	9,325.00	134,178.00
Aug 88	144,381.00	9,540.00	134,841.00
Sep 88	144,833.00	9,755.00	135,078.00
Oct 88	145,027.00	9,970.00	135,057.00
Nov 88	144,540.00	10,185.00	134,355.00
Dec 88	144,677.00	10,400.00	134,277.00
Jan 89	139,605.00	10,615.00	128,990.00
Feb 89	138,587.00	10,830.00	127,757.00
Mar 89	137,454.00	11,045.00	126,409.00
Apr 89	138,968.00	11,260.00	127,708.00
May 89	140,489.00	11,475.00	129,014.00
Jun 89	142,103.00	11,690.00	130,413.00
Jul 89	142,633.00	11,905.00	130,728.00
Aug 89	143,205.00	12,120.00	131,085.00
Sep 89	144,432.00	12,335.00	132,097.00

Month, year	Total	Revolving	Nonrevolving
Oct 89	141,472.00	12,550.00	128,922.00
Nov 89	140,864.00	12,765.00	128,099.00
Dec 89	138,858.00	12,980.00	125,878.00
Jan 90	138,453.00	13,195.00	125,258.00
Feb 90	136,479.00	13,410.00	123,069.00
Mar 90	134,945.00	13,625.00	121,320.00
Apr 90	134,949.00	13,840.00	121,109.00
May 90	134,847.00	14,055.00	120,792.00
Jun 90	134,791.00	14,270.00	120,521.00
Jul 90	137,389.00	14,485.00	122,904.00
Aug 90	137,649.00	14,700.00	122,949.00
Sep 90	138,788.00	14,915.00	123,873.00
Oct 90	139,215.00	15,130.00	124,085.00
Nov 90	136,329.00	15,345.00	120,984.00
Dec 90	133,394.00	15,560.00	117,834.00
Jan 91	131,249.00	15,775.00	115,474.00
Feb 91	128,806.00	15,990.00	112,816.00
Mar 91	126,862.00	16,205.00	110,657.00
Apr 91	127,463.00	16,420.00	111,043.00
May 91	127,762.00	16,635.00	111,127.00
Jun 91	127,477.00	16,850.00	110,627.00
Jul 91	127,316.00	17,065.00	110,251.00
Aug 91	128,868.00	17,280.00	111,588.00
Sep 91	124,407.00	17,495.00	106,912.00
Oct 91	123,320.00	17,710.00	105,610.00
Nov 91	122,356.00	17,925.00	104,431.00
Dec 91	121,563.00	18,140.00	103,423.00
Jan 92	118,915.00	18,355.00	100,560.00
Feb 92	120,808.00	18,570.00	102,238.00
Mar 92	118,916.00	18,785.00	100,131.00
Apr 92	118,677.00	19,000.00	99,677.00
May 92	116,511.00	19,215.00	97,296.00
Jun 92	116,981.00	19,430.00	97,551.00
Jul 92	117,440.00	19,645.00	97,795.00

(continued)

Month, year	Total	Revolving	Nonrevolving
Aug 92	117,972.00	19,860.00	98,112.00
Sep 92	117,476.00	20,075.00	97,401.00
Oct 92	117,069.00	20,290.00	96,779.00
Nov 92	117,450.00	20,505.00	96,945.00
Dec 92	118,052.00	20,720.00	97,332.00
Jan 93	116,815.00	20,935.00	95,880.00
Feb 93	113,386.00	21,150.00	92,236.00
Mar 93	112,398.00	21,365.00	91,033.00
Apr 93	112,923.00	21,580.00	91,343.00
May 93	108,268.00	21,795.00	86,473.00
Jun 93	110,302.00	22,010.00	88,292.00
Jul 93	111,904.00	22,225.00	89,679.00
Aug 93	110,743.00	22,440.00	88,303.00
Sep 93	110,733.00	22,655.00	88,078.00
Oct 93	111,343.00	22,870.00	88,473.00
Nov 93	113,379.00	23,085.00	90,294.00
Dec 93	116,134.00	23,300.00	92,834.00
Jan 94	117,157.00	23,515.00	93,642.00
Feb 94	117,701.00	23,730.00	93,971.00
Mar 94	119,772.00	23,945.00	95,827.00
Apr 94	122,457.00	24,160.00	98,297.00
May 94	121,848.00	24,375.00	97,473.00
Jun 94	123,954.00	24,590.00	99,364.00
Jul 94	122,830.00	24,805.00	98,025.00
Aug 94	124,818.00	25,020.00	99,798.00
Sep 94	130,010.00	25,235.00	104,775.00
Oct 94	131,168.00	25,450.00	105,718.00
Nov 94	132,472.00	25,665.00	106,807.00
Dec 94	134,421.00	25,880.00	108,541.00
Jan 95	137,051.00	26,095.00	110,956.00
Feb 95	134,333.00	26,310.00	108,023.00
Mar 95	135,358.00	26,525.00	108,833.00
Apr 95	137,364.00	26,740.00	110,624.00
May 95	139,185.00	26,955.00	112,230.00
Jun 95	141,289.00	27,170.00	114,119.00

Month, year	Total	Revolving	Nonrevolving
Jul 95	141,701.00	27,385.00	114,316.00
Aug 95	145,052.00	27,600.00	117,452.00
Sep 95	145,724.00	27,815.00	117,909.00
Oct 95	148,196.00	28,030.00	120,166.00
Nov 95	148,265.00	28,245.00	120,020.00
Dec 95	152,123.00	28,460.00	123,663.00
Jan 96	152,099.00	28,675.00	123,424.00
Feb 96	153,850.00	28,890.00	124,960.00
Mar 96	152,515.00	29,105.00	123,410.00
Apr 96	154,339.00	29,320.00	125,019.00
May 96	156,071.00	29,535.00	126,536.00
Jun 96	153,864.58	29,749.87	124,114.71
Jul 96	156,221.48	29,896.81	126,324.66
Aug 96	155,518.93	29,010.93	126,507.99
Sep 96	155,838.52	29,164.27	126,674.24
Oct 96	153,028.52	29,252.15	123,776.38
Nov 96	153,064.84	29,410.18	123,654.66
Dec 96	154,897.33	31,955.55	122,941.78
Jan 97	156,412.65	31,635.81	124,776.84
Feb 97	156,616.90	31,489.84	125,127.05
Mar 97	157,596.00	33,260.60	124,335.40
Apr 97	156,874.11	34,248.17	122,625.94
May 97	159,528.94	34,182.69	125,346.25
Jun 97	161,670.69	33,788.71	127,881.98
Jul 97	161,865.54	32,296.87	129,568.67
Aug 97	163,000.74	32,289.65	130,711.09
Sep 97	164,693.95	33,582.04	131,111.91
Oct 97	163,551.74	33,284.51	130,267.23
Nov 97	164,077.38	33,266.97	130,810.41
Dec 97	167,541.75	36,996.79	130,544.97
Jan 98	167,431.17	35,901.90	131,529.27
Feb 98	164,030.11	35,060.25	128,969.86
Mar 98	165,253.36	34,732.86	130,520.50
Apr 98	169,681.80	34,591.16	135,090.64

(continued)

Month, year	Total	Revolving	Nonrevolving
May 98	169,347.13	34,618.01	134,729.13
Jun 98	170,363.30	33,805.55	136,557.75
Jul 98	172,532.11	33,087.85	139,444.27
Aug 98	176,422.98	33,236.36	143,186.63
Sep 98	176,173.69	31,710.60	144,463.09
Oct 98	179,663.09	33,194.45	146,468.64
Nov 98	181,112.38	32,834.44	148,277.94
Dec 98	183,344.83	31,943.76	151,401.06
Jan 99	182,235.88	31,617.85	150,618.03
Feb 99	184,647.83	30,945.05	153,702.78
Mar 99	183,843.73	30,484.16	153,359.56
Apr 99	186,600.31	30,533.53	156,066.78
May 99	185,359.85	30,410.64	154,949.20
Jun 99	190,986.63	31,513.93	159,472.70
Jul 99	191,192.43	31,893.60	159,298.83
Aug 99	195,578.46	31,983.83	163,594.63
Sep 99	191,458.47	29,446.89	162,011.58
Oct 99	193,084.38	30,131.56	162,952.81
Nov 99	194,679.08	29,033.27	165,645.81
Dec 99	201,641.62	32,483.27	169,158.34
Jan 00	205,458.36	32,971.42	172,486.94
Feb 00	207,819.94	31,308.56	176,511.38
Mar 00	204,990.09	29,687.96	175,302.13
Apr 00	205,800.87	30,104.45	175,696.42
May 00	209,769.87	29,693.18	180,076.69
Jun 00	212,963.38	31,142.39	181,820.98
Jul 00	221,008.60	32,472.85	188,535.75
Aug 00	226,338.79	33,363.81	192,974.98
Sep 00	229,054.84	34,166.56	194,888.28
Oct 00	235,720.69	36,140.94	199,579.75
Nov 00	235,312.67	37,171.48	198,141.19
Dec 00	234,448.64	38,724.98	195,723.66
Jan 01	230,393.55	37,428.89	192,964.66
Feb 01	233,369.44	37,595.47	195,773.97
Mar 01	234,693.81	36,649.88	198,043.94

Month, year	Total	Revolving	Nonrevolving
Apr 01	241,761.88	37,369.05	204,392.83
May 01	244,337.22	39,111.57	205,225.66
Jun 01	243,266.30	39,109.11	204,157.19
Jul 01	246,990.41	38,839.88	208,150.53
Aug 01	256,931.82	38,604.09	218,327.73
Sep 01	257,163.63	38,709.47	218,454.16
Oct 01	262,924.78	31,467.64	231,457.14
Nov 01	279,919.43	33,409.47	246,509.95
Dec 01	279,970.22	34,833.69	245,136.53
Jan 02	275,973.81	33,291.77	242,682.05
Feb 02	281,526.63	32,555.25	248,971.38
Mar 02	283,077.21	31,811.36	251,265.84
Apr 02	284,378.41	33,713.96	250,664.45
May 02	287,993.56	34,283.89	253,709.67
Jun 02	294,055.16	36,525.10	257,530.06
Jul 02	303,156.49	41,146.88	262,009.61
Aug 02	303,579.85	41,288.57	262,291.28
Sep 02	312,437.98	42,223.39	270,214.59
Oct 02	307,904.77	42,477.58	265,427.19
Nov 02	300,522.33	42,323.74	258,198.59
Dec 02	307,518.48	44,440.36	263,078.13
Jan 03	310,592.14	44,459.96	266,132.19
Feb 03	314,439.76	43,805.04	270,634.72
Mar 03	309,920.86	42,375.67	267,545.19
Apr 03	319,867.35	43,833.88	276,033.47
May 03	321,142.61	40,905.99	280,236.63
Jun 03	327,925.55	41,198.93	286,726.63
Jul 03	350,249.04	42,209.91	308,039.13
Aug 03	364,673.62	44,357.09	320,316.53
Sep 03	374,642.75	44,424.07	330,218.69
Oct 03	382,962.97	45,025.66	337,937.31
Nov 03	387,735.86	47,473.02	340,262.84
Dec 03	393,043.94	45,265.69	347,778.25
Jan 04	402,125.31	47,148.59	354,976.72

(continued)

Month, year	Total	Revolving	Nonrevolving
Feb 04	406,048.30	46,378.11	359,670.19
Mar 04	411,969.73	45,825.32	366,144.41
Apr 04	418,162.34	46,119.16	372,043.19
May 04	429,357.75	46,258.50	383,099.25
Jun 04	436,237.99	48,675.96	387,562.03
Jul 04	444,923.20	50,356.57	394,566.63
Aug 04	455,209.59	50,475.43	404,734.16
Sep 04	471,117.78	54,717.81	416,399.97
Oct 04	484,519.84	57,187.43	427,332.41
Nov 04	496,400.47	60,157.34	436,243.13
Dec 04	492,345.95	50,382.20	441,963.75
Jan 05	487,185.16	50,825.07	436,360.09
Feb 05	491,460.39	52,471.52	438,988.88
Mar 05	493,381.47	52,048.41	441,333.06
Apr 05	494,545.57	53,267.14	441,278.44
May 05	494,926.22	54,268.41	440,657.81
Jun 05	495,057.84	55,481.37	439,576.47
Jul 05	496,333.11	56,646.27	439,686.84
Aug 05	501,462.84	56,696.40	444,766.44
Sep 05	508,424.50	57,690.82	450,733.69
Oct 05	512,461.04	58,934.45	453,526.59
Nov 05	514,384.58	60,123.45	454,261.13
Dec 05	516,533.57	66,307.45	450,226.13
Jan 06	517,114.48	65,627.83	451,486.66
Feb 06	501,406.78	64,801.59	436,605.19
Mar 06	499,499.27	63,746.59	435,752.69
Apr 06	501,788.66	65,315.54	436,473.13
May 06	497,050.32	67,466.16	429,584.16
Jun 06	504,985.31	69,466.81	435,518.50
Jul 06	512,586.20	70,589.32	441,996.88
Aug 06	523,095.38	71,552.03	451,543.34
Sep 06	526,167.97	72,156.91	454,011.06
Oct 06	527,169.53	74,246.03	452,923.50
Nov 06	529,729.81	76,606.75	453,123.06
Dec 06	534,353.95	79,874.45	454,479.50

Month, year	Total	Revolving	Nonrevolving
Jan 07	531,945.04	77,810.16	454,134.88
Feb 07	527,114.34	75,595.77	451,518.56
Mar 07	532,001.35	72,947.35	459,054.00
Apr 07	535,220.03	73,595.16	461,624.88
May 07	540,479.16	74,453.66	466,025.50
Jun 07	542,641.09	75,083.09	467,558.00
Jul 07	554,017.27	76,378.02	477,639.25
Aug 07	566,484.30	77,455.39	489,028.91
Sep 07	567,631.73	78,347.48	489,284.25
Oct 07	569,719.94	80,562.06	489,157.88
Nov 07	574,026.04	82,947.66	491,078.38
Dec 07	584,055.60	86,046.01	498,009.59
Jan 08	579,490.84	84,894.59	494,596.25
Feb 08	576,953.88	83,447.13	493,506.75
Mar 08	580,715.45	82,065.36	498,650.09
Apr 08	583,920.07	83,073.38	500,846.69
May 08	584,492.28	83,897.69	500,594.59
Jun 08	581,772.70	84,035.26	497,737.44
Jul 08	586,523.53	83,856.41	502,667.13
Aug 08	592,375.80	83,627.40	508,748.41
Sep 08	596,256.52	83,310.09	512,946.44
Oct 08	585,813.58	77,007.02	508,806.56
Nov 08	580,708.83	75,490.02	505,218.81
Dec 08	575,764.31	74,418.27	501,346.05
Jan 09	555,504.93	61,429.32	494,075.61
Feb 09	546,880.43	55,810.86	491,069.56

NA = not available
Source: Federal Reserve Board

Appendix 5

Mortgage Debt Outstanding
(millions of dollars, end of period)

Type of holder and property	2004	2005	2006	2007Q4	2008Q1	2008Q2	2008Q3	2008Q4
All holders	10,663,749	12,101,261	13,487,850	14,568,485	14,695,367	14,736,703	14,706,022	14,639,295
By type of property								
One- to four-family residences	8,269,026	9,380,898	10,433,398	11,128,203	11,192,416	11,180,238	11,124,499	11,033,793
Multifamily residences	617,866	688,533	744,002	843,123	861,838	878,333	892,939	895,796
Nonfarm, nonresidential	1,679,986	1,930,313	2,208,975	2,489,380	2,532,503	2,568,690	2,578,301	2,598,552
Farm	96,872	101,518	101,475	107,778	108,610	109,442	110,283	111,154
By type of holder								
Major financial institutions	3,926,324	4,396,243	4,780,819	5,067,153	5,129,005	5,113,578	5,072,173	5,036,033
Commercial banks	2,595,605	2,958,042	3,403,052	3,645,724	3,685,963	3,662,246	3,850,431	3,836,865
One- to four-family	1,580,992	1,793,029	2,084,510	2,208,229	2,217,309	2,157,985	2,287,714	2,250,629
Multifamily residences	118,710	138,702	157,555	168,407	172,942	176,145	210,224	209,852
Nonfarm, nonresidential	860,670	989,372	1,123,210	1,228,490	1,254,801	1,286,891	1,310,951	1,334,526
Farm	35,233	36,939	37,777	40,598	40,911	41,225	41,542	41,858
Savings Institutions	1,057,395	1,152,738	1,073,967	1,095,256	1,111,766	1,115,558	883,637	860,265
One- to four-family	874,199	953,819	867,831	878,958	884,834	884,534	691,595	666,381
Multifamily residences	87,545	98,352	95,792	92,705	94,588	96,924	65,202	65,230
Nonfarm, nonresidential	95,052	99,951	109,604	122,711	131,434	133,187	125,949	127,736
Farm	599	616	740	882	910	913	891	918
Life insurance companies	273,324	285,463	303,800	326,173	331,276	335,774	338,105	338,903
One- to four-family	7,874	7,746	11,028	10,991	11,227	11,385	11,372	11,397
Multifamily residences	40,453	42,440	46,078	51,837	52,498	52,908	52,974	53,000
Nonfarm, nonresidential	214,085	224,258	235,402	252,193	256,313	260,157	262,348	263,007
Farm	10,912	11,019	11,292	11,152	11,238	11,324	11,411	11,498

Source: Federal Reserve Board

Appendix 6

Residential Mortgage Originations

Year	Amount (trillions of dollars)
1990	0.46
1991	0.56
1992	0.89
1993	1.02
1994	0.77
1995	0.64
1996	0.79
1997	0.83
1998	1.51
1999	1.29
2000	1.02
2001	2.03
2002	2.48
2003	3.81
2004	2.77
2005	2.78
2006	2.82
2007	2.31
2008	1.61

Source: MortgageDaily.com

Bibliography

Altman, Edward I. "Financial Ratios, Discriminant Analysis and the Prediction of Corporate Bankruptcy." *Journal of Finance* (September 1968): 189–209.

Anders, George. *Merchants of Debt: KKR and the Mortgaging of American Business.* New York: Basic Books, 1992.

Baskin, Jonathan B., and Paul J. Miranti. *A History of Corporate Finance.* New York: Cambridge University Press, 1997.

Bird, Edward J., Paul A. Hagstrom, and Robert Wild. "Credit Card Debts of the Poor: High and Rising." *Journal of Policy Analysis and Management*, Vol. 18, No. 1: 125–134.

Block, Kenneth M., and Jeffrey B. Steiner. "Usury: Voiding Criminally Usurious Loans Under the Civil Usury Law." *New York Law Journal*, Vol. 228, No. 10 (July 17, 2002): 1–3.

Brown, Tom, and Lacey Plache. "Paying with Plastic: Maybe Not So Crazy." *The University of Chicago Law Review*, Vol. 73, No. 1 (Winter 2006): 63–87.

Caldor, Lendel. *Financing the American Dream: A Cultural History of Consumer Credit.* Princeton, NJ: Princeton University Press, 1999.

Canner, Glenn B., and Wayne Passmore. "Credit Risk and the Provision of Mortgages to Lower-Income and Minority Homebuyers." *Federal Reserve Bulletin*, Vol. 81, No. 11 (November 1995): 989–1017.

Chandler, Lester D., Jr. *The Visible Hand: The Managerial Revolution in American Business.* Cambridge, MA: Harvard University Press, 1977.

Cisneros, Henry G. "Achieving the American Dream." *Christian Science Monitor*, November 28, 1995.

Culp, Christopher L. *Structured Finance and Insurance: The ART of Managing Capital and Risk.* Hoboken, NJ: John Wiley & Sons, 2006.

Cunningham, William H., and Isabella Cunningham. "Consumer Protection: More Information or More Regulation." *Journal of Marketing,* Vol. 40, No. 2 (April 1976): 63–69.

El-Erian, Mohamed. *When Markets Collide: Investment Strategies for the Age of Global Economic Change.* New York: McGraw-Hill, 2008.

Evans, David S., and Richard Schmalensee. *Paying with Plastic: The Digital Revolution in Buying and Borrowing.* Cambridge, MA: MIT Press, 1999.

Fabricant, Solomon. "Toward a Firmer Basis of Economic Policy: The Founding of the National Bureau of Economic Research." National Bureau of Economic Research, 1984, http://www.nber.org/nberhistory/sfabricant.pdf.

Flannery, Mark J. "Supervising Bank Safety and Soundness: Some Open Issues." *Economic Review*, Vol. 92, No. 1/2 (2007): 83–101.

Friedman, Benjamin, ed. *The Changing Roles of Debt and Equity in Financing U.S. Capital Formation.* Chicago: University of Chicago Press, 1982.

Geisst, Charles R. *Undue Influence: How the Wall Street Elite Put the Financial System at Risk.* Hoboken, NJ: John Wiley & Sons, 2005.

―――. *Visionary Capitalism: Financial Markets and the American Dream in the Twentieth Century.* New York: Praeger, 1990.

General Accountability Office (GAO). "Information on Recent Default and Foreclosure Trends for Home Mortgages and Associated Economic and Market Developments." GAO-08-78R (October 16, 2007), http://www.gao.gov/products/GAO-08-78R.

―――. "Credit Cards: Customized Minimum Payment Disclosures Would Provide More Information to Customers but Impact Could Vary." GAO-06-434 (April 2006), http://www.gao.gov/new.items/d06434.pdf.

―――. "Credit Cards: Increased Complexity in Rates and Fees Heightens Need for More Effective Disclosures to Consumers." GAO-06-929 (September 2006), http://www.gao.gov/highlights/d06929high.pdf.

Gosselin, Peter. *High Wire: The Precarious Financial Lives of American Families*. New York: Basic Books, 2008.

Graham, Ann. "Deposit Insurance Reform: What's on the Table and What Will It Cost?" *Texas Banking*, Vol. 91, No. 5 (May 2002): 48–49.

Greenspan, Alan. *The Age of Turbulence: Adventures in a New World*. New York: Penguin Books, 2007.

Heatherly, Charles L., ed. *Mandate for Leadership: Policy Management in a Conservative Administration*. Washington, DC: Heritage Foundation, 1981.

Hendrickson, Robert A. *The Cashless Society*. New York: Dodd, Mead, 1972.

Kaufman, Henry. *On Money and Markets: A Wall Street Memoir*. New York: McGraw-Hill, 2000.

Krainer, John. "The Separation of Banking and Commerce." *Economic Review*, Federal Reserve Bank of San Francisco, 2000, http://www.frbsf.org/econrsrch/econrev/2000/article2.pdf.

Langley, Monica. *Tearing Down the Walls*. New York: Simon & Schuster, 2003.

Lobell, Carl D. "State Usury Laws." *The Banking Law Journal*, Vol. 102, No. 4 (July 1985): 349–361.

Mandell, Lewis. *Credit Card Use in the United States*. Ann Arbor: University of Michigan, 1972.

Mann, Ronald. *Charging Ahead: The Growth and Regulation of Payment Card Markets Around the World*. New York: Cambridge University Press, 2007.

Manning, Robert D. *Credit Card Nation: The Consequences of America's Addiction to Debt*. New York: Basic Books, 2000.

Markowitz, Harry. "Portfolio Selection." *Journal of Finance*, Vol. 7, No. 1 (March 1952): 77–91.

Meltzer, Allan. *A History of the Federal Reserve, 1913–1951*. Chicago: University of Chicago Press, 2004.

Modigliani, Franco, and Merton H. Miller. "The Cost of Capital, Corporation Finance, and the Theory of Investment." *American Economic Review*, Vol. 48, No. 3 (June 1958): 261–297.

———. "Dividend Policy, Growth and the Valuation of Shares." *Journal of Business*, Vol. 34, No. 4 (1961): 411–433.

Nader, Ralph. "Don't Privatize the GSEs—Federalize." *American Banker*, Vol. 170, No. 48 (March 11, 2005): 10.

Post, Mitchell A. "The Evolution of the U.S. Commercial Paper Market Since 1980." *Federal Reserve Bulletin*, Vol. 78, No. 12 (December 1992): 879–891.

Reagan, Ronald. *The Reagan Diaries*. New York: Harper Collins, 2007.

Seligman, Joel. *The Transformation of Wall Street: A History of the Securities and Exchange Commission and Modern Corporate Finance*. Boston: Houghton-Mifflin, 1982.

Seltzer, Lawrence H. *A Financial History of the American Automobile Industry*. Boston: Houghton-Mifflin, 1928.

Sharpe, William F. "Capital Asset Prices: A Theory of Market Equilibrium Under Conditions of Risk." *Journal of Finance*, Vol. 19, No. 3: 425–442.

Soros, George. *The New Paradigm for Financial Markets: The Credit Crash of 2008 and What It Means*. New York: PublicAffairs, 2008.

Stanton, Thomas H. "The Life Cycle of the Government-Sponsored Enterprise: Lessons for Design and Accountability." *Public Administration Review*, Vol. 67, No. 5 (September–October 2007): 837–845.

———. *Government Sponsored Enterprises: Mercantilist Companies in the Modern World*. Washington, DC: AEI Press, 2002.

———. *A State of Risk: Will Government-Sponsored Enterprises Be the Next Financial Crisis?* New York: Harper Business, 1991.

Sullivan, Teresa, Elizabeth Warren, and Jay Lawrence Westbrook. *The Fragile Middle Class: Americans in Debt*. New Haven, CT: Yale University Press, 2000.

———. *As We Forgive Our Debtors: Bankruptcy and Consumer Credit in America*. New York: Oxford University Press, 1989.

Thatcher, Margaret. *The Downing Street Years*. New York: Harper-Collins, 1993.

Thomas, D. L., and N. E. Evans, "John Shakespeare in The Exchequer." *Shakespeare Quarterly*, Vol. 35, No. 3: 125–137.

United States Department of Commerce. *Historical Statistics of the United States: Colonial Times to 1957*. Washington, DC: U.S. Government Printing Office, 1957.

Warren, Elizabeth. "Unsafe at Any Rate." *Democracy*, No. 5 (Summer 2007): 1–4.

Watro, Paul. "The Bank Credit Card Boom: Some Explanations and Consequences." Federal Reserve Bank of Cleveland, *Economic Commentary*, March 1, 1988.

Zweig, Phillip L. *Wriston: Walter Wriston, Citibank, and the Rise and Fall of American Financial Supremacy.* New York: Crown Publishers, 1996.

Index

A&P (Great Atlantic & Pacific
    Tea Co.), 36
Abbey Building Society Ltd., 156
Adams, James Truslow, 207
adjustable rate mortgages (ARMs),
    9–10, 76–77, 122, 134–140,
    149
Alliance & Leicester, 156
Alternative-A and subprime
    mortgage market, 137, 144,
    145–147
alternative mortgage product
    (AMP), 148–149
Altman, Edward, 70
American Bankers Association
    (ABA), 29, 39, 105
American Dream, use of term, 207
American Express Co. and card,
    55–56, 62, 85, 87, 90, 110,
    111, 200, 202
    Optima Card, 98
American Rediscount Corp., 44
Ameriquest Mortgage Co., 146
Annunzio, Frank, 97
antipredatory law, 189–190
asset-backed security (ABS),
    100–102, 112–115, 212
    in the United Kingdom, 157

AT&T (American Telegraph and
    Telephone Co.), 38
automobile industry
    financial subsidiaries, 90
    following World War II, 61
    in the 1920s, 36, 42, 43

baby-boomer generation, 163–166
balloon mortgages, 138
balloon payments, 9
BankAmericard (Visa), 62, 88, 93
bankers, popular views of, 37–38
Bankers Trust Co., 97
Bank for International Settlements
    (BIS), 80–81, 127, 129,
    185, 199
Bank Holding Company Act, 86, 103
Banking Act (1933), 72
banking houses, 6
banking industry
    failure of banks and thrifts in
        the 1980s, 80
    financial subsidiaries, formation
        of, 89
    financial subsidiaries, relocation
        of, 95–98
    international, 73–74
    interstate, 90

banking industry (*continued*)
    investment and insurance
        businesses, 106
    in the 1920s, 41
    in the 1950s, 60
    savings and loan (S&L) crisis,
        127–130
Bank of America, 41, 48, 62, 93, 105,
    110, 111, 144
Bank of Italy, 41
Bank of New York, 96–97
Bank of United States, 48
bankruptcy, statistics on, 221
Bankruptcy Abuse Prevention
    and Consumer Protection
    Act, 108
bankruptcy laws
    changes in the 1970s and 1980s,
        77–78
    early, 15–16
    reforms, 107–111
bankruptcy remote, 102
bankruptcy risk, Z ratio for
    predicting, 70
Barclays, 157
Bear Stearns, 143–144
Bellamy, Edward, 85–86
Belmont & Co., 14
Belmont family, 14, 37
Bernanke, Ben, 184
Bernard of Clarveaux, St., 75
beta coefficients, 69–70
Biggins, John, 62
Blair, Tony, 208
bonds
    collateral backing, 100–102
    covered, 132, 157
    following World War II, 63–64
    junk, 80, 128–129
    subprime-backed, 112–113
    zero-coupon, 23, 120
Book of Calculations (Fibonacci), 46
Book of Squares (Fibonacci), 46
Bradford & Bingley, 156

Brazil, 172
Britain, 110, 155–159, 208
Brown, Gordon, 208
Bush, George H. W., 129, 180
Bush, George W, 4, 119, 137,
    181, 208

call money market, 64
cannibal consumption, 10, 13
capital asset pricing model (CAPM),
    69–70, 71
capital gains, 142, 166, 185, 189
Capital One, 111
caps, 76–77
Carey, Hugh, 94
Carnegie Steel Co., 54
carry trade, 167–170
Carte Blanche, 87
Carter administration, 90–91, 110
certificates of auto receivables
    (CARs), 99
Chandler Act (1938), 77
Chao, Elaine, 166
Chapter 7, 78, 108–109
Chapter 11, 77, 78
Chapter 13, 78, 108, 109
charged-off debt, 105, 106, 108
Charg-It, 62
Chase Manhattan Bank, 72, 93,
    96, 110
chattel mortgage, 190
Chaucer, Geoffrey, 2
check cashing services, 16–17
Chemical Bank, 97
Chicago School of Economics, 68
Christmas clubs, 41–42
Chrysler, Walter, 54
Chrysler Corp., 54
Cisneros, Henry, 137
Citibank, 38, 48, 87, 93–95, 97, 109,
    110, 160
Citicorp, 89–91, 95–96, 97
Citigroup, 107, 111, 114, 144, 162
Citroën, 43

Clearing House Interbank Payments System (CHIPS), 203
Clinton administration, 4, 136–137, 142, 164
collar, 77
collateral, concept of, 42
collateralized debt obligations (CDOs), 132–134, 212
collateralized mortgage obligations (CMOs), 129–132, 144–145, 212
college students
  See also student loans
  preapproved credit card offers to, 104–106
commercial paper, 8, 89–90
  asset-backed, 101–102
Commodity Futures Modernization Act (2000), 195
Commodity Futures Trading Commission (CFTC), 163, 195
Community Reinvestment Act (CRA) (1977), 136
computers, role of, 63
conspicuous consumption, 12–13, 14, 37
consumer credit
  based on future ability, 54
  following World War II, 59–65
  historical development, 3–5, 13–18
  in the 1920s, 35–56
  Regulation Z, 73
  statistics, 219, 223–237, 239–253
consumer debt
  See also debt
  extent of problem, 28–33
  historical increase in, 10
consumerism
  changes covering four genera-tions, 18–23
  following World War II, 60–61
  in the 1920s, 35–56

Consumer Protection Act, 73
Cooper, Kent, 187
corporate bonds, 64
corporate credit, 36
corporate interest, 19
corporate taxes, first, 36
cost of equity, 70
Countrywide Financial Corp., 137, 144, 146, 148, 156
covered bonds, 132, 157
Cox, Christopher, 143, 163
CQMoneyLine, 187
Cramer, Jim, 123
Cranston-Gonzalez Affordable Housing Act (1990), 135
credit
  See also consumer credit; installment credit
  changing views toward, 7–8, 13–14
  as a commodity, 13
  debt, extent of problem, 28–33
  democratizing and lax extending of, 103–107
  need to change policies, 189
  politics and, 153–177
  revolving, 19, 88, 123–127
credit cards
  annual fees, 27, 91–92
  denying credit, 27–28
  early use of, 86–88
  fees and minimum payments, 24–27, 30, 91–95
  finance and credit card subsidiaries, relocation of, 95–98
  first, 62, 85
  funding needed for the development of, 89–91
  government regulation of, debate, 31–32
  impact of computers on, 63, 105–106
  increased use of, 16, 18

credit cards (*continued*)
    indebtedness, extent of problem,
        28–33
    issuers, top ten, 111
    late payment fees, 27
    minimum payment option,
        24–27, 30, 92–95
    payments system, 107
    payment system, privatizing the,
        200–204
    preapproved offers, 104–106
    rise of, 85–115
    securitization, 9, 81, 99–103
    statements, 28
    transaction costs and zero
        interest, 92
    Wall Street, role of, 33
credit default swaps (CDSs), 133, 192
credit enhancement, 102
credit rating agencies, reliance on,
    198–200
Czech Republic, 172

Dante, 5
Dean Witter Reynolds, 107
debit cards, 110, 201, 202
debt
    acceptance of, 7
    charged-off, 105, 106, 108
    changing attitudes toward, 14
    crisis, first, 15
    following World War II, 65–71
debt service ratio (DSR), 28–29
debt-to-equity ratios, following
    World War II, 66
Delaware, 96–97
Depository Institutions Act (DIA),
    127, 128
Depository Institutions
    Deregulation and Monetary
    Control Act (DIDMCA)
    (1980), 75–76, 80, 94, 121,
    127, 128, 195
deposit rates, 72

Depression of 1929, 56
derivatives, 24, 176, 191–193
Deutsche Bundesbank, 182
Dickens, Charles, 121
Dillon, Clarence, 53, 54, 55
Diners Club International, 62, 85, 87
Discover Card, 98, 107, 111, 200
diversification, theory of, 69, 70, 71
Dodge Brothers Co., 54
Dodge family, 53
Dreiser, Theodore, 207
Drexel Burnham Lambert, 128–129
Duer, William, 15
DuPont, 96
Durst family, 4

Edward III, 1–2, 184
E.F. Hutton & Co., 97
Eisenhower, Dwight D., 64, 125
Employee Retirement Income Secu-
    rity Act (ERISA), 165, 198
Enron, 113, 118, 162, 210
Esso, 88
European Central Bank (ECB), 182
"Everyone Ought to Be Rich"
    (Raskob), 37

Fannie Mae, 9, 60, 76, 81, 99, 124,
    126, 137, 143, 144, 147, 148,
    185, 186, 187
Federal-Aid Highway Act (1956), 61
Federal Deposit Insurance Corp.
    (FDIC), 135, 194–195
Federal Home Loan Bank Board,
    99, 126
Federal Housing Administration
    (FHA), 99, 124, 126
Federal Reserve
    formation of, 36
    policy differences between
        European policies and those
        of the, 182–183
Fedwire, 202, 203
Feldstein, Martin, 149

Fibonacci, Leonardo, 46–47
financial architecture, 23
financial crisis
    fixing, 190–194
    privatizing the payments system,
        200–204
    rating agencies, reliance on,
        198–200
    reform, levels of, 209–213
    safety net, 194–197
financial engineers, 23
Financial Institutions Recovery,
    Reconstruction and
    Enforcement Act (FIRREA)
    (1989), 129
financial obligations ratio (FOR),
    28–29
Financial Products Safety
    Commission, 210
financial services
    See also banking industry
    following World War II, 62, 65–66
    reform, levels of, 209–213
Financial Services Modernization
    Act (1999), 113, 136
financial subsidiaries
    formation of, 89
    relocation of, 95–98
Financial Times, 168, 174
First Boston, 100
Fisher, I., 40
Fitch's, 198
Flegenheimer, Arthur. *See*
    Schultz, Dutch
float, 55–56
floating-rate debt, 121
Ford Motor Co., 43, 67, 71
Franklin, Benjamin, 17
Franklin National Bank, 62
Freddie Mac (Federal Home Loan
    Mortgage Corp.), 9, 76, 81,
    99, 126, 144, 147, 148, 185,
    186, 187
Friedman, Milton, 160

Garn—St. Germain Act, 76, 80, 127
gas credit cards, 88
General Electric Capital, 90, 103
General Electric Co., 38, 44
General Motors Acceptance Corp.
    (GMAC), 43, 61, 71, 89, 101
General Motors Corp., 38, 43, 61
Germany, 68
Giannini, A. P., 41
Gilded Age, 13, 14
Ginnie Mae, 9, 81, 99, 124, 125–126,
    137, 186
Glass-Steagall Act (1933), 72, 142,
    160–162, 179, 194
global crisis, 155–177
Goldman Sachs, 143–144
Goodyear Tire & Rubber Co., 96
Government Accounting Office
    (GAO), 28, 30, 148, 149
government-sponsored enterprises
    (GSEs), 99
Gramm, Phil, 161, 195, 196
Gramm-Leach-Bliley Act (1999),
    136, 142, 147, 160, 161–162,
    179, 194
Greenspan, Alan, 106, 114, 144,
    160–162, 179, 195, 196, 203
Group of 20, 211

HBOS (Halifax Bank of Scotland),
    156
hedge funds, 168–169
home equity lines of credit
    (HELOCs), 141
home equity loans (HELs), 79, 113,
    122–123, 139–140, 141, 189
home ownership. *See* mortgage
    industry (mortgages)
Household Finance Corp., 52,
    53, 90
Housing and Urban Development
    (HUD), 137
HSBC Bank USA, 111
Hyde, Henry, 107

IBM, 63
Iceland, 168, 169
income tax, first, 36
indebtedness, acceptance of, 8
individual retirement accounts
    (IRAs), 165
Industrial Acceptance Corp., 44
installment credit, 19, 42
    following World War II, 61, 62
installment credit companies, 40,
    43–44
Intel, 173
interest
    abolition of tax deduction on
        consumer, 79
    charging of, 7
    quoting in payment terms, 13
    Fibonacci on, 46–47
interest rates
    See also mortgage rates
    adjustable, 72–73, 74–75, 79–80
    Fed regulations in 2008, 184
    freezing the yield curve following
        World War II, 63–65
    Regulation Q, 72, 75–76
    structural changes, 71–73
    Truth in Lending Act, 73
    zero, 92
international banking, 73–74
International Match, 100
Interstate Branching Act (1994), 90
inverse floater, 133–134
Islamic financing, 188

Japan, 68, 168, 170–171
JC Penney, 97
JP Morgan Chase, 93, 97, 111,
    144, 212
junk bonds, 80, 128–129

Kazakhstan, 172
Kennedy administration, 124
Knights Templar, 2
Krueger, Ivar, 100, 172

LaGuardia, Fiorello, 51–52
layaway plans, 41–42
Lee, Higginson & Co., 53
Lehman Brothers, 143–144, 196
Levittown, 60
Liberty War Bonds, 40–41
loan sharks, 44–53, 60
lobbying, 186–187
London interbank offered rate
    (Libor), 73–74
Looking Backward: 2000–1887
    (Bellamy), 85–86

Major, John, 208
Mandate for Leadership, 159–160
Manufacturers Hanover Corp., 96
manufacturing, following World
    War II, 66–67
manufacturing securities, 174
Marconi device, 41
Markowitz, Harry, 69, 70, 71
Massachusetts, 97
MasterCard, 96, 98, 107, 200–202
MasterCharge, 88
Maxwell Motor Car Co., 42
McFadden Act (1927), 60
Mercantile Agency, 198
merchants, credit extended by,
    41–42
mergers, valuing in the 1920s, 53–54
Merrill Lynch, 143–144
Miller, Merton, 7, 67–68
Minnesota, 97
Mitchell, Charles, 38, 94, 174
MM theory, 67–68, 71
Modigliani, Franco, 7, 67–68, 71
moneylenders, views toward, 5–6
money market mutual funds, 74–75
money orders, 11
Montgomery Ward & Co., 36, 97
Moody, John, 198
Moore, Gordon, 173, 177
Moore's Law, 173–174
Morgan, J. P., 37, 53–54, 160–161

Morgan Stanley, 107, 143–144
mortgage-backed securities (MBS),
    112, 126
mortgage industry (mortgages), 9
    adjustable rate mortgages
        (ARMs), 9–10, 76–77, 122,
        134–140, 149
    alternative mortgage product
        (AMP), 148–149
    asset-backed security (ABS),
        100–102, 112–115
    balloon, 138
    borrow now, pay much later
        syndrome, 140–142
    in Britain, 155–159
    chattel, 190
    collateralized debt obligations
        (CDOs), 132–134
    collateralized mortgage
        obligations (CMOs), 129–132,
        144–145
    debt, statistics, 255
    extent of problem, 28–33
    following World War II, 60, 119
    funding, 130–134
    home ownership, growth of,
        118–119
    hybrids, 138
    impact of computers on,
        105–106
    lump sum variant, 121–122
    negative amortization, 138
    negative equity, 119–120
    in the 1920s, 42–43, 118–119
    private-label residential-
        mortgage-backed securities
        (RMBs), 144
    real estate mortgage investment
        conduits (REMICS), 130–134
    revolving mortgage credit,
        123–127
    savings and loan (S&L) crisis,
        127–130
    second, 123

securitization, 99–100,
    145–146, 148
signs of problems, ignoring,
    142–150
statistics, 255, 257
subprime market, 137, 144,
    145–147
usury laws, demise of, 134–140
veterans', 60
mortgage rates
    caps on adjustable, 76–77
    changes covering four
        generations, 19–23
    collar, 77
    fixed-rate, thirty-year, 20
Mortgage Reform and Anti-Predatory
    Lending Act (2007), 189

Nader, Ralph, 93, 187
naked shorting, 196–197
Nasdaq (National Association of
    Securities Dealers Automated
    Quotations), 193
National City Bank, 38, 48,
    146, 174
National City Co., 38
national debt, introduction of
    concept, 4
National Homeownership Strategy,
    136–137
National Settlement Service, 202
NationsBank Corp., 138
Nationwide Building Society, 156
negative amortization loans, 9, 138
New Century Financial Corp., 146
New York Stock Exchange,
    173–174, 193
Nilson Report, The, 108
Northern Rock, 156

Office of Thrift Supervision, 135
O'Neill, Paul, 195
online currency trading services, 170
Optima Card, 98

Packard, Vance, 62
Paine Webber, 161
Panic of 1907, 37
pass-through securities, 124–125, 126
pawnbrokers, 16–17, 44, 50, 52
payday loans, 16–18, 51–52
payments system, 107
    privatizing the, 200–204
pay-through securities, 126–127, 144
period of distribution capital, 35
period of production capital, 35
Pfandbrief, 132
policy and regulations
    coordination, need for, 181–188
    fixing, 190–194
    overcomplexity, 188–190
    privatizing the payments system, 200–204
    rating agencies, reliance on, 198–200
    reform, levels of, 209–213
    regulation, debate over, 179–181
    safety net, 194–197
Ponzi, Charles, 43
poor, changing definition of being, 16
Poor's Publishing Co., 198
portfolio diversification, theory of, 69, 70, 71
post office savings banks, 40
prime rate, introduction of, 72
Prince, Charles, 114
principles-based system, 183, 185, 199
private-label residential-mortgage-backed securities (RMBs), 144
private mortgage insurance (PMI), 149–150
Prohibition, 39

queuing system, 197

radios, tabletop, 41
Raines, Franklin, 141, 143, 187

Raskob, John J., 37
RCA Corp., 41
Reagan administration, 128, 159, 180, 194
real estate mortgage investment conduits (REMICS), 130–134
redlining, 136
Reed, John, 98
Regulation Q, 72, 75–76, 80, 128
regulations. *See* policy and regulations
Regulation Z, 73
reform, levels of, 209–213
Reformation, 6, 48
Reich, Robert, 166
Renaissance, 6, 75
residential mortgage-backed securities (RMBS), 156–157
Resolution Trust Corp., 135
reverse mortgages, 9
revolving credit, 19, 88
revolving mortgage credit, 123–127
Reward of Thrift, The, 39
Riegle Community Development and Regulatory Improvement Act (1994), 136
risk
    bankruptcy, Z ratio for predicting, 70
    systematic versus specific, 60–70
Rogers, Will, 181
Romania, 169
Roosevelt, Franklin D., 59
Rubin, Robert, 164–165
Russell Sage Foundation, 48, 50, 52
Russia, 172

salary buying, 51–52
Sallie Mae, 104
Salomon Brothers, 160
Sarbanes-Oxley Act (2002), 180
Sarnoff, David, 41
savings and loan (S&L) crisis, 127–130

savings bank industry, 41
Schultz, Dutch, 44–45
Sears, Roebuck and Co., 36, 42, 96, 201–202
Discover Card, 98, 107
Securities and Exchange Commission (SEC), 101–102, 143–144, 162–163, 211
Securities Exchange Act (1934), 64
securitization, 9, 81, 99–103, 145–146, 148
fixing financial problems and, 190–194
global, 171–172
reform, levels of, 209–213
in the United Kingdom, 156–157
Shakespeare, John, 49
Shakespeare, William, 6
Sharpe, William, 69–70, 71
Shaw, George Bernard, 165
Shays, Christopher, 187
small loan market, 47–48
Smith, Adam, 6
Smith, Ian, 85
Smith Barney, 160
Social Security, 194
Soros, George, 208–209, 212
South Dakota, 95–96
special-purpose vehicles (SPVs), 101–102
Spectator, 170
Standard Oil Co., 56
Stevin, Simon, 47
Stiglitz, Joseph, 199
stock brokerage firms, following World War II, 62
stock market
following World War II, 62
lending money, 56
structured finance, 23–24, 191
student loans, 20
default rates, 104
introduction of, 61

subprime mortgage market, 137, 144, 145–147
swap market, 8, 24, 191–192, 195–196
Swiss National Bank, 182
synergy, 54
synthetic securities, 130–134, 191–192

Tappan, Lewis, 198
Taxpayer Relief Act (1998), 144
Tax Reform Act (1986), 79, 117, 165
technology, role of, 173–177
Telegraph, The, 30
televisions, 61
Tennessee Valley Authority, 185
Thatcher, Margaret, 158, 159
Theory of the Leisure Class (Veblen), 14
Third World Debt Crisis, 74
Thoreau, Henry David, 159
thrift movement, 39–40
travelers' checks, 55
Travelers Insurance, 160
Trust Indenture Act (1939), 100
Truth in Lending Act (1968), 28, 51, 73, 93
Turkey, 172
Twin City Savings and Loan Association, 97

UBS, 161, 182
Ukraine, 172
Uniform Small Loan Law (USLL), 52–53
United Air Lines, 96
United Kingdom, 110, 155–159
U.S. Bancorp, 111
U.S. Steel, 54
unlicensed lenders (loan sharks), 44–53
usury
changes in definition of, 7, 14–15
civil versus criminal, 49
following World War II, 60

usury (*continued*)
    laws, demise of, 134–140
    loan sharks, 44–53, 60
    moral, 50
    need for, 213–216
    statutory versus legal rates, 49–51
    ways around, 51–52

value-at-risk approach, 199
Veblen, Thorstein, 14, 37
Veterans Administration (VA), 60, 99, 124
Visa, 62, 88, 96, 98, 107, 200–202
Vitagraph Studios, 39
Volcker, Paul, 74, 90

Wachovia Corp., 156
Wallich, Henry, 182
Wal-Mart, 201–202

war loans, 7
Warren, Elizabeth, 210
Washington Mutual Incorp., 111, 144, 146, 156
watering down assets, 54
Weill, Sanford, 160
Wells Fargo, 111, 144
Wilson, Woodrow, 40
WorldCom, 113, 118, 162
World Economic Forum, 179
World War II, industries and markets following, 59–65
Wriston, Walter, 93, 95, 98

yield curve, 63–65

zero-coupon bonds, 23, 120
zero interest, 92
Z ratio, 70

About the Author

CHARLES R. GEISST is the author of seventeen other books, including *Wall Street: A History* and *Undue Influence: How the Wall Street Elite Put the Financial System at Risk.* He has appeared on many television and radio programs commenting on the financial markets and has written about the markets for many financial magazines and newspapers. He holds the Ambassador Charles A. Gargano Chair at Manhattan College.

About Bloomberg

BLOOMBERG L.P., founded in 1981, is a global information services, news, and media company. Headquartered in New York, Bloomberg has sales and news operations worldwide.

Serving customers on six continents, Bloomberg, through its wholly-owned subsidiary Bloomberg Finance L.P., holds a unique position within the financial services industry by providing an unparalleled range of features in a single package known as the Bloomberg Professional® service. By addressing the demand for investment performance and efficiency through an exceptional combination of information, analytic, electronic trading, and straight-through-processing tools, Bloomberg has built a worldwide customer base of corporations, issuers, financial intermediaries, and institutional investors.

Bloomberg News, founded in 1990, provides stories and columns on business, general news, politics, and sports to leading newspapers and magazines throughout the world. Bloomberg Television, a 24-hour business and financial news network, is produced and distributed globally in seven languages. Bloomberg Radio is an international radio network anchored by flagship station Bloomberg 1130 (WBBR-AM) in New York.

In addition to the Bloomberg Press line of books, Bloomberg publishes *Bloomberg Markets* magazine.

To learn more about Bloomberg, call a sales representative at:

London:	144-20-7330-7500
New York:	11-212-318-2000
Tokyo:	181-3-3201-8900